PSYCHIC
DETECTIVES

PSYCHIC DETECTIVES

The Mysterious Use of Paranormal Phenomena in Solving True Crimes

JENNY RANDLES and PETER HOUGH

Published in 2002 by Silverdale Books
an imprint of Bookmart Ltd
Registered number 2372865
Trading as Bookmart Ltd
Desford Road
Enderby
Leicester LE9 5AD

A catalogue for this book is available from the British Library.

ISBN 1-85605-696-1

Editorial and design by
Amber Books Ltd
Bradley's Close
74–77 White Lion Street
London N1 9PF

Project Editor: Jill Fornary
Design: Floyd Sayers
Picture Research: Lisa Wren

Printed in Portugal

011908789

Contents

Psychics and Criminals

U NFORTUNATELY, CRIME IS an unavoidable part of modern society. As recently as 50 years ago, it was considered safe to let our children play freely in the streets, and offences such as vandalism were rare enough to merit attention when they occurred. These days, accounts of robberies, missing persons, and murder regularly fill our newspapers and television screens. People fit alarms to their most precious belongings, take great care to know where their offspring are going – especially at night – and are more aware of the darker side of human nature than ever before.

Fascination with crime is also widespread. Newspapers, movies and television fill our heads with images of violence and portray all aspects of the justice system, from police methods to court proceedings. We all want to know how crimes happen and, more importantly, how they are solved.

Yet the process of investigating crimes is often less sensational than it appears in the movies or in television drama series. It is less about shoot-outs and sudden breakthroughs and more about persistence, hard work, and sheer luck. Sometimes a case will be cracked immediately by a team of dedicated specialists following clues and working on forensic evidence with scientific precision. On many other occasions, however, it can take years for a criminal to be brought to justice because that one vital lead never comes.

Today's police forces employ ever more sophisticated techniques, including DNA testing, psychological profiling, and computerized data analysis. Nonetheless, success in solving crimes is not always the result of conventional

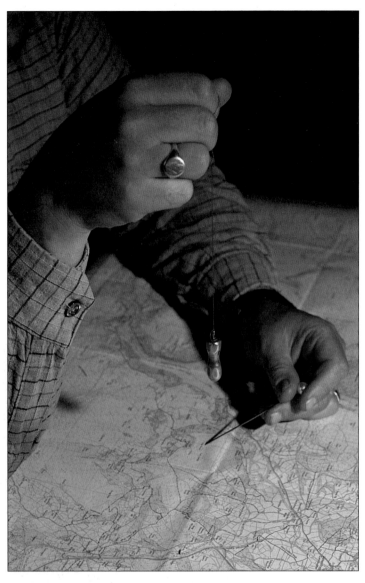

Dowsing – usually with a pendulum over a map – has been widely used by psychic detectives in their search for suspects, clues, and even bodies.

investigative work. Many detectives admit that they rely to some degree on 'hunches' – but is a hunch simply inspired guesswork based on a wealth of experience, or an illustration of some other, inexplicable, type of insight at work? The validity of this sort of 'intuition' is widely accepted, as it is seen as a form of professional wisdom and follows in the familiar tradition of famous fictional detectives that began with Sherlock Holmes.

What is less well recognized is that the police have often received help from individuals offering information obtained from sources that clearly lie beyond our rational world. The unexplained paranormal powers of these so-called 'psychic detectives' have sometimes provided the key to unravelling the most perplexing criminal cases. Their help can take many forms – many psychics receive visions while in an altered state of consciousness; some uncover significant facts by dangling a pendulum over a map; still others discover the fate of missing persons in their dreams, or claim to be able to contact the dead. This book will explore some of the most fascinating real-life cases from around the world, in which psychic forces have played a part in solving crimes and apprehending culprits.

Yet because of a general reluctance to acknowledge the existence (and the reliability) of psychic phenomena, the role of these supernatural crime-busters has often gone unsung. It was not always so. Ancient civilizations routinely turned to seers, known as 'shamans' or 'oracles', to decide matters of justice; these people were held in great esteem for their extraordinary insights and powers of divination. The paranormal was not only accepted, it was fully integrated into everyday life. By the Middle Ages, however, many societies had come to view the supernatural with suspicion and fear, and many individuals who today might be called 'psychic' were persecuted as witches. Nevertheless, over the next few centuries, it was not unheard of for crimes to be resolved by testimony received through apparitions or visions.

In today's high-tech world, the very notion of consulting 'spirits' seems alien to our concept of modern crime investigation. Yet the task of hunting criminals and preventing crimes is a daunting one for police, and relies on the co-operation of many different people working as a team and using their combined skills for the common good. In cases where ordinary detection methods have failed, why should we dismiss the help of anyone who claims to have some information – even if we cannot explain precisely where that knowledge comes from? Only prejudice and superstition stands in the way – considerations that should be set aside if a dangerous criminal can be removed from the streets more quickly. Police investigators who have been receptive to offers of assistance from self-confessed psychics have adopted this open-minded attitude on the basis of 'no stone unturned'.

Yet what do senior police officers really think of 'psychic detectives', and how successful has their collaboration been? How has media coverage affected

The oracle of Delphi was the most influential medium of the classical world. The oracle would receive guidance while in a trance-like state; the messages were often ambiguous and enigmatic.

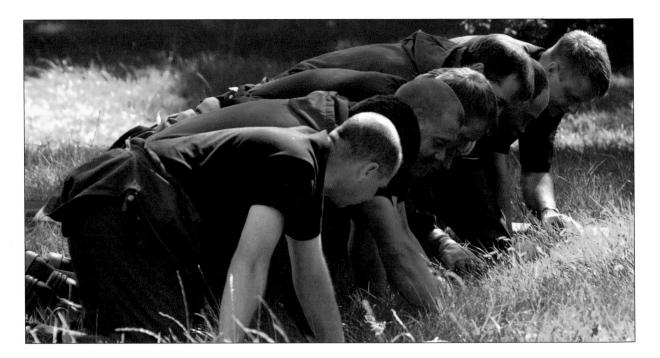

Conventional methods of criminal investigation used by the police include meticulous searches based on information provided by members of the public. Many law-enforcement officers have received useful leads from people claiming to have psychic abilities.

the role of psychics in crime investigations? And how do the psychics themselves regard their work? In this book, these attitudes and issues are explored through interviews and case histories.

The evidence for psychic phenomena is also assessed by presenting the results of scientific experiments conducted to determine the truth about phenomena such as clairvoyance and dowsing. Are extrasensory abilities part of our genetic inheritance, and do psychics have access to unique areas of the brain denied to most of us? And how valid are the criticisms of sceptics who scoff at the notion of paranormal powers?

If psychic abilities truly exist, how can we distinguish the genuinely gifted individual from the scores of would-be psychics attracted to high-profile cases, who in reality are either deluded or frauds? The statements of many law-enforcement officers suggest that there have been some very successful cases of psychic detection, yet useful leads have sometimes been disregarded or overlooked amid a flood of false information.

To complicate matters still further, even the most respected supernatural sleuths, with established reputations, cannot always supply straightforward insights to order. Before they can be of assistance to police, psychics must first learn to interpret their own often enigmatic impressions.

The struggle to yield practical leads and hard evidence can be both frustrating and emotionally traumatic for anyone working as a psychic detective. And when a person's life hangs in the balance or a criminal is at liberty, the pressure to 'perform' can become unbearable.

The prospect of facing scepticism or ridicule places a great burden on psychic detectives. Yet there are other dangers to face. Some psychics have offered information, only to be suspected of having committed the crime themselves. Others, in their pursuit of justice, have even accepted life-threatening risks. By pointing the finger at a criminal, they may also be placing themselves in the firing line. And that takes just as much guts as it does special powers.

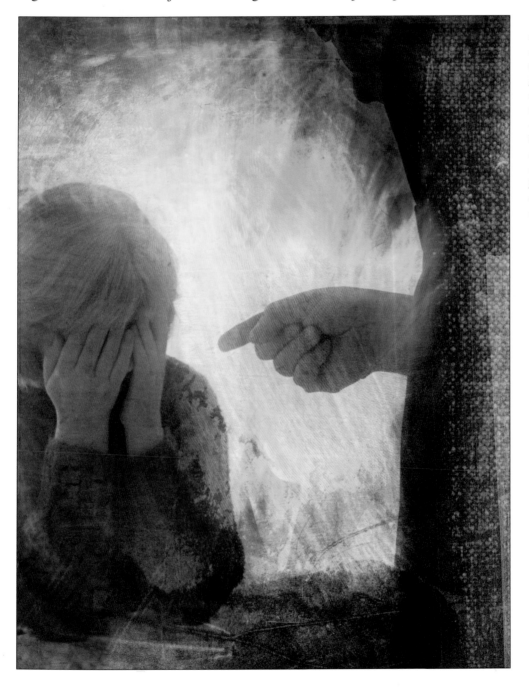

When someone's life is hanging in the balance, psychics are under enormous pressure to provide a crucial lead that may solve the case. For a psychic detective, the burden of responsibility is immense, and the pressure can be intolerable when all efforts to help fail.

The First Psychic Detectives

THE BELIEF THAT CERTAIN individuals are able to foresee events, or to understand things that cannot be fathomed using the known senses, is a time-honoured one. Many early civilizations, from tribal cultures to the ancient Greek and Roman societies, not only acknowledged that such powers existed, but elevated those who possessed them to positions of great authority and influence. The concept of the 'oracle' is also present in the Bible, which contains many accounts of visions received as messages from God. In the Middle Ages, the self-proclaimed mystic, Nostradamus, produced a volume of prophecies that is still examined today, while nowadays interest in the paranormal is reflected in countless books, films, and television shows.

Similarly, the use of alleged psychic phenomena to help solve crimes is not merely the product of a modern-day 'new age' mentality. Centuries ago, without the benefit of today's sophisticated police methods and forensic science techniques, the quest for justice was often difficult, and supernatural assistance was not discounted. In medieval times, culprits were sometimes convicted not on the basis of organized investigation and evidence-gathering, but through the testimony of 'spirits'. In the Victorian era, as the new 'spiritualist' movement gathered force, adherents communicated with the dead during seances. With the infamous case of Jack the Ripper came the first major involvement of psychics in a serial murder enquiry, and the emergence of the contemporary 'psychic detective'.

Humankind has always had a desire to see the future, and has often chosen to do so by consulting with ghosts or spirits. Around the globe, very few cultures emerged that did not have their own 'wise men', or 'shamans', whose paranormal insights from beyond known science directed everyone from tribal leaders to humble citizens. Their pronouncements empowered decisions of law, condemned criminals to their fate, and dictated battle tactics that risked the future of an entire civilization.

Even today, there are tribal cultures that rely upon what we would consider to be 'psychic inspiration'. They can be found all over the world in areas that have been less touched by the march of rationalism that dominates our technology-driven cities. While we may term these indigenous tribal peoples as 'primitive', this label belies the richness and sophistication of many of their societies, as well as their familiarity with the hidden forces that we once all accepted as factual reality. Science may tell us that these things are simply a figment our

Most tribal societies had shamans. These leaders and spiritual guides were often chosen because they experienced visions and had intuitive knowledge beyond what others could glimpse. Among humanity's first recognized psychics, shamans still exist in some cultures.

imagination, yet thousands of years of human experience have often suggested otherwise. Perhaps we have not evolved from the days of mere superstition, but instead have fled from the truth. Otherwise, why do we still seek out fortune-tellers and psychics, with so many sources of information and means of communication at our disposal?

POWER OF THE ORACLES

The ancient Greek and Roman empires had their own shamans in the form of oracles. From unknown ages – certainly before 1000 BC – these women (as most of them were) became revered as priestesses for their ability to see the future and for the guidance they offered to both kings and paupers.

Oracles such as the Sibyl, in a volcanic grotto near Naples, Italy, or those at the famed temple of Delphi, in Greece, passed their skills on to their descendants over many generations. They had both innate powers – to see visions inside their minds – and superstitious divination methods, which ranged from interpreting leaves rustling in the trees to reading the symbols in blood and guts spilled from sacrificed animals. But what the oracles said was rarely ignored; they wielded real power.

In 500 BC, the (then) holder of the Sibyl priesthood, Herophile, produced scrolls setting out the entire future history of the empire. From the scraps that have survived through the centuries, these visions seem to have painted an impressive picture of the rule of the last Caesars – despite these events lying many years in the future. According to legend, the prophetess, using her gift of

Oracles uttered their pronouncements while in a trance-like state. Here, the oracle at Delphi relates what she is seeing, and a scribe writes down the prophecy. Visions received during an altered state of consciousness are often used by many modern-day psychic detectives.

foresight, was able to map out in some detail all the major court intrigue, assassination attempts, and battles that would bring an end to more than 1,000 years of empire. Her warnings were carefully followed, and are believed to have been behind several decisions to execute 'traitors'.

As the centuries rolled by, other 'oracles', even within the Christian era, have performed surprisingly similar duties. Almost 900 years ago, the Catholic scholar Malachi set out a series of visionary insights into the reign of every pope. Many of his verses were remarkably apt; for example, one decreeing that the Holy Father would be 'of the half moon' was dedicated (hundreds of years ahead of time) to the priest who was to hold the shortest papal office and who died between one moon and the next! The description of the last pope of the twentieth century as 'of the labour of the sun' also proved appropriate, in two ways. First, the labour movement in his

CRIME FILE:
Jeanne Dixon: Assassination foreseen

Could President Kennedy's life have been saved by heeding psychic warnings?

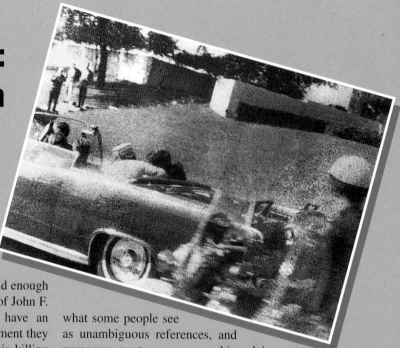

It is said that people who are old enough to remember the assassination of John F. Kennedy in November 1963 have an image in their minds of the moment they first heard the news. Just as this killing seems to have caused shock waves in the human consciousness, it also reportedly caused an unprecedented number of visions and was foreseen by many. There are apparent allusions to the murder in the readings of psychics over several centuries. Nostradamus's writings contain what some people see as unambiguous references, and numerous contemporary psychics claim to have seen the tragedy ahead of time and tried to warn the president.

Among these was celebrity psychic Jeanne Dixon. A doyenne of Washington society, she mixed in influential circles and often gave readings to the rich and famous. Her books and magazine columns were avidly read and, when she correctly predicted Kennedy's victory in the 1960 election (against the odds), her fame was at its height.

But Dixon saw catastrophe looming soon after and had a vision of the dead president shortly before his assassination. Although she tried to get word to the White House, the die was cast. Of course, we cannot assume that by acting we will stop the tragedy; the very action we take may unexpectedly lead to it. Yet politicians often have their lives threatened and cannot be seen to change their plans in response to a psychic warning. When Kennedy died in a hail of bullets, many psychics were shocked, saddened, and unsurprised in equal measure.

President John F. Kennedy slumps forward into the arms of his wife, Jacqueline, seconds after being shot by a sniper's bullet as his motorcade passed the Texas Book Depository in the city of Dallas.

Psychic Jeanne Dixon was well known for many successful predictions, including Kennedy's assassination. However, she also incorrectly claimed that the 1990s would see a female president in the White House and a giant comet strike the Earth.

native Poland signalled the end of Communism and inspired a spiritual revolution across eastern Europe. Second, the labours of the real sun, thanks to a newly discovered hole in the ozone layer and the build-up of greenhouse gases in the Earth's atmosphere, were causing rising temperatures which threatened to bring ecological doom to the planet.

During the sixteenth century, more prophecies were written by a mystical French doctor called Michel de Nostredame (Nostradamus). He wrote cryptic stanzas in Sibyl-like terms that he claimed would set out all major future events in the history of the world. It is not easy making sense of Nostradamus's anagrams and riddles, and their predictive success is usually hailed only after the fact, making them contentious, at best, as visionary material. But they do forewarn, some experts say, every major political act. Numerous crimes over the centuries, from the alleged murder of the young princes by Richard III in England, to the assassinations in the United States of John and Robert Kennedy (called 'two brothers of the new land' in the verses), can be read here if a liberal interpretation is adopted.

Either way, the enduring fascination of these prophecies remains. Apart from the Bible, the visions of Nostradamus are the only work of non-fiction to have been constantly available in book form since the invention of the printing press. Even in the cynicism of today's Space Age, an entire cottage industry

This eighteenth-century woodcut depicts the French doctor and mystic Nostradamus, whose amazing verses written centuries ago purport to document the future from the mid-sixteenth century to the end of world, more than 2,000 years from now.

Dreams of the future are recorded in the Old Testament of the Bible and are among the earliest para-normal phenomena known to humankind. Here, Jacob, while sleeping, has a vision of steps leading up to heaven and attended by angels.

exists around this form of 'oracle', with countless books regularly offering new interpretations, and the production of big-budget movies and television drama series such as Francis Ford Coppola's 'First Wave' (1998), inspired by the verses.

DREAMS AND VISIONS

Naturally, it is difficult to make sense out of the enigmatic centuries-old verses written by Nostradamus or Malachi, but this in itself is not an unusual problem. The unconscious mind operates through dreams and symbols, not logical imagery, and often delivers messages to the conscious mind through analogies.

This is seen readily in the world of dreams, where bizarre events may occur each night and are usually dismissed as flights of imagination. However, they form the raw material from which supernatural experiences have always been drawn. It may be that oracles and shamans of past times, like mediums and psychics today, simply learned to read their dreams and visions in the same way as fortune-tellers might read tea leaves.

History has many examples of the power that can be found within dreams. Indeed, the Bible is full of such visions, sent to prophets by God as warnings of coming events such as plagues and famines. Joseph, for example, would today be deemed a great psychic whose frequent dreams were perceived to be messages from Heaven. In his day, he was used as a political tool to guide the Egyptian Pharaoh, who elevated his visionary to a position of trust and authority. Psychic detectives operate much like this.

In the ancient world, it was never thought wise to trifle with the abilities of a psychic. You were grateful that they were on your side, and you used them to steer your administration in healthy directions. Indeed, widespread doubts by the powers-that-be, sensing that it was not possible to look beyond the boundaries of time and space, are a relatively recent phenomenon. These suspicions were born both of the age of reason and the triumph of science that began in the seventeenth century. Even until shortly before then, a vision was treated with reverence and could – indeed, often did – bring about swift retribution for any wrongdoer.

SUPERNATURAL JUSTICE

An early well-recorded case of psychic detection in Britain, connected with a tragic crime, was simply a continuation of practices dating back to the Sibyl. It was September 1631, and Christopher Walker lived in a brooding house overlooking Chester Moors, just south of Chester-le-Street in County Durham. His niece Anne, a pretty teenager, had arrived to take over the care of his home after the death of his wife, but talk was soon rife among the villagers of the small community of Great Lumley that the relationship between Anne Walker and her step-uncle was rather closer than it ought to have been.

Tongues were silenced when the niece was sent to live with another relative in Chester-le-Street. Indeed, the ploy seemed to have succeeded at the time, as the young girl quietly disappeared from both the sight and the minds of Great Lumley's villagers.

Yet, as Christmas approached, a local miller named James Graham had an extremely strange and unsettling experience. As he worked late into the night in his locked mill, he heard muffled sounds from the floor below and caught a brief glimpse of an intruder. Steeling himself for confrontation, Graham calmly climbed down and prepared to face the unwelcome visitor, but was relieved to discover that it was simply a young girl who seemed to be in need of shelter. She looked dirty and dishevelled, with her dress torn and her hair matted with blood across gaping cuts that slashed her forehead. As Graham stared at her shocking appearance, a chill ran through his body.

This stained-glass window at Lincoln Cathedral in England commemorates an ancient example of a psychic dream. The Egyptian Pharoah foresaw in symbolic terms the coming years of famine when he dreamt of seven lean cattle alongside seven fat ones.

There was something not quite right about the girl's gaze: it was clouded by an ethereal look. Her eyes stared right at him, yet they seemed somehow vacant. In those days of superstition and widespread belief in witchcraft and demons, one answer seemed obvious – this was some form of apparition.

The spectral girl began to talk. She explained that her name was Anne Walker and insistently related a tale of the terrible crime she had endured. As she described her trauma, the miller's head was filled with images. He could now see the scene unfolding in his mind. He watched – and felt – the terror, as the girl related her awful fate. She reported how she had become unexpectedly pregnant by her step-uncle. Fearful that the scandal would destroy his reputation, Christopher Walker had sent her away. But he knew that, as the birth grew near, her physical condition would become obvious, and something had to be done. So, telling his niece that he had arranged lodgings far away in Lancashire until after the child was born, she was put into the care of a miner returning to work across the bleak moors, and she said goodbye to her guardian.

But Mark Sharp, the miner, had no intention of taking her to Lancashire. He had other orders. Once they were on desolate moorland west of the village, he struck the girl violently with his pick, killing her in a bloodied frenzy. The miller watched all this unfold inside his mind's eye, and he winced as he felt the pain of her violent death.

The 'spirit' of Anne Walker described the means by which the miner completed his conspiracy of murder. He did this by tossing her body into a coal pit, burying his pick, and hiding his stockings, having failed to clean off the spurting blood. But now, with a burning need for justice, the ghostly image of the dead teenager pleaded with the miller to go to the town elders and help them to find her body, in order to make her killers pay. Having spoken her piece, the spectral girl then disappeared.

Aware of Christopher Walker's standing in the community, Graham decided that he could not go to a magistrate with this extraordinary story. To do so would earn the wrath of those upon whom his livelihood depended. But

The bleak Durham moorland, where young Anne Walker was brutally murdered in the seventeenth century. This was the scene of one of the first 'psychic detective' cases in which a criminal was allegedly brought to justice from beyond the grave.

he bargained without the persistence of the murdered woman. She returned in visions and in dreams twice more over the next few days, telling the miller that she could never rest until he had acted.

On December 21, Graham took the news to Thomas Liddell, who was chief justice for the area. Even in this age, there was a sense of equity, and the maxim 'innocent until proven guilty' applied in Britain, especially for the well-to-do. Unable to simply accept his story, two magistrates subjected the miller to intense questioning before concluding that he was sincere. Investigations further revealed that Graham had never met Anne Walker and that he had no motive to invent this story. This was deemed sufficient grounds for the law to act, and a search party was mounted.

GRIM DISCOVERY ON THE MOORS

As had been feared, the dead woman's body was found where Graham told them it would be. The pick and the bloodied stockings were also unearthed. Both Christopher Walker and Mark Sharp, who had now somewhat foolishly returned to the area, were arrested and committed for trial in Durham.

The trial was driven by suspicion and fear, but little beyond circumstantial evidence existed to associate Walker with Sharp's widely accepted crime. However, as the proceedings wound on, one of the witnesses told, with a look of horror, that he could see the spirit of Anne Walker standing in the courtroom identifying her own uncle as the man who had ordered her death! After this moment of high drama, there was little doubt what the jury would decide. Both Walker and Sharp were convicted of murder. It seems likely that this was the first guilty verdict to be brought at a murder trial in which the main prosecution witness was the victim.

The belief that the dead could return briefly to life to ensure that justice was done has never completely left society, despite the march of rationalism. Several

Since the invention of photography, there have been pictures reputed to reveal ghosts. This one, taken in a church in Sussex, England, appears to show the figure of a priest at the altar. Stray light or film faults may be the real cause of such phantom-like images.

Poltergeist effects have long been reported. This video footage shot in 1967 at Rossenheim, in Germany, shows a ceiling lamp swinging violently inside a lawyer's office. This inexplicable phenomenon was believed to be the violent 'outburst' of a poltergeist connected with a young woman who worked there.

opinion poll surveys taken in Britain and the United States in 1999 revealed that 35 percent of people believe that ghosts are real, and that more than two-thirds are tolerant of the possibility. These findings help to explain why, in a very different world today, the use of psychic detection to aid the authorities is still remarkably common.

Indeed, the birth of modern psychic research owes itself to a case of supernatural criminology. In 1847, John Fox, a farmer and devout Methodist, moved into a home in Hydesville, New York, with his two Canadian-born daughters aged 12 and 14. These two became the focus of a poltergeist attack. Unusual rapping sounds were heard, and objects began to move around the house of their own accord with no obvious cause. Soon the girls announced that the phenomena resulted from the spirit of a dead man called Charles Rosna. They claimed that he told them, by means of various raps, that he had been killed in the old Fox house by blacksmith John Bell.

Following this ghostly advice, the Foxes dug up their cellar and found bones. The dead man was thought to have been a tinker who had been killed during the previous century. However, there was no record of his murder, and justice was not to be served by this case of psychic detection.

Rather more remarkably, the Fox sisters started a craze for communicating with the dead using intermediaries, or mediums as they came to be called, using such knocking sounds – one knock for 'yes', two for 'no' being the agreed basis of the resulting contact. The craze spread to Europe, in particular to Britain, as early as 1852, and the United Kingdom soon became the home of the new 'spiritualist' movement that thrives even into the twenty-first century. Modern mediums such as Doris Stokes have become entertainers and television stars.

The explosion of popular interest in clairvoyance and spiritualism during the twentieth century has resulted in many publications devoted to the field. Prediction *magazine, the October 1939 edition of which is shown here, is one of the oldest still in print today.*

CRIME FILE:
Alan and Clara: Till death us do part

Foreseeing their own murders did not save this tragic couple, yet justice still triumphed from the grave.

For young lovers planning to elope in eighteenth-century England, there was just one place to go – Peak Forest, a village in north Derbyshire, set amid the white limestone moors. At that time, there was special dispensation for people to marry instantly in Peak Forest, in the same fashion as Las Vegas today. Young couples regularly fled there from miles around when circumstances prevented an ordinary betrothal.

Alan and Clara were escaping the wrath of Clara's rich parents, who had declined to accept her intended spouse. So, the couple fled on horseback from Yorkshire, across the Pennine mountains. On the first night of their journey, Clara suffered a terrifying dream. In it, she saw Alan being attacked as they picked their way through an unfamiliar rock-strewn pass. She saw him fall down dead as the assailants then turned on her. At that point, she woke up screaming. Afraid that her brothers might be in pursuit to prevent Alan marrying her at any cost, the pair hastened on their journey, and they spent the night before their wedding at Castleton, in an inn surrounded by the caverns of the area. Peak Forest was only a short ride from there.

But, as they left the inn in cheerful spirits, relieved that prior threats made by her brothers had not been fulfilled, they were directed by a gang of miners to take a short cut through Winnats Pass, a notorious path that would speed them toward Peak Forest. Little did the lovers

The eerie winter isolation of Winnats Pass in Derbyshire's Peak District, scene of the murderous assault on young lovers Alan and Clara in the 1700s. Do their spirits still haunt this lonely spot, where they wreaked a supernatural revenge on their killers?

know that the four men, having joined up with a fifth, had gone ahead to ambush the evidently wealthy young couple as they edged through the rocky outcrops.

By now a terrified Clara had recognized the horrific scene from her dream, but it was too late to turn back. As the mass of the High Peak rose up all around them, they could only go forward without great danger to themselves. Then, out of nowhere, the brigands struck, dragging the pair from their horses and gleefully snatching the money that they had brought with them to Derbyshire in order to start a new life.

As Alan pleaded with the men for their release, Clara was bundled into a nearby shack. She watched in horror as they beat her fiancé to death with heavy mining tools. When finished, they then turned on her. This time there was no means of escape by waking from the nightmare. She was helpless as they murdered her before fleeing with £200 in gold coins – a not inconsiderable fortune at that time.

Sadly, the forewarning vision of death had not saved these tragic lovers. However, the killers never recovered from the horrors they had inflicted in Winnats Pass and were haunted, both figuratively and literally, by the two people whose lives they had so violently ended. Two of the men, Nicholas Cook and John Bradshaw, died soon afterward in mysterious accidents in the very pass where the murder was committed – one falling from a rocky perch and the other smashed to death when a heavy rock inexplicably came loose and crashed onto his head. Rumours soon grew that Alan and Clara were seeking some sort of spectral revenge.

As for the other two men, now constantly plagued by their own demons, Thomas Hall hanged himself to escape the torment, and Francis Butler was

driven insane by visions of the couple whose life he had so brutally terminated. The final survivor was James Ashton. He quickly lost his share of the money, which he had invested in horses, when all of his stock died in a mystery plague. Driven by despair, and fearing his own imminent retribution, he confessed to the murders and named the other guilty men in the hope that their souls might be eased by this admission.

Ten years later, the remains of the young couple were recovered from an old mine shaft, where James Ashton had dumped the bodies. The story of their deaths has become legend in the Peak District, and the preserved saddle from Clara's horse – recovered when the animal fled riderless from the scene of the murder back to Castleton – can be seen at the now popular tourist attraction of Speedwell Cavern nearby.

The saddle recovered from Clara's horse after it fled the scene of her murder is now on public display in the museum at Speedwell Cavern, Castleton, Derbyshire.

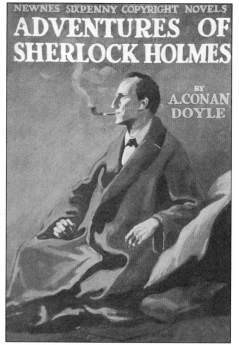

The character of Sherlock Holmes, conceived by Sir Arthur Conan Doyle, was a detective with near-supernatural flashes of insight. Doyle was deeply interested in the paranormal and devoted much of his life to investigating such phenomena.

A horned devil presides over the Sabbat, as demons and witches dance frenziedly around him. In the Middle Ages, Christians demonized those with psychic powers, claiming that clairvoyance was Satan's 'gift' in exchange for a human soul.

Ironically, long after the Fox sisters left Hydesville, when they were old ladies and had been discredited by many critics as tricksters, the complete skeleton of a man was found under their old house. A tinker's tin was buried next to the remains. It seems that the murder of Charles Rosna had been real after all.

Victorian melodramas were written around this new fascination for psychic phenomena, and the role that the supernatural could play in crime was swiftly recognized. For example, writers such as Charles Dickens (who had been a court reporter) were aware of the way in which old beliefs and new materialism were clashing head-to-head. The fictional stories of 'Sherlock Holmes' by Sir Arthur Conan Doyle, himself a spiritualist, saw his great detective bring murderers to book by employing intuitive powers that deliberately bordered on the realms of the psychic. A number of supernatural elements, such as phantom hounds and omens, fill these tales.

Things are little different today, with various 'high-tech' television dramas and big-budget movies featuring visions seen from the spirit world or mediums who help police to track serial killers. Psychics still see crimes before they happen. Murder victims still return as apparitions or in dreams to plead that their killers be brought to justice. And in real-life crime investigations, despite the wonders of forensic science and new methods of empirical detection, an incredible number of police forces worldwide have used and continue to use supernatural aids in their quest for the truth. Indeed, psychic detection, arguably one of the oldest servants of justice in the world, is very much alive and well amid the computers, DNA testing, and satellite surveillance techniques of our sophisticated modern civilization.

THE SPECTRE OF WITCHCRAFT

There was once a time when those deemed to possess special powers, and who offered psychic insights, were feared and hated. The result was almost 300 years of persecution, during

FACT FILE:
Film phenomena

In recent years, Hollywood has been quick to translate public interest in the paranormal into box-office success.

In the blockbuster film *The Sixth Sense*, a young boy claims that he can 'see the dead'. He even acts as a psychic detective when the spirit of a girl who supposedly died of natural causes guides him to a videotape showing that she was poisoned.

For some actors, paranormal experiences are not confined to the big screen. Years ago, Anthony Hopkins, star of *Hannibal*, signed for a role in the film version of the novel *The Girl from Petrovka*, but could not find a copy of the book to research his character. After a fruitless tour of London bookstores, he found himself at Leicester Square underground station. There, to his amazement, Hopkins saw a discarded copy of the novel on a platform seat. He was so pleased that he didn't mind the curious notes written in the margins.

He went abroad to make the film and for the first time met the author, George Feife. Feife was upset because his own copy of the novel, complete with annotations, had been lost by a friend while in London. It was, of course, the same copy that Hopkins had found 'by chance'.

In the film The Sixth Sense, *a boy is 'cursed' with the ability to see the dead. He conquers his fear by helping these tortured souls to find peace.*

which anything from 200,000 to one million men, women, and children were put to death in continental Europe, Britain, and the United States. People that today might be deemed 'psychic' are, in fact, very much yesterday's 'witches'.

Witchcraft grew out of the ancient pagan religions. Our forefathers worshipped the dark and light forces that controlled their lives. Much later, the wise woman of the village was someone skilled in the use of healing herbs, knowledgeable in ritual magic, and possessed of the ability to foresee the future. She could also detect things by what today we might call ESP (extrasensory perception). In the days before scientific enquiry, these powers instilled the great fear that the devil was their paymaster.

During the Middle Ages, paganism was outlawed, giving impetus to a more violent conflict. Anyone caught practising pagan rituals or dabbling with supernatural forces was deemed by implication to be challenging the Christian God. In the terror that followed, Catholic and Protestant witchfinders alike created a veritable blood bath that lasted for years.

*Joan of Arc was both
clairvoyant and clair-
audient. Today, she
would be a media star,
but in fifteenth-century
France only one fate
awaited her – burning.*

MEDIEVAL WITCH-HUNTS

Perhaps the most famous 'witch' to be tried and then burnt at the stake was Joan of Arc. This 'Maid of Orleans', daughter of a well-to-do peasant in fifteenth-century France, appeared to be an extraordinary clairvoyant and clairaudient. She had premonitions and, from the age of 13, claimed to hear voices under a 'fairy tree' near her home. She identified the voices with a number of saints,

who encouraged her to remain pure in body and in thought. When news reached Lorraine that Orleans was under siege by the English, these same voices ordered Joan of Arc to save the city!

Despite her success in relieving Orleans, the young heroine was handed over to the English on May 23, 1430 by the Burgundian commander. She became the subject of a show trial designed to discredit Charles VII of France. For political reasons, the trial's conclusion was preordained. Joan of Arc was executed as a witch a week later.

Central to the ensuing witch-hunt that obsessed medieval Europe were two Dominican friars who conducted the inquisition of suspected witches with a fanatical fervour. Their paranoid beliefs included the view that many bishops and cardinals practised the 'black arts'. With twisted logic, they concluded that anyone who opposed the execution of 'witches' must also themselves be a follower of Satan. Even children did not remain immune from this terror. Many were tortured and executed, while others were granted immunity from prosecution on the provision that they implicated their elders.

Although this paranoia gripped much of medieval Europe, by far the worst atrocities were committed in Germany. In a period of 13 years, 300 alleged sorcerers were executed in the state of Bamburg alone. Nothing matched the cruelty exhibited by their German prosecutors. This savagery became a massive industry, lining the pockets and fattening the bellies of judges, clerks, witchfinders, jailers, torturers, executioners, and the merchants who provided the scaffolding and wood for the fires to burn the so-called 'witches'.

The 'Witchfinder General', Matthew Hopkins, was paid generously to go from village to village seeking witches. Although torture was outlawed in England, Hopkins devised many 'tests' to obtain confessions.

Torture was prohibited in England except by special Act of Parliament. Although burnings did take place in Scotland, by and large the punishment for convicted witches was hanging. Yet, although torture was not officially allowed, pressure was applied in more subtle ways. Suspects were often 'swum', a process that involved shackling their arms and legs together, and then tossing them into a river. If they sank, they were judged to be innocent. However, if they floated, invisible demons were thought to have supported them, and they were summarily executed as disciples of the devil.

CRIME FILE:

Maria Marten: When the dead tell tales

Did the spirit of a murdered girl enter her mother's dreams to explain her mysterious disappearance?

William Corder was a pig farmer and landowner in Polstead, near Sudbury in Suffolk, England. In 1827, as a 24-year-old, he had inherited the business from his father and brothers, all of whom had succumbed to illness within a few months. In this tiny community, William Corder had inherited rather more than property. His older brother, Thomas, had had an affair with local teenager Maria Marten, and now William was sharing in her favours, too. Indeed, they had had a child together. Forced by the Victorian morals of the day to consider marriage, William advised the girl's mother, Anne, that on May 19 they would go to Ipswich to be wed.

Instead, Maria was smuggled out of her home dressed as a boy, since, as William had said, she was afraid that she might be arrested for previous minor indiscretions. Her family were bemused, but this was the last Anne Marten ever saw – or heard – of her daughter.

When asked why the wedding had not taken place and where Maria was,

The infamous Red Barn in Polstead, Suffolk, where the body of Maria Marten was found in 1828. Did her ghost return to identify the killer, or was the supernatural used as a ploy to catch the most logical suspect?

William insisted that there had been legal difficulties that were slowly being overcome, but that the girl was in Ipswich waiting for her fiancé and all would be well. After six months had passed, doubts began to grow.

In November, Corder stunned locals by placing an advertisement in the *Sunday Times* asking for a wife! A girl called Mary Moore replied, and the two very quickly married. They then moved to Essex, where Corder announced that he was giving up farming to become a teacher.

Meanwhile, Anne waited and waited to hear from her estranged daughter, who was to be welcomed home now that her marriage to Corder would not be taking place. His vague promises before leaving the area had suggested that something was wrong.

At the turn of the year, Anne Marten shocked the local community by insisting that she had been visited twice in nightmares by visions of Maria. In her dreams, her daughter was showing her her own murder scene. Anne urged her husband, Tom, to visit the now-empty Corder farm, in particular its Red Barn, where the girl's body had been left by Corder after he had killed her. She knew this because Maria had told her.

It was necessary to obtain a court order to search the Red Barn, but by April 1828, Tom Marten had finally succeeded. Almost immediately the badly decomposed body of Maria was discovered there – exactly where his wife had insisted that it would be found, hastily buried under a makeshift pile of stones and decaying corn.

Maria had been brutally murdered, both shot and stabbed, and then put into a sack. Only one man was sought in connection with this crime – William Corder. He was duly arrested, tried, and quickly convicted. Sentenced to death, he was hanged at Bury St Edmunds, Suffolk, on August 11, 1828.

As was common in that day, Corder did not die easily on the scaffold. It took many minutes to force his final breath after numerous attempts. Hundreds watched the scene, and interest in the case was so intense that souvenir hunters stripped the Red Barn, while ghoulish entrepreneurs actually sold pieces of the killer's skin and lengths of the hangman's rope! Part of Corder's skin was even used to bind a book telling the story, and this is still on show at the 800-year-old Moyses Hall in Bury.

There are persistent doubts about what really happened regarding Anne Marten's supposed visions of her murdered daughter. Crime writer Colin Wilson suspects that Anne may have picked up a telepathic message from the teenager at the point of her death – although this presumes that the youngster was alive for seven months after her disappearance and died only around Christmas 1827. Another possibility is that Maria's ghost returned in a dream to ensure that her killer was caught. A more mundane explanation is that Anne, convinced that Corder had harmed Maria, merely invented the dream as a dramatic means of persuading the authorities to act. Maria Marten was last seen heading toward the Red Barn; therefore, it was not too unlikely to suspect that she had met her end there.

Interestingly, at the time that she had her dream, Anne Marten had owned a copy of a popular novel called *The Old English Baron*, in which a man finds his missing daughter's body thanks to directions given to his wife in a dream. Perhaps, then, it was not the spirit of the dead girl that exposed her killer, but her mother's clever manipulation of the public mood and the Victorian fascination for melodrama and the supernatural.

THE PENDLE WITCHES

The best-documented witch trials were probably those of 19 men and women in Lancashire, England, in 1612. This came out of a number of disputes between 'witch' families in the Pendle Forest area near Burnley, Lancashire. In this case, the accused claimed to have psychic powers that they used to harm their neighbours.

The bizarre episode began in 1595 when Christopher Nutter and his son, Robert, died within a short time of one another. The family claimed that they had been bewitched by an old lady called Chattox and her daughter, Alizon. Various members of the community had been grumbling for months about their alleged witchcraft practices, but it was an incident occurring on March 18, 1612 that attracted the attention of the authorities.

The self-confessed Pendle Witches of Lancashire are pictured casting spells around a burning cauldron. There is no doubt that the two families involved in this case believed they had psychic powers, which they admitted using to harm their neighbours.

Alizon was travelling along the road to Trawden when she met a peddler called John Law. The young woman asked him for some pins, but he refused to undo his pack. Alizon became angry with him, and, as he turned away, a stroke overcame him. He was taken to a nearby alehouse, and his son Abraham arrived from Halifax. Alizon was found, and, now with his speech restored, the peddler accused her of bewitching him and bringing about his sickness. She admitted this was indeed the case, but begged forgiveness, which the victim granted.

Abraham Law was not satisfied, however, and Alizon went before a magistrate to repeat her confession. She then described her initiation into witchcraft by her grandmother and implicated both families in the possession of such powers. Arrests were made, and neighbours were found to testify against the accused. Their confessions revealed how they consorted with demons and murdered people using 'sympathetic magic'. One man readily admitted to murdering Christopher and John Nutter in this way. In August 1612, no fewer than 19 'witches' from the area went up for trial before a jury in Lancaster. The majority of them died on the gallows.

The notorious Salem witch trials were held in 1692. This illustration appeared in the magazine Harper's *in 1892. It shows one of the accusing girls pointing at the suspect and crying out that she could see a flock of birds circling around her head.*

THE SALEM WITCH TRIALS

Another well-documented case of mass hysteria resulting from accusations of witchcraft occurred in the village of Salem, Massachusetts. During February 1692, the juvenile female population went into fits and began to act like animals. They claimed they had been bewitched by three women in the village, including a West Indian slave called Tituba. As had been the case in Europe, others soon became implicated as the contagion spread, and there were 50 executions before the madness was brought to an end.

Most modern commentators believe that those accused of witchcraft had no real psychic powers, but were either self-deluded or totally innocent, and merely caught up in the fear and paranoia. Certainly, most of those charged with the crime were victims of an hysteria that was taken advantage of and used for political advantage, to purge certain 'undesirables' from society. However, evidence of clairvoyance, the mainstay of today's psychic detective, was often seen in some of the women deemed to be witches.

An artist's rendition of the murdering spectre who became known as 'Jack the Ripper'. The grisly case gripped the British nation and attracted the attentions of many would-be psychic detectives.

PSYCHIC SEARCH FOR JACK THE RIPPER

In the annals of criminology, no case has gripped the public imagination more than the ghastly murders of five women in the East End of London, England, attributed to one assailant – known as 'Jack the Ripper'. Ever since they were first committed in the autumn of 1888, these still-unsolved killings have attracted many bewildering theories, spawning numerous films and books. The case has also attracted the attentions of psychic investigators, themselves keen to throw light on what became the first widely touted occult murder hunt.

Jack the Ripper was the first recognized serial killer of the modern era. The exact number of victims in his murder spree has been difficult to ascertain. Up to 14 were credited to him by the press, but in fact the police accepted only five. Psychic Pamela Ball, during her recent investigations into the crimes, chose to include a sixth victim, Martha Tabram, because she fitted in with the time frame, although she was not mutilated as the others had been.

JACK'S FIRST VICTIMS

Martha Tabram was 39 when she died. She had married Henry Tabram on Christmas Day 1869 and bore him two sons, but he left her six years later, allegedly because of her heavy drinking. By all accounts, she had a very forceful character and loved a good time. Although it was assumed that she had supplemented her income through prostitution, this was never proven.

According to prostitute Mary Ann Connoll, known as 'Pearly Poll', Martha Tabram had been drinking with two soldiers on the night of her murder, August 7, 1888. She told the inquest that at around 11:45 p.m., Tabram had taken one of the guardsmen into George Yard, presumably for sex. At 3:30 a.m., a cab driver noticed what he assumed to be a sleeping form on the first-floor landing of George Yard Building. Just over an hour later, a dock labourer on his way to work found Martha Tabram's bloodied body.

She had been the victim of a frenzied attack involving 39 stab wounds, all of which, except for one, could have been inflicted by a penknife. The focus of the attack was her breasts, stomach, and genitals. It was estimated that she had died approximately two hours before the examination. If this was correct, then the cab driver had just missed seeing the murderer flee.

Police Constable Barrett reported that he had spoken to a young Grenadier Guardsman at about 2:00 a.m. that night in nearby Wentworth Street. The guardsman claimed that, at the time, he had been waiting for a friend. When an identity parade was organized, Pearly Poll failed to attend. She then later wrongly identified two Coldstream Guards as the soldiers she and Tabram had met. Had someone threatened the prostitute with reprisals? Had Martha Tabram spent all of that time with the soldier? If not, and he was innocent, why did he never come forward?

The second murder took place on August 30. Mary Ann Nichols, known as 'Polly', was the daughter of a locksmith. Just a few months before her death, she wrote to her father and told him she had found herself a job as a domestic servant. In July, however, she ran away with some clothes belonging to her employer and moved into a lodging house with a woman called Ellen Holland.

On the night of her death, Nichols returned at 1:20 a.m. after leaving The Frying Pan public house, but she was

Believed to be the second victim, Mary Ann Nichols had her throat cut and her abdomen sliced open. The women killed by Jack were among the first murder victims to be photographed.

CASE FILE:

Who was Jack the Ripper?

The mystery of Jack's identity was never solved, although over the years many candidates have been proposed.

It is possible that Mary Kelly's lover, Joe Barnett, was responsible for her murder. He disliked her working as a prostitute, and the couple had a very volatile relationship, although it was often Mary who was the aggressor.

Several commentators have focused on the apparent anatomical knowledge of the killer, implying that he was a medical doctor. Sir William Withey Gull fitted this profile. Gull, who treated patients for insanity, came from a poor background, but had worked his way up. After receiving his degree in medicine, he worked at Guy's Hospital in London and, by 1861, had a practice in London's prestigious Mayfair. Gull was made a baronet and was also appointed Physician Extraordinary to Queen Victoria and Physician Ordinary to the Prince of Wales. Gull had a mild stroke aged 72 and reportedly died in January 1890. Some believe, however, that he was secretly incarcerated in a lunatic asylum in north London, under the name of Thomas Mason. Mason died in 1896.

Curious as to why the string of murders had suddenly stopped, senior police officer Sir Melville Macnaghten considered Montague John Druitt as a suspect. Though not a doctor, Druitt had disappeared three weeks after Mary Kelly's murder, and his drowned body was found in floating in the River Thames on December 31. Macnaghten also claimed that Druitt's family thought he was the killer, and further that Druitt was 'sexually insane'.

James Maybrick was a cotton merchant born in Liverpool on October 24, 1838 who had married an American woman called Florence. She was later imprisoned for his murder at the close of an unsatisfactory trial. Maybrick became a Ripper suspect in 1991 when his alleged diary was revealed to the public. It had reputedly been passed down through the family of his estranged wife.

There are doubts surrounding the authenticity of the diary. Nevertheless, this document does contain information that had not been common knowledge. For example, the writer refers to Elizabeth Stride's red hair, a detail not widely known, and mentions that she may have been killed with her own knife. The diarist further alleges that the murder of Emma Smith was also carried out by the Ripper.

The Maybrick diary begins in March 1887 and details the writer's pathological hatred of his wife, who had been having an affair. He refers to her as

The police considered Montague Druitt to be a prime suspect, and his own family believed he was capable of the crimes. He vanished shortly after Jack's last murder, and his body was subsequently found in the Thames.

Jack's butchering of his victims suggested that he was familiar with anatomy. This theory turned the spotlight on Sir William Withey Gull, Queen Victoria's doctor. Although his involvement was never proven, some believe that he was later admitted to a mental institution under a false identity.

a whore, and this may have been the catalyst for the murder of prostitutes. There are many cryptic references in the book that seem to correspond with elements concerning the Ripper affair.

Surgeon Robert Donston Stephenson was another Jack the Ripper suspect. It was said that he possessed a box of blood-stained ties used to conceal organs removed from the scene of the murders. Mabel Collins, associate editor of the Theosophical Society's magazine *Lucifer*, befriended him, and Stephenson told her many tall tales about his supposed exploits. It was Baroness Vittoria Cremers who uncovered the bloodied ties and Stephenson responded by claiming that he had met Jack the Ripper in the hospital and that the killer had described his methods to him.

Another suspect emerged in 1993 with the discovery of a letter written by then-retired Chief Inspector John Littlechild. Dated September 23, 1913, it was a response to a journalist's enquiry. In it, Littlechild names Dr Francis J. Tumblety as 'a very likely suspect'.

Tumblety was born in 1833 to an American mother and Irish father. He was a solitary type and, at the age of only 15, sold pornography in his home town of Rochester, New York. Two years later, he left the area, and in 1858 his activities as a physician led to suspicions of charlatanism. The death of one of Tumblety's patients was blamed on gross malpractice.

Nevertheless, he prospered as a medical doctor in Detroit. During the Civil War, he made a number of outrageous claims, allegedly telling a certain Colonel Dunham that he had collected specimens of 'the wombs of every class of woman'. He had apparently developed a hatred of women after falling in love with one, only to discover that she was a prostitute. After the war, Tumblety took to travelling and spent time in Liverpool and London. There he was arrested on November 7, 1888 – just before the last murder – and charged with eight counts of gross indecency and indecent assault against four men. Tumblety was bailed awaiting trial at the Old Bailey, but fled the country and was pursued by British police in America. However, Tumblety had covered his tracks well. When he died in 1903, a collection of preserved uteri were found among his belongings.

In the Ripper case, even the British Royal Family was not above suspicion. Prince Albert Edward, the Prince of Wales, had been involved in several sexual scandals. The prince was named in the Mordaunt divorce case of 1869–70, although the other party in this affair, Lady Mordaunt, was subsequently declared insane.

In the early 1970s, a Dr Thomas Stowell implicated Prince Albert Victor, son of the Prince of Wales, as being Jack the Ripper. Two years later, the illegitimate son of the artist Walter Sickert claimed that Prince Albert Victor had secretly married his grandmother and that the child of that union had married his father. Mary Jane Kelly had witnessed the marriage, and author Stephen Knight suggests that she was murdered as part of a Masonic conspiracy. There were indeed ritualistic elements to several of the murders. The Earl of Crawford speculated in the *Pall Mall Gazette* in 1888 that, when plotted on a map, the murder sites conform to the shape of a cross or a five-pointed star, a magical symbol called a 'pentagram'. Crawford also wrote that the sexual organs of a prostitute have been used in rituals to evoke demonic spirits.

Prince Albert Victor, son of Edward VII, was accused of the murders nearly a century after they were committed. Author Stephen Knight postulated that Mary Kelly had been killed because she knew of incestuous marriages within the Royal Family.

refused admission because she did not have the four pence to pay for her lodging-house bed. Just over one hour later, she was seen by her roommate on the corner of Osborn Street and Whitechapel Road. Holland suggested that they return to their lodgings, but Nichols refused. As far as it is known, apart from the murderer, Holland was the last person to see her alive.

At around 3:45 a.m., Charles Cross and Robert Paul found Mary Ann Nichols's body in Bucks Row. A doctor reported that five of her teeth were missing and that there was bruising to her face. Her throat had been cut down to the vertebrae with 'a long-bladed knife, used with great violence'. There were also cuts to the lower abdomen that ran in a downward direction and which may have been carried out by a left-handed person.

Annie Chapman was the next victim. About one week before her murder, she complained of feeling unwell and spent most of her meagre earnings from hawking crochet work on drink. A postmortem later showed that she was suffering severely from tuberculosis.

Around 1:50 a.m. on September 8, she was turned away from her usual lodging house and went to find some money to buy a bed elsewhere. She was found at 6:00 a.m. just a quarter of a mile away, at the back of 29 Hanbury Street, by John Davis, as he was leaving for work. The passageway at the side of the building was used regularly by prostitutes and their clients. Davis had been unable to sleep that night, but had heard nothing unusual. However, at around 5:30 a.m., a neighbour reported hearing a commotion, with a woman's voice crying out 'No!' and then the sound of something falling against a fence.

Annie Chapman had been partially suffocated before her throat was cut. After her death, exceptionally gruesome mutilations had been carried out. Her brass rings were missing, and two farthings had been laid out beside her. These factors fuelled a growing belief that the murderer had some anatomical knowledge, with the suggestion that the killings were being carried out as part of a bizarre ritual.

KILLER STRIKES TWICE IN ONE NIGHT

The next two murders both occurred within an hour of one another on the night of September 30. Elizabeth Stride was born in Sweden and had started work as a domestic, but was then registered as a prostitute. On the evening of her murder, she was seen kissing and cuddling a short dark man near the Bricklayers Arms public house at around 11:00 p.m.

Three-quarters of an hour later, William Marshall spotted her in Berner Street talking to a man in a short, black cutaway coat and a sailor's hat. At 12:35 a.m., Stride and a young man were seen by a police constable opposite the International Workmen's Club. The man was aged around 28 and wearing a black cutaway coat with a hard deerstalker hat.

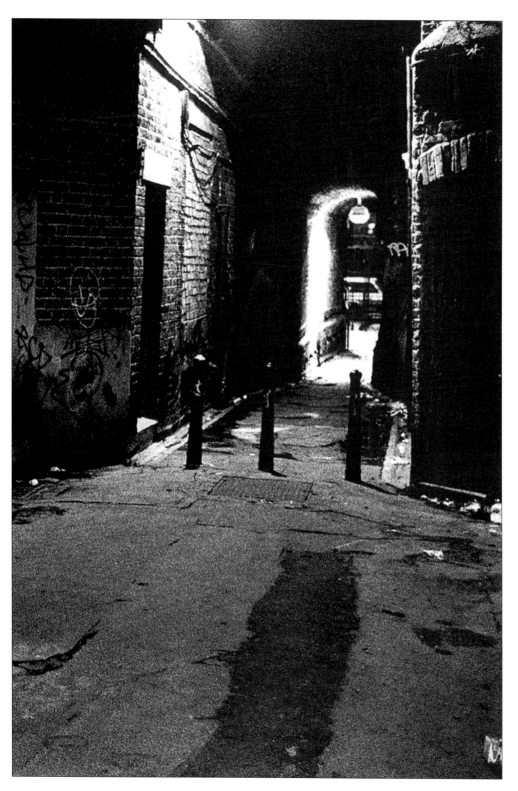

Jack seemed well acquainted with the grim backstreets and dark alleyways of Whitechapel, which made it an ideal territory for him to stalk his prey and then escape undetected. Even today, the brooding atmosphere of Victorian times still lingers in this east London neighbourhood, which has become forever identified with these notorious unsolved crimes.

The grotesquely mutilated body of Mary Jane Kelly, shockingly discovered in her own bed. The killer had cut away both breasts, the vagina, and even the young woman's heart. She was left legs akimbo; this may have had some sexual or childbirth significance for her depraved murderer, who must have fled the scene covered in blood.

Just minutes later, a man witnessed an argument between a man and a woman near the gateway to Dutfield's Yard, where the body of Elizabeth Stride was later found, at 1:00 a.m., when Louis Diemschutz drove his pony and cart into the yard. The animal shied at a bundle on the ground, which on closer inspection proved to be a woman's body. Her throat had been cut.

The second victim that same night was Catherine Eddowes, a very popular woman, described by the deputy of the lodging house where she usually stayed as 'very jolly, always singing'. She died in the early hours of September 30, but it was not until October 2 that the police learned her true identity. By 8:30 p.m. on her last evening, she had become so drunk that she was locked up by the police for her own welfare. They released her at about 1:00 a.m., and she made the comment that she would get a 'damn fine hiding'.

Eddowes's throat had been cut to the bone, bringing about immediate death, after which she had been mutilated. The walls of the abdomen were laid open from a cut that began at the breasts. Some internal organs had been removed. According to witnesses, Eddowes apparently believed that she knew the identity of the Ripper and, on the night of her death, was obviously in a hurry to meet someone.

It was on November 9 that the Ripper struck last. Mary Jane Kelly, born in Limerick, Ireland, had moved to Wales while still a child. In Cardiff, she became a prostitute, later taking up residence in a high-class London brothel. On the day of her death, Kelly spent the early evening with her friend Lizzie Aldbrook. Ironically, she had warned Aldbrook about the dangers of working the streets. Later, Kelly was seen in the company of a shabby, blotchy-faced man wearing a stiff felt hat, called a 'billycock'. He was carrying some beer, and Kelly appeared to be drunk. Later, between midnight and 1:00 a.m., she was heard singing loudly in her lodgings.

At 10 o'clock the following morning, a rent collector called on Mary Kelly to collect several weeks' arrears. When his knocks went unanswered, he peered through the window and was confronted by the horrific murder scene.

According to the doctor who assisted in the postmortem, Kelly's death occurred between one and two o'clock in the morning. However, other residents in Miller's Court reported cries of 'Oh, murder!' just before 4:00 a.m. The postmortem examination showed that the victim's throat had been cut. Her face had

Media coverage of the gruesome string of murders was intense, as police struggled to catch the killer. This illustrated newspaper describes details of the case, including the assertion that Elizabeth Stride's sister dreamt of her death at precisely the hour when she fell victim to Jack.

also been slashed and mutilated, with several facial features partly removed. Both of her breasts were also removed, as was the vagina, and skin and muscles from the thighs. Her heart had been excised and taken away.

JACK AND THE PSYCHIC DETECTIVES

Mediumship in the late nineteenth century was still in its infancy, but the Ripper case engendered enormous media speculation and inspired spiritualists to hold sittings in an attempt to reveal the killer. Some of these sessions were reported in the press. One group in Cardiff even claimed to have discovered that the man who had murdered Elizabeth Stride was

41

DETECTIVE FILE:
Robert James Lees: Royal clairvoyant

Did this 'spirit adviser' to Queen Victoria foresee in grisly detail Jack the Ripper's fourth killing?

According to his alleged diary, Lees claimed that, some time after the third murder, he had been writing in his study when he suddenly experienced a vision of a narrow court with a gin-palace nearby. He could see the bar's clock, which read 12:40 a.m. – closing time. In Lees's strange reverie, a man then entered a dark corner of the court, accompanied by a woman who was very drunk. The man placed a hand over her mouth, then slit her throat, before stabbing her repeatedly.

Lees went to the police with the story, but they were predicably sceptical – until the next murder happened exactly as he had described it. The face of the killer was etched on Lees's mind, and he recognized it instantly when he accidentally encountered chief suspect Dr William Withey Gull. Again, his claims led nowhere.

Despite the apparent accuracy of Lees's vision, there is some doubt as to the authenticity of the diary. In 1931, it was claimed that it had been a hoax perpetrated by a journalist at the *Daily Express*.

Lees's diary may have been a fake, but the medium independently stated that he did indeed corner Jack the Ripper – none other than Dr William Withey Gull.

middle-aged and lived in Commercial Road, or Commercial Street, and had been one of a gang of 12.

In Bolton, Lancashire, a sitting produced the information that Jack had 'the appearance of a farmer, though dressed like a labourer, with a strap around his waist and peculiar pockets'. He had a dark moustache and 'scars behind the ears and in other places'. The medium claimed that the killer would be caught carrying out a further murder. This patently did not happen. Other alleged psychics, including a clergyman, contributed information that they had received in dreams, but it all came to nothing.

A leading clairvoyant at the time of the murders was Robert James Lees. He is said to have displayed psychic abilities from infancy. It was rumoured that Queen Victoria consulted Lees about her dead husband, Prince Albert. Apparently, it was also said that the queen had authorized him to assist the police in the Ripper case, although there is no evidence for this.

Lees was serious about spirituality and wrote a number of books to increase public knowledge and understanding. These works, he claimed, were dictated by his spirit guides. Lees had long been receiving random images in his mind which he felt were connected with the Ripper murders. In October 1888, he offered his services to the police, as many psychics do with major crimes today, but the authorities showed little interest in employing him to help track this killer. He then contacted Scotland Yard.

Lees's involvement was not made public until April 1895, when an article appeared in the *Sunday Times Herald*. On three separate occasions, Lees had apparently received clairvoyant information relating to the case. In the first instance, he 'saw' one of the murders being committed and noted that the culprit was wearing a dark tweed suit and a light-coloured overcoat. He reported that the sense of evil had affected him so much that he had been forced to flee abroad for a time.

On another occasion, Lees was riding in a horse-drawn cab with his wife when he suddenly felt compelled to dismount and follow someone whom he was convinced was the murderer. He stopped a policeman, and then an inspector, who treated his claim with derision. The man in question was prime suspect Dr William Withey Gull. Later, he followed a psychic trail that led the police to the house of a 'prominent physician' whose wife worked at the Royal Court. Lees neither denied nor confirmed the story and did not name the physician, although he did say that the couple had a young boy. When questioned, however, Lady Gull confirmed that they had been visited by a medium and a police officer who had asked 'impertinent questions'.

After Lees's death in 1931, his diary was given wide publicity in the national press. This was one of the earliest examples of mass-market interest in psychic detection, although Lees's contributions are contentious in the context of psychic research.

THE HUNT CONTINUES

In 1998, a new book was published about the Ripper case, written by psychic Pamela Ball. *Jack the Ripper: A Psychic Investigation* was the result of her own attempts to contact both the victims and suspects by supernatural means. She describes herself as 'a psychic therapist, healer, and medium with over 20 years' experience'.

In her book, Ball states that she came to the case with no preconceptions or pressure to solve the mystery. Two assistants carried out conventional research into the case, and their findings were largely kept from the psychic as she worked. Ball used a number of paranormal methods, including astrology, dowsing, psychometry, and channelling.

Psychic Pamela Ball compiled astrological profiles of both victims and possible perpetrators, to try to learn more about their characters. She hoped to uncover some pattern in the killings, but was unsuccessful using this method.

Where there was sufficient detail regarding place, date, and time of birth, Ball was able to cast astrological charts to assess the personalities of the main players. She wondered if this would reveal common factors among the victims that had eluded conventional investigators, but perhaps had attracted the murderer. Unfortunately, her attempts failed to establish any significant links.

Pamela Ball and her assistants, Fiona Ball and James Eden, employed a pendulum as they dowsed, to ascertain the truth of certain information. While the questioner held the pendulum, it would swing in a circular motion, or back and forth, to denote 'yes' and 'no' respectively.

Psychometry was also used to try to glean information from objects associated with the crimes. By holding such a 'charged' item, a psychic can supposedly pick up 'vibrations' which can then be interpreted. In addition, Ball attempted to communicate directly with the spirits of both Ripper victims and suspects through alleged channelling from the afterlife. Once she had relaxed

and put herself into an altered state of consciousness, her assistants made notes while she spoke in this auto-hypnotic condition; an audio tape was also used to record the sessions.

Pamela Ball had begun her psychic quest by visiting a number of places associated with the murders in east London's Whitechapel. A brewery now stands on the site where Annie Chapman was killed in Hanbury Street. There, the psychic picked up a strong sense of resignation, which was repeated when she attempted to contact Annie's spirit. In the area that was once Miller's Court, where Mary Kelly was murdered, Ball experienced a feeling of nausea and strong pressure on the shoulders, along with the presence of a small, moustached man.

29 Hanbury Street, before it was demolished in 1963. Annie Chapman was murdered at the back of the building. She had been partially suffocated before her throat was cut. More than 100 years later, psychic Pamela Ball felt an unmistakable air of suffering endured at the site.

Consulting the Victims

In another experiment, Ball visualized the pages of a calendar turning backward. In this way, she was able to drift back to the late nineteenth century. On July 22, 1997, Pamela Ball found herself in touch with the spirit of Catherine Eddowes. More accurately, Ball says that the contact was primarily with the 'Akashic Record' of the deceased – a giant recording library of that person's entire life which she says is lodged in the 'ether'. Thus, it is not a matter of receiving straight answers, but rather a matter of picking up information, and then attempting to make sense of it.

Ball believes that Eddowes was murdered 'because she knew something'. The poor woman went to meet her murderer. Ball received the impression of a

In the wake of the murders, the terrified community formed the Whitechapel Vigilante Committee, chaired by a Mr Lusk. He is mentioned in the newspaper article below, having allegedly received a box from Jack the Ripper that contained a piece of Catherine ('Kate') Eddowes's kidney.

stocky man in his early 30s, with what she described as 'a strong, dark energy'. An image of a furtive figure she dubbed 'The Catcher' then came into her mind. She felt a discomfort in her neck and felt the man slash at Catherine Eddowes with a knife. Then Ball described how the killer had been disturbed.

One week later, contact was made with Elizabeth Stride. Ball felt Stride's anger flood into her, as well as her desperation as she hurried to meet 'somebody special'. The psychic reported: 'The feeling is that she was careless.' Ball said that she felt pains in her neck and leg as the murderer spun his victim around before finally pulling her to the ground.

The killer was described as tall, probably because of the hat he wore. Ball sensed that this man was considerably thinner than the one who had murdered Catherine Eddowes. Clearly, they were two different men. This one had a 'cultivated moustache' and 'very funny, very weird' eyes, and was in his early 40s. Ball commented: 'If this truly is Jack the Ripper, he doesn't feel terribly evil.'

Annie Chapman was contacted on August 5, and was said to be 'a gentle person, light at heart, and with a sense of humour'. Ball felt that Chapman was living on borrowed time when she was murdered. This impression was reinforced when the psychic suddenly began coughing and experienced difficulty breathing. As recalled, Chapman had, indeed, been seriously ill.

Ball felt that Chapman had been very unhappy most of the time, but was not a prostitute, although she may have supplemented her income in this way from time to time. She thought that she had been totally surprised by the attack and did not even see her killer. The psychic also sensed that he was a small, stocky man, with some sort of brain condition that was affecting his behaviour.

In a session held two weeks later, Mary Ann 'Polly' Nichols presented herself to the medium. During this contact, Ball experienced a number of physical sensations. They began with severe backache

SKETCHES IN CONNECTION WITH THE WHITECHAPEL AND ALDGATE MURDERS.

DETECTIVE FILE:
Pamela Ball: Psychic sleuth

Many 'psychic detectives' have attempted to crack the case of Jack the Ripper, which has resisted all conventional investigative methods.

One of the latest psychics to delve into the long-unsolved Jack the Ripper murders, Pamela Ball regards herself as a therapist and healer. With many years of experience as a medium, she says that she came to the case with 'no preconceived notions or ready-made suspects'. She claims that she merely wanted to adopt a fresh angle, 'to see whether a different approach to the conundrum, using psychic tools of investigation, could shed new light on the mystery'. Pamela Ball calls her method of investigation 'evidential mediumship'.

In the course of her experiments, employing techniques such as dowsing and psychometry, Ball had hoped to gain unique insights that could reveal new facts, offer some evidence for alternative theories, and perhaps explode a few well-established myths. However, she realizes that not everyone will share her views. As she explains: 'There are those who will find the methods used suspect, there are those who will disbelieve me, and there are those who will call me mad – that is their privilege.'

Like many other psychics, Pamela Ball employed a pendulum in her quest for new information about the Ripper murders. Crystals, which are often used in psychic investigations, are believed to possess energies that are attuned with the paranormal world.

down one side of her body (Nichols's spinal cord had been cut), followed by the sensation of a heavy weight pressing down on her left shoulder, and then a shortness of breath, as if she were being strangled. Ball believes that this woman was murdered by a different man than the others. This killer was short and worked quickly: 'It's so cold, not even cruel,' Ball says, 'it's something to do with his mother. He doesn't feel old, I would have thought early 30s. We can discount Gull, at least for this one.'

A few days later, the team conducted another session, this time involving Mary Tabram. Immediately, the medium felt that her hands were burning and sore, and her stomach churned. Ball saw a child born on March 28, 1863, with thyroid deficiency, and given the name 'Joseph'. Then the name 'Jenny Mountford' came to the psychic, indicating a married woman aged around 32 who had given birth to another man's child. Was this the same Lady Mountford associated indirectly with the case at the time?

Pamela Ball felt that all of the women who were murdered – except for Elizabeth Stride – shared knowledge of a secret concerning criminal activities and that this secret had a political dimension. She concluded from her research that 'Jack' was impotent, and blamed his mother for this. He wanted to have sex with his mother, who had abandoned him as a child; this explained why he singled out older women. The mutilations, she sensed, were intended to destroy his victims totally as women.

Ball and her assistants tried in vain to find firm evidence to support any of the information she had received psychically. They trawled the registers of births and deaths, searching for evidence of the baby and its mother, Jenny, looking under the name 'Mountford' and variations of it, all to no avail. The records of London hospitals were also perused, but produced nothing.

Ball also attempted to contact the various murder suspects. First was Montague John Druitt, whom Ball felt was a dreamer with a serious temper, and afflicted by terrible migraines. According to Ball, Druitt was dismissed from his teaching post because he broke down in front of his class, then took to wandering off on his own. She also had the impression that he may have been homosexual and afraid of women, but was too sensitive to have committed murder.

Ball then channeled James Maybrick, and experienced a sense of voyeurism, as if Maybrick had witnessed one of the killings but had not actually taken part. He seemed to have some first-hand knowledge about the murders of Stride and Eddowes. Aiming to explore another lead, Ball next tried to channel the Victorian psychic Robert James Lees. Lees seemed to be blocking something, a connection between the Ripper case and the Royal Family that he did not want revealed.

HANDLING THE EVIDENCE

Pamela Ball was given the opportunity to examine several relevant objects – the so-called 'Maybrick Diary', a knife supposedly left at one of the murders, and a shawl believed to have belonged to Catherine Eddowes.

On handling the diary, Ball experienced nausea and foreboding, but the vibration connected with the writer did not feel the same as that of Maybrick. Through the further use of the pendulum, Ball ascertained that the diary had been transcribed from the original by Maybrick's son, also called James. Ball asked whether Maybrick was associated with any of the murders. The answer came back as 'No', except for Elizabeth Stride.

The knife was thought to have been left beside the body of Annie Chapman, although there are no police records to verify this. It has been identified as of the type used for amputations, and manufactured in the 1870s. However, Ball could detect no connection with the murder. In contrast, when she held the shawl, the psychic had an overwhelming feeling that it was genuine, and that indeed it had been the property of Catherine Eddowes.

CRIME FILE:
Spring-Heeled Jack: Supernatural fiend

Tales of demonic serial killers were rife in the 19th century, fuelling a new fascination for the paranormal.

The bizarre figure of 'Spring-Heeled Jack' allegedly first appeared in Britain in September 1837. A tall man had assaulted a London woman by inflicting brutal slashes across her body with what she described as sharp claws. Similar attacks spread across southern East Anglia, but they were focused particularly in the capital's eastern suburbs.

Eyewitnesses soon reported that Jack was not human, but was instead a winged being with glowing red eyes and could leap huge distances, including from one rooftop to another, in order to escape being caught. Speculation was rife, and psychics claimed to know the identity of Jack. Theories ranged from the spawn of the devil to a deformed member of the aristocracy. In several ways, the saga paralleled the case of Jack the Ripper, which was to occur half a century later.

Only one murder was known to have been committed by Spring-Heeled Jack. In 1845, he was seen to attack a prostitute in east London and to breathe blue fire into her face before throwing her body into an open sewer, then leaping prodigiously out of the grasp of shocked witnesses.

Despite the clues given to police, Jack was never caught. Colourful tales about his appearance and behaviour developed, from the initial view that he was a madman wearing a disguise, into modern tales of a mythological creature.

Similar stories appeared in the eastern United States in January 1909, when the 'Jersey Devil' created havoc in farming communities. The leaping beast was said to have the jumping abilities of a kangaroo, the wings of a bat, and a monstrous bipedal body. It was even cornered in a Pennsylvania barn by pursuing police, but when the doors were forced open, the monster had disappeared like an apparition.

The last accepted sighting of Spring-Heeled Jack was in Everton, Liverpool, in 1904, where a possible imitator was chased across city rooftops, having frightened a number of women. A tall man with a red face was also reported in east London in 1975 as leaping in one bound across an entire street intersection. In a sign of the times, witnesses reported Jack as most probably being an alien!

In the nineteenth century, the supernatural 'man-beast' Spring-Heeled Jack terrorized London and has been seen sporadically in parts of Britain ever since. The fantastic claims made for his attacks have inspired many legends, yet no explanation has ever been reached for these incredible eyewitness accounts.

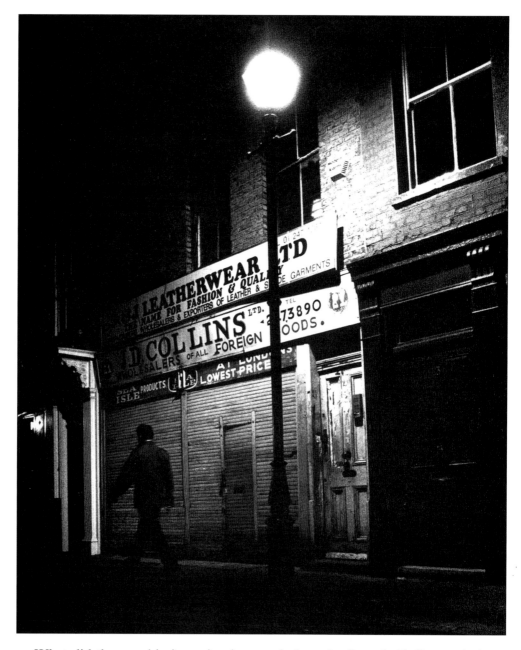

Spitalfields, the stamping ground of the mysterious serial killer (or killers) known as Jack the Ripper. By night, desolate streets such as this still echo with the sinister footsteps of the notorious murderer, whose identity may never be known.

What did the psychic investigation carried out by Pamela Ball reveal about the identity of Jack the Ripper? From the beginning of the contact sessions, she had felt that there were two independent murderers involved. One of them, she became convinced, was James Maybrick, whom she believed was responsible for the death of Elizabeth Stride; the other killings attributed to the Ripper had been carried out by someone else. She felt strongly that the women had not been targeted because they were prostitutes, but because they were mothers. Ball felt that the killer had been seeking revenge on his own mother by murdering and mutilating other women who were mothers themselves.

She commented on the mysterious character who presented himself to her under the image of 'The Catcher'. Ball had received the impression that this was a shadowy figure who regularly visited the East End and was known to all of the women. Was this 'Jack'? The psychic names James Maybrick as The Catcher.

Ball's final analysis was that all of the women held pieces of a jigsaw that had put them in danger and that Catherine Eddowes was trying to blackmail the Ripper when she was killed. Martha Tabram, she concluded, was murdered because she knew of an illegitimate child possibly fathered by the Prince of Wales. But she also puts Joe Barnett, Mary Kelly's common-law husband, in the frame because she had sensed psychotic elements in his personality.

MYSTERY STILL UNSOLVED

In the end, while Ball's psychic investigation had been a fascinating exercise, it revealed little that could be satisfactorily verified. Perhaps the only piece of information that we can rely upon was the answer to the question that she posed into the ether: 'Will we ever discover who Jack the Ripper was?' Pamela Ball's pendulum told her 'No'.

Pamela Ball's reservations about the authenticity of the Maybrick diary may be well founded, although others have challenged her views regarding its true author. In June 1994, it was alleged that a Michael Barrett wrote the 9,000-word document himself and had it copied into an old photographic album using Diamine Black manuscript ink containing nigrosine, a very unusual patent dye. If this is so, then Ball had been right when she said that the original author was not the man who had actually written the account into the diary. However, the debate has never been resolved, and some still believe the diary to be genuine.

One of the main criticisms of psychics is that they are often quite wishy-washy in their pronouncements, or simply wrong. If truly in touch with the dead, why are they apparently unable to give straight, factual answers to direct questions? Sceptics say this is because so-called psychics are either deluded or fraudulent. Psychics, however, have a different explanation.

Mediums and clairvoyants will say that their information is invariably correct, but is usually presented in a very obtuse way – not in words, but as impressions or emotions. These vague 'feelings' must then be analyzed and interpreted as best they can. Some mediums are better than others at decoding this data, and each individual's skills can vary from day to day, depending on his or her frame of mind at the time. Unfortunately, paranormal phenomena do not perform to order and can be rather slippery to pin down. This dilemma has always been the primary challenge of all psychic detectives, who continually struggle to make sense of their extraordinary gifts.

Tools of the Trade

W HEN FACED WITH DANGEROUS criminals, police defend themselves with anything from a baton to a gun. But what kind of weapons are at the disposal of the psychic detective? In fact, there is a wide assortment of tools with which they claim to be able to see beyond the realms of known science. Some of these techniques exploit phenomena that occur spontaneously, such as dreams or visions. Others, including dowsing and psychometry, require skills that must be refined with experience. All have one goal in mind – to help the police catch the perpetrators of crime. However, although the operating methods of psychic detectives can sometimes prove effective where traditional policework has failed, these paranormal aids are not easily harnessed, while the evidence uncovered is often very hard to decipher.

VISIONARY DREAMS

Dreams that foresee the future, or that provide extrasensory information, have always existed. They are the most common paranormal experience to be reported throughout history and are involved in most cases of psychic detection. Some incidents occur 'out of the blue', when a person not usually considered psychic has a dream that informs him or her about something extraordinary. Seasoned psychic detectives have regular experiences of this kind, and those that have often been found to 'dream true' can actively assist in police investigations. Unfortunately, when things are 'seen' in dreams ahead of time, or across vast distances, the messages received are invariably difficult to interpret, since dreams operate on a symbolic level.

Here, a forked branch is used as a dowsing rod, to find hidden mineral deposits or sources of water. Although dowsing is a technique that must be honed by practice, its effectiveness still relies on the innate abilities of the practitioner. The rods simply aid the process by magnifying the natural reactions of the body.

53

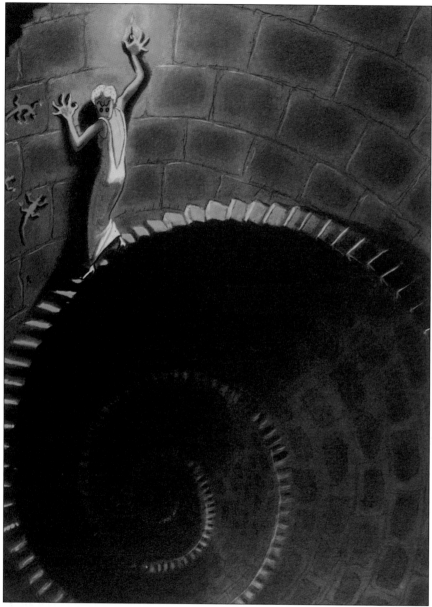

We all dream, even those of us who claim we never do so. In fact, every night, several hours or more are given over to our subconscious mind, which creates mental images as our bodies and conscious selves are on 'low power'. However, dreams are not added to our long-term memory; after we have woken, the dreams we had dissolve and are rapidly forgotten. We need to make a specific effort to recall them, by describing them to others or by writing the details down in a 'dream diary' within moments of waking. If we do not do this on waking, they become more and more fragile, and are often gone completely before we have left the bedroom.

DREAM LANGUAGE
Dreams also use a very different 'language' from waking consciousness, employing symbols to represent root human feel-

In dreams, vivid images and symbols reflect our innermost fears and phobias, such as being scared of heights. The significance of some dreams can often be difficult to decipher.

ings deep within our unconscious mind. They contract time and shift realities with apparent ease, and they are made up of a vast array of interwoven sources. Some dreams take memories of recent events and replay them. Others act as 'dry runs', testing out what it might be like to experience an event, such as getting married. Yet others are pure fantasy, exercising the strong creative faculties found in the parts of the brain involved in dreaming.

The major ongoing scientific controversy revolves around whether the dreaming mind can ever truly reach beyond the boundaries of time and space to add information to a dream plot involving events that have either not yet happened or are currently happening well beyond our normal range of awareness. Such dreams would inevitably be very useful in solving crimes. In less dramatic circumstances, dreams have been known to help hone one's intuition when pondering a baffling matter – working around the known facts and visually dramatizing a possible solution. Problem solving via dreams is an accepted phenomenon and implies no supernatural powers. For example, the scientist Friedrich von Kekule had been struggling to comprehend the form of

Eighteenth-century composer Tartini dreamt of Satan playing the music he needed for the final passage of a piece. From this inspiration, he transcribed the 'Devil's Trill Sonata'.

a complex chemical molecule. He puzzled over this so much that, as he slept, his dreams offered an answer! In them, he visualized a snake curling back on itself. On waking, the vivid imagery conjured by von Kekule's sub-conscious mind alerted him to the precise shape and structure of the benzene molecule, a mystery that had long baffled scientists.

It is quite likely that the process of intuition or 'hunches' – exer-cised, for example, by a number of police officers and other law enforcement officials – works in a similar way. A dramatic insight that might lead to a break-through in a case may arise as a result of their minds working on the facts of the problem and then sending a message in the form of an intuitive flash or

Scientists explore the mysteries of dreaming with an EEG (electro-encephalograph) to record brain-wave patterns, as seen here at a sleep study laboratory at the University of Loughborough. The tracings are then compared to the images seen in the subjects' dreams.

waking dream. Dreams during sleep may operate in a similar fashion, but are frequently more 'apparent'.

Our dreams take place while our brain rhythms alter phase. These go through a natural cycle during sleep and provoke changes in body chemistry, such as the release of certain hormones. It is possible that these changes play a role in how some people manage to access data from beyond the known senses.

Alterations to the electro-chemical transmission of nerve impulses are proving to be significant, as scientists begin to fully map these patterns. MRI (magnetic resonance imaging) techniques can now be used to highlight the significant changes that take place in the brain of a conscious or unconscious person as they think or dream.

INTERPRETING DREAMS

To most of us, dream recall is a confused mass of conflicting images, symbols, emotions, bizarre plots, and fragmented elements which can appear convincingly real. Learning to recall one's dreams, and then to decode them, is often the greatest challenge faced by anyone planning to become a psychic detective. It is likely that errors will be made in the translation process, and what may simply be fantasy or guesswork will sometimes be taken for a genuine paranormal vision. Equally, some true insights may seem so fanciful and unlikely that the dreamer simply dismisses them as imagination.

Psychic Michael Bentine – who had a number of 'unusual' experiences – once related how he struggled to decide whether he was 'dreaming true' or simply fantasizing: 'How does one tell if a dream is imagination or reality? All I can say is that I felt when something was real. The emotions were very strong. But there is little difference between imagination, intuition, and ESP. They are all part of the same process.'

Experiments carried out in sleep laboratories have convinced some scientists that, at the unconscious level, the mind can indeed gain access to information from beyond time and space. Results show this capability to be above the level of chance expectation – although not to any sufficiently high degree. This still leaves the probability that some dreams, believed to be psychic, are in fact only imagination. It may be the case, however, that some dreamers are so gifted at 'seeing true' that they vastly expand the level of success normally found in these sleep laboratory studies.

Automated equipment at this dream lab in Montpellier, France, incorporates a radar beam that reacts when the subject falls asleep. This triggers a video camera, which then records images of body movements during all the dream phases of sleep.

Dr Keith Hearne, a psychologist who has studied hundreds of reputedly paranormal dreams, emphasizes that the dreamer needs to be specific in their prediction. If a person dreams of a plane crash and predicts such an event, this cannot be considered useful evidence if a plane crashes a month later. Hearne

Dreams that appear to foresee the future often relate violent or tragic events, as if these deeply emotional scenarios somehow 'ripple' ahead of time with heightened energy, just as a large rock disturbs the water's surface when tossed into a pond. Plane crashes are a frequent subject of nightmares, although these visions generally do not mirror real events. Still, traumatic accidents can be vividly described in dreams that do come true.

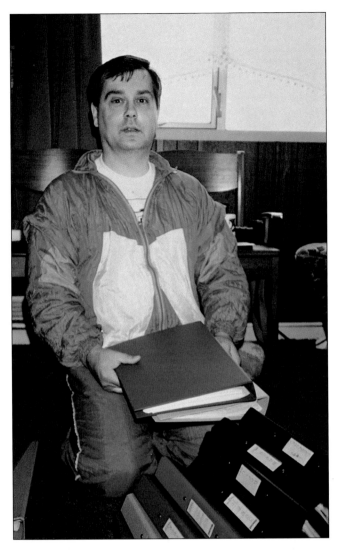

explains: 'Statistics show that there is one major plane crash in the world somewhere every two weeks. So a premonition about a plane crash has to be very specific for me to be interested in it.' In other words, the dream has to describe the aircraft type, the location, or other features that match extremely closely for chance to be relevant.

Upon waking, psychic dreamer Chris Robinson records his visions in notebooks, and then analyzes the symbol-laden images. If his interpretations suggest that a crime may be committed, he informs the local police, who, after Robinson's success with several cases, have accepted him as their most unusual informant.

All too often, what are viewed as premonitions are merely coincidences; billions of dreams are experienced every night. Chance matches with future events can be taken literally by the dreamer because many dreams have emotional significance. It is rather like winning the lottery. The odds of winning are enormous, yet many of us dream of it, and inevitably someone will succeed. If it occurs after a wish-fulfillment dream, then it may appear to that person that the dream has predicted their win.

Given the vast number of dreams that are dreamt every night, it is inevitable that a few will appear to resemble coming events. As Dr Hearne says, only when the specific details of these dreams go well beyond what coincidence should comfortably accommodate can we be sure that something more is taking place.

PSYCHIC DREAMING

One man who discovered how his dreams could help the police was Chris Robinson, from Luton, Bedfordshire, England. In 1989, he first realized that he was seeing local crimes in his dreams. He relates: 'I dream like everybody else. It's a mixture of pictures that you can recognize as being reality and

CRIME FILE:

Chris Robinson: Visions of a catastrophe

Tragedy could not be averted when dream warnings of a bomb appeared to direct police to the wrong city.

On June 1, 1996, Chris Robinson began to have a series of dreams warning of a terrible atrocity. Through symbolic images such as meat, concrete boots, and tall buildings with express elevators, Robinson became aware that a major city was soon to be bombed by terrorists. Could he use his experience as a psychic detective to prevent lives being lost?

As the dreams continued during early June, Robinson saw further images, including dogs, which he knew from past visions symbolized an attack by the IRA. Convinced that the bombing would be in London, he passed this information on to the authorities via his MI5 contacts.

However, Robinson was missing something that he did not recognize as significant. Many of the puzzling things that he was being shown began with the letter 'M': maps, mountains, the name 'McKinley', and so on. He knew that his dreams often directed him to the location of a crime by giving the letters of the town's postcode. Indeed, he guessed that the mysterious concrete boots meant CB – or Cambridge. Robinson entered in his notes the question: 'Who is M?', speculating whether the letter stood for the surname of a victim or perhaps that of the bomber. In fact, it represented neither.

By June 10, Robinson had been called by a woman in Kent named Jeanette (who declined to disclose her second name, as she feared she would become an IRA target if she aided in their capture). Jeanette had had dreams of future events and wanted to tell the more experienced police informant that she was now dreaming of a bomb attack on a city. A vision of Piccadilly in London, a place with which she was familiar, appeared in these dreams. This convinced her that the IRA was planning an attack on the capital.

Since this seemed to confirm the interpretation that Robinson was giving for his own dreams, it now seemed clear that a major terrorist outrage was imminent in London. The authorities were duly warned, and security was stepped up – an act that Robinson now feels might have led to a last-minute change of plans by the bombers, who, perhaps frightened out of the capital, may have turned elsewhere.

A few days later, a bomb was planted in a car outside a shopping centre in the northern city of Manchester. It was a Saturday morning, and the streets were crowded with shoppers. After a coded warning from the IRA, the police desperately directed several thousand people away from the area, to the edge of Piccadilly Gardens. Moments later, one of the largest terrorist bombs in peacetime detonated, exploding with such ferocity that, even in the safe haven to which these people were ushered, some were knocked to the ground. Closer to the blast site, hundreds of people were injured by flying debris. Only one person was killed, thanks both to good fortune and to a well-executed and calm evacuation of the crowded complex. Had the bomb detonated minutes earlier, it is likely that hundreds would have died inside the twisted metal and collapsing

The horrific aftermath of the IRA bomb that devastated the centre of Manchester in June 1996. The Victorian postbox that survived the blast was later brought back into service as the area was rebuilt. After the blast, the box was emptied and all the letters delivered as normal, and it now carries a small plaque marking its extraordinary history.

concrete walls of the cavernous shopping mall. The devastation was so immense that a vast area in the heart of the city was demolished, with the damage sustained resembling that suffered during raids by Hitler's bombers in World War II. It took four years and millions of pounds to restore the site, and scars can still be seen. The adjacent bus station was so badly damaged that it was never deemed safe enough to reopen.

The dreams of Chris Robinson and Jeanette had been remarkably accurate. Indeed, Chris was even able to narrow the date and time down to within a two-hour window on that Saturday morning. Yet, he had been so sure that London was to be the target that he had turned down flat a request by a German television channel to do an interview there the day before. His timing had been precise, but his perceived target was 200 miles (322km) away from the real danger. However, details described from his dreams about the focal point of the attack, the high number of injuries, and other items were all correct. In retrospect, the answer to his question 'Who is M?' was obvious: M is the postcode for Manchester. And Jeanette had been right to identify Piccadilly as the target. She was simply unaware that the Piccadilly in question was in this case at the centre of another major British city.

Time in the dream state does not seem to flow as it does in waking reality. The past, present, and future all intertwine, making it possible to 'see' a crime even before it is committed. The question is: can it then be prevented? On a literal level, psychic detectives such as Chris Robinson have learned that certain recurrent dream symbols, such as clocks, have specific meanings for them.

pictures that really could not exist.' He adds that he sees these images in the form of symbols, and that only gradually did he come to appreciate what the appearance of a 'bee' or a 'clock' in one of his dreams would signify. This makes him very much more like the ancient oracles than might be appreciated, although psychic dreaming is not generally the literal seeing of an event unfolding before one's eyes, as was allegedly practised at Delphi. Instead, Robinson sensed that his powerful and intense dream vision was a warning of a disaster or crime yet to happen.

After he had offered the Bedfordshire police several clues from decoded dreams that helped with pending cases, Robinson became registered as an official informant. This was crucial when, in May 1990, he had a vivid dream in which dogs were scuttling through a graveyard to a location where cameras and ticking clocks were significant. He deduced from these dream symbols that terrorists were going to bomb a Royal Air Force (RAF) base in Stanmore, Middlesex, and he promptly informed the guards on duty. Still unsure if they would take him seriously, Robinson followed this up by driving to the base and insisting on giving a statement.

Fortunately, his status with the Luton police ensured that the baffled military authorities listened in earnest. A month later, the event that Robinson had warned of did indeed occur, when terrorists sneaked onto the base via an adjacent graveyard and blew up the photographic stores. Thankfully, nobody was hurt in the attack.

Despite his successful prediction, Robinson had not been precise enough about the timing to act as a deterrent. Seeing a crime before it happened did not, in this case, serve to prevent it. Detective Sergeant Richard McGregor explained that the biggest problem police face when dealing with these unconventional informants is that their dreams 'resemble cryptic clues in a crossword'. They usually make sense after an event has occurred, but are rather more difficult to interpret beforehand. Sadly, that is true of many psychic dreamers.

PROVING DREAM PREDICTIONS

Psychic dreamers have tried to prove their abilities in a number of ways, and Chris Robinson agreed to blind tests performed in front of live cameras. In October 1994, he appeared on a British morning television show; the night before, a member of the television crew had secretly locked an item in a sealed box. Robinson announced that he thought the contents was likely to be a child's toy because, during the hours before the show, he had dreamt of a telephone box, a postman's sack with Christmas presents, and a childhood friend nicknamed 'Dolly'. He was right. As the box was opened, the stunned audience saw a teddy bear revealed. Even more extraordinary was that the toy had been placed inside by a production worker whose family ran a post office and who had been born on Christmas Day. Robinson's dream had seemingly portrayed all of this in symbolic form.

Dave Mandell, another psychic dreamer, has assisted police in fighting terrorist crimes, but uses a different method to establish his credentials. He sketches the graphic images that he sees in a dream, then photographs himself holding the sketch while standing in front of a bank or other building which has a clock displaying both the date and time in full view. When the event witnessed in his dream occurs, the photo offers proof that he really did foresee the event, often just a few days before it happened.

On March 8, 1994, Mandell went even further, when he appeared on the television news show 'London Tonight' to display an image, drawn from a series of dreams, in which a shower of lights, similar to fireworks, rose from a line of parked cars before falling to the ground. He wrote on the sketch (again, filmed using his usual method in front of a clock at a local bank) that the lights seemed to fall onto a 'river or runway'. After tens of thousands of people had witnessed Mandell's prediction on television, his grim warning came true the very next day. IRA terrorists shelled the runway at London's Heathrow Airport,

Police inspect a burned-out car at a hotel near London's Heathrow airport, after it was used to launch mortars at the runway. Hours earlier, psychic Dave Mandell had dramatically predicted the attack on television. His dream of a shower of lights rising from a row of parked cars and falling onto a 'river or runway' proved uncannily accurate.

launching mortar bombs from a line of parked cars. Fortunately, no injuries were involved in this intriguing case of psychic detection.

THE PRICE OF FAILURE

Psychic dreamers do not always succeed in averting disaster. When they fail to convince the authorities to act, the outcome can be devastating.

Chris Robinson had a series of dreams in the summer of 1993, in which a man, surrounded by bees, was being attacked and killed. It appeared to be a scene in Africa. The following day he met an American woman, Kathy Eldon, whose son Dan was a news photographer in Somalia. His award-winning photographs had appeared in *Time* and *Newsweek*.

Robinson's dreams clarified as the weeks went by and culminated on July 10, when he 'saw' four people being brutally attacked by water and other apparently symbolic items, including cameras. He was certain that this meant

CRIME FILE:
Foiled hold-up in Arizona

Dorothy Nickerson had occasionally dreamt of events before they happened, but never imagined that her visions would one day prevent a crime.

One November night in 1982, Nickerson awoke in the early hours in a cold sweat, with a scene being played out in the dark bedroom before her eyes. She saw a grocery store in shadow, a clock that read a quarter after midnight, and two men carrying out an armed raid on the terrified women manning the counter.

Sure that this was just a bizarre nightmare, she went downstairs to make coffee, trying to forget what she had just witnessed. But that proved very difficult, especially once she realized that the store she had seen was the Circle K supermarket in the nearby small town of Cottonwood.

Throughout the day, Nickerson tried to put this weird dream behind her by watching television, but she could not focus on the daytime soaps. Instead, she suddenly saw the scene on her television screen shimmer, to be replaced by a rerun of the robbery. Now she could see it all in detail. A customer left, leaving two women alone in the store. Then two men walked in, one a big moustached man who looked Mexican, the other smaller and not Hispanic. The pair had guns and threatened the shopkeepers with violence. Before she could see if they opened fire, the scene vanished and her usual television show reappeared.

All day, Dorothy Nickerson trembled and was uncertain what to do. Should she call the police? Would they think she was a crank? Surely this event could not really happen … Yet, overwhelmingly, she felt certain that it would – and tonight.

When her husband returned from work that evening, she shared her dilemma with him. He agreed that, if she felt so strongly, then she ought to contact the store's owner. So she made the call, suggesting that the owner empty the cash box before midnight and employ someone to protect her staff, since she was sure there was going to be a robbery. The bemused owner merely acknowledged the information politely and hung up. However, minutes later, a night-duty sergeant phoned Nickerson, saying that he had just been called by the concerned owner of the Circle K and wished to know more about the robbery. She duly explained what she knew.

As the night wore on, she hovered by the telephone, unsure which would be preferable – news that the robbery had occurred (meaning she was not going crazy) or that it had never materialized (in which case, she had no doubt that the Cottonwood police would view her with understandable suspicion).

At 1:00 a.m., the police called again. They had posted a patrol car outside the store and, just after midnight, had seen a man loitering outside an adjacent building, acting strangely. As he matched the description of one of the two men Nickerson had described, they questioned him. The police discovered that he was indeed carrying a gun and arrested him before he could carry out his intended plan to rob the convenience store. The 'Mexican' man was not with him, but Dorothy Nickerson was convinced that, if the police had acted a few minutes later and struck at 12:15 a.m., both culprits would have been apprehended.

For centuries, dowsing has been used to locate underground mineral deposits, as shown in this illustration from De Re Metallica, *1556.*

danger for Dan Eldon and attempted to warn the man's mother to act. However, she was sure that her son was safe.

On July 12, Dan and three other journalists were brutally attacked and killed on the Somalian coast at Mogadishu. Many of the images seen in Robinson's dreams fitted precisely with the events that unfolded.

Robinson was devastated by his inability to prevent this tragedy, despite sensing what was going to happen. 'It was all there and we did not stop it. I felt that I had failed', he said. Indeed, he felt as if he had not done enough and shouldered the responsibility for an event that was clearly beyond his control. Many psychic dreamers have assumed this heavy burden, feeling that they should have acted more vigorously to ensure their concerns were heard. However, without the benefit of hindsight, it is very difficult for others to heed such warnings.

THE ART OF DOWSING

Dowsing, which is also known as divining, is the apparent ability to locate water, minerals, and other objects psychically, by means of a pendulum or a pair of hand-held rods which act as indicators. Dowsing – usually with a pendulum over a map – has been commonly used by psychic detectives in their search for suspects, clues, and even bodies.

Chinese accounts from the Hsia dynasty record that Emperor Ta Yu, born around 2205 BC, was a dowser. There is a picture of the emperor holding a forked rod, with an inscription which reads: 'Yu of the Hsia dynasty was a master in the science of the earth and in those matters concerning water veins and springs; he was well acquainted with the Yin principle, and when required built dams.'

German mining expert Georgius Agricola wrote one of the first major European books on mining and metallurgy in the sixteenth century. His work *De Re Metallica* (which translates as 'On Metals') contains illustrations of dowsers finding locations for miners to dig for ore.

Dowsers who use rods will customize any item for the job. Traditionally, a forked hazel twig is used, but lengths of wire in a single 'Y' form, or two L-shaped rods, can also be utilized. These are often fashioned from wire coat hangers. As the dowser walks slowly across the search area, the ends of the rods are held loosely in the hands at chest height, tilted slightly forward. At the same time, the dowser concentrates on what he or she is looking for. When the rods react – usually by swinging sharply downward, inward, or outward – this indicates where the material or object should be found.

Map dowsing is the form usually adopted by psychic detectives. Here, the dowser moves a pendulum around a map, in an effort to locate people or objects.

German artist and dowser Peter F. Strauss taking part in an experiment using a special metal rod. Dowsers find that certain instruments work better for them than others; it is a matter of trial and error. Here, as Strauss approaches the item that he is searching for, the rod flips violently upward to indicate its presence.

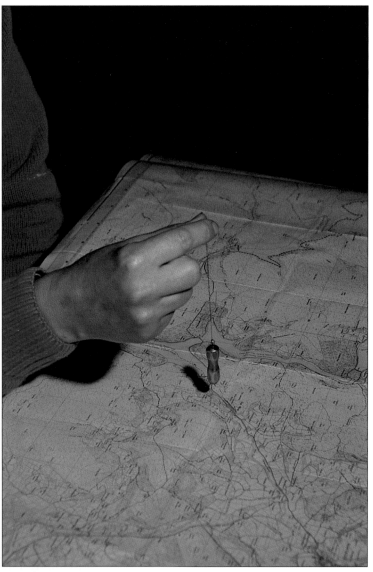

The pendulum consists of a weight on the end of a cord and allegedly responds to questions, circling or swinging back and forth, with one movement meaning 'no' and the other 'yes'. The orientation varies from dowser to dowser, and the chord length may also be altered to detect different substances. Some dowsers simply move a hand over the map until they feel a reaction.

Both methods can also be combined. Oil dowser Greg Storozk told researcher Chas Clifton: 'I won't go out of my house on any dowsing job unless I dowse the map first.' He added: 'When I map dowse, I think of my spirit flying over the ground the map represents. I put my eyes in the tip of the pen or pencil that I'm moving over the map.'

HOW DOES IT WORK?

There are a number of theories to explain how dowsing works. Although the scientific community tends to deny that the phenomenon even exists, some empirical research supports its validity. In the 1970s, Czech-born physicist Dr Zaboj V. Harvalik attempted to explain how

Map dowsing for leys, reputed to be invisible lines of energy that criss-cross the Earth. It is said that the ancients built their temples along leys, which we can plot on maps by locating Christian churches built on top of these pagan ruins.

the body reacts to the presence of underground water and minerals. He set up networks of buried wires and sought to determine how small a current of electricity flowing through them could be detected by dowsers. He also shielded various areas of dowsers' bodies with metal sheets, to establish which parts of their body were sensitive to detecting electrical fields. He concluded that there were dowsing sensors around the kidneys and near the pituitary and pineal glands of the brain.

Archaeologist Tom C. Lethbridge was one of the first to carry out studies into pendulum dowsing in the 1930s. Through dowsing, he found the ancient hill carvings of the Gog and Magog just outside Cambridge, England. Initially,

Lethbridge was certain that the pendulum was responding to electromagnetic fields present in nature. Then he found that the length of the cord could make a difference, as well as the emotional state of the dowser. The pendulum would even react differently when discovering male and female human remains.

Experiments were carried out on a number of dowsers, including Storozuk, during the September 1982 annual convention of the American Society of Dowsers. They were hooked up to a device to read brain wave signals – a multi-channel electroencephalograph called a 'mind mirror'. When the participants detected a signal, the mind mirror recorded bursts of alpha and delta waves, reflecting the states of altered consciousness associated with deep dreaming.

However, some dowsers opt for a metaphysical explanation. They suggest that the 'higher self' receives information by interfacing with a 'collective unconscious'. This theory was first put forward by the Swiss psychologist Carl Jung, who proposed the existence of a 'super mind' containing every thought

There is a strong commercial application for dowsing. Clayton McDowell discovered oil in Edwards County, Illinois, in 1983 using this technique.

CASE FILE:
Paul Smith:
Money talks

Blessed with a talent he can explain only as God-given, Paul Smith had no doubt that he would triumph in the ultimate dowsing contest.

Farmer Paul Smith had the gift of dowsing and had successfully located water and oil on land around his native Texas. Then, in the spring of 1985, Smith received a circular advertising a meeting sponsored by the Seven Continent Dowsers, to be held toward the end of May in Glenwood, Illinois. The leaflet invited readers to a challenge. A certificate was to be hidden on a five-and-a-half acre estate, and contestants would have just 20 minutes to find the piece of paper, which was redeemable for a gold coin worth around $800.

As Smith read the circular, he felt a current of energy rise through his arm and intuitively knew that he would be the one to locate the certificate. Despite the fact that Elizabeth, his wife, was pregnant with their second child and there were plenty of things to do around the farm, Smith felt he had no choice but to attend the meeting. He told his wife that he was certain the child would not be born until after his return. Elizabeth was used to her husband's strange premonitions and implicitly trusted him. So Smith duly called fellow dowser Edwin Sarnachi, who was organizing the contest, and made arrangements to travel to Illinois. Sarnachi was quickly charmed by Smith's enthusiasm and his assertion that the $800 gold coin would be his.

Smith arrived early, and he listened as the older dowsers talked about their methods and gave advice to newcomers. Sarnachi then explained to the competitors that the certificate had been hidden somewhere in the trees around a lake. Several false clues had been planted, and the find had to be handed to Sarnachi within 20 minutes of the start of the search. He estimated there was a one-in-a-thousand chance of anyone locating the piece of paper in time.

As the contenders scattered in the woods, the hunt began. Smith followed the others, then sat down on a stump and sketched a map of the area, dividing it in half – north and south. By holding his hand over the map, he determined that the object lay in the south. He then divided that portion into east and west. Smith ran his hand over it until he felt a tickle, and then stopped. A surge of energy travelled up his arm, and he knew that the certificate lay hidden somewhere in the southwest quadrant.

Smith made his way through the trees by the lake and came across a creek, and he immediately felt that this was where the certificate was hidden. As he moved down a bank, he discovered a metal sluice gate. He examined his feelings and then decided that he should investigate further. Smith put his arm through the metal bars of the gate and his fingers closed around a roll of paper. He had found the certificate – and within the 20-minute deadline.

On Sunday May 26, 1985, Paul Smith was presented with his prize – a solid gold Liberty Head coin dated 1877. He declined numerous offers to buy it and chose to keep the coin as proof of his dowsing skills. Smith believes that dowsing is a gift from God.

He was right about the baby, too. His son was born on June 10.

that everyone has ever had. Allegedly, a dowser can obtain information from this super mind in the same way that some psychics claim to be able to read a gigantic record of all life history. This data is then relayed to the unconscious, which moves the rods or pendulum appropriately to alert the conscious mind.

SCIENTIFIC EVIDENCE FOR DOWSING

In the early 1920s, influential researcher Abbé Mermet suggested that dowsing worked because objects gave off radiation, and that when the human body entered such fields they were picked up by the nervous system, which then caused muscular movements in the hands. A considerable amount of research was carried out to identify the nature of these supposed radiation fields, particularly by the De la Warr Laboratories. It was concluded that they were linked

The famed Swiss psychologist Carl Jung, pictured front right, proposed the idea of a 'collective unconscious' or 'super mind', which dowsers and other psychics may be able to tap into. Jung's novel theories on the subconscious conflicted with those of his one-time mentor Freud, seen here seated on the far left.

to 'new worlds beyond the atom'.

At the time that Mermet was writing, the complete but paradoxical quantum theory was just emerging. Quantum mechanics postulates that energy can exist as a wave or a particle depending on the circumstances. It has been shown that subatomic particles can react to one another, even though there is no apparent causal relationship. Parapsychologists point to quantum theory as a possible explanation for paranormal phenomena in general and dowsing in particular.

More recently, Professor Hans-Dieter Betz published the results of his dowsing research, carried out over several years in 12 different countries. The 73-page analysis was reported in *The Journal of Scientific Exploration*. Betz found that dowsers' success rates were often twice as great as those that could be expected using orthodox methods of water exploration.

Martyn Taylor, of the Association for the Scientific Study of Anomalous Phenomena (ASSAP), carried out a dowsing experiment at the Fortean Times UnConvention in London during April 2000. He hid a live electrical circuit, together with other unconnected wires, in a ladder-shaped lattice. Participants had to dowse for the live wires without any visible clues, and to determine in which direction the current flowed. Four people not only discovered the live wire, but also correctly dowsed the direction of the current flow.

GOLD DIGGERS

The famous Uri Geller has dowsed on the Solomon Islands for both gold and diamonds, finding deposits that were later successfully mined. Merely driving over an area was often enough for him to pinpoint a location.

Best-selling fiction writer Stephen King has had his own brush with the phenomenon of dowsing. He recalls how, as a boy of 12, he would dowse with his Uncle Clayton. King's uncle used a wishbone-shaped piece of applewood because it worked best for him.

That particular summer, the well where his aunt and uncle drew their water was running dry. One day, Uncle Clayton grabbed hold of his nephew and told him they were going to dowse for a new well. King was sceptical. Clayton walked apparently aimlessly around the back garden, along the drive, and up onto a hill. The writer remembers how his uncle talked about all sorts of things while he was doing this, then occasionally stopped, and the applewood fork would tremble, just a little. He would then continue.

At this point, Stephen King was sure that his uncle was making the twig vibrate. As they crossed the front lawn, the twig began to quiver again, then suddenly twisted and pointed downward. The motion was so violent that King could not see how his uncle had made it happen. Now he wanted to try! Uncle Clayton stepped back to the edge of the lawn and handed the youngster the divining rod. This is how Stephen King described what happened:

Stephen King is the world's most prolific and successful horror writer. His stories often embrace the pararnormal, which he himself experienced at first hand when as a boy he had a dramatic dowsing experience.

'I started walking toward the spot where Uncle Clayton had been when the rod dove, and I'll be damned if that applewood stick didn't seem to come alive in my hands. It got warm, and it began to move. At first it was a vibration that I could feel but could not see, and then the tip of the rod began to jiggle around … At one moment it was upright, and at the next it was pointing straight down. I can remember two things very clearly about that moment. One was a sensation of weight – how heavy that wooden wishbone had become … the other [was] a combined feeling of certainty and mystery.'

It was three or four years before the well was dug. A hole was drilled 100ft (30m) into the ground – less than a yard (1m) from where they had dowsed. They had discovered a huge quantity of water.

LOST AND FOUND

Dowsing has also been used successfully to locate missing persons. In one notable case during the 1980s, in Bath, Maine, Baptist Minister Robert Ater used his dowsing skills to find two students who were lost. One cold April evening, Ater heard on the news that two University of Maine students had not

How does a pendulum work? Some believe that an ethereal power causes it to swing. Another, rather more mundane, explanation is that tiny, sub-conscious muscle movements are responsible. In any event, a pendulum is merely an indicator – like the hand on a watch or the needle of a compass – by which information may be passed to the conscious mind.

returned from a hiking trek into New Hampshire's White Mountains, which were then being swept by blizzards.

In practice, Ater dowses with a pencil and map, which involves two procedures. The first he calls 'dropping in', where the point of the pencil hits the map. The pencil then begins to follow a trace, which Atar calls 'channelling'. When this occurs, he says: 'It's as if my pencil is travelling in a well-defined groove.'

Robert Atar, like many other dowsers, stresses the importance of consciousness in the process: 'State exactly to yourself what you wish to find. Become involved in it personally. Dowsing is a natural function of man. Ancient peoples knew this. Primitives in our own time demonstrate powers of the brain that are occluded in so-called civilized persons.'

When he heard about the two missing students, Atar thought about his own two teenage boys while he spread a road map out on the table. He located Mount Washington, the goal of the walkers, and held his pencil over Crawford Notch, where it was thought they had parked their car. He asked himself: 'Exactly where is the trail the hikers took as they began their ascent?' The pencil moved back and forth erratically, then Atar 'felt' along a path, settling on Pinkham Notch, eight miles (13km) from Crawford. The dowser knew that Pinkham was the place where the students had left their car.

The pencil moved around Mount Clay, across the bottom of Mount Washington, then stopped abruptly at a point between Mount Adams and Mount Jefferson. Atar was certain that this was the place where the boys had sheltered from the storm and phoned weatherman Jonathan Lingol at the observatory on Mount Washington. Lingol did not dismiss the information and wrote down the dowser's coordinates, mainly because it was some distance from the walkers' supposed route and had not been searched.

Just as Robert Atar had predicted, the students were found in a crude shelter midway between Mount Adams and Mount Jefferson. They were discovered alive by the Appalachian Mountain Club one week after being reported missing. Atar received an appreciative letter from Jonathan Lingol. 'Mr Lingol [thanked] me for my effort and affirm[ed] that the two hikers were found exactly where I predicted, and their car had indeed been parked at Pinkham, rather than Crawford Notch'.

POWER OF THE PENDULUM

One of the most successful dowsers of missing persons was Captain Vo Sum of the South Vietnamese Navy. He had been introduced to pendulum dowsing by his father, who had himself dowsed to find Vo Sum's elder brother. The young man had disappeared in France, and his father was informed by the pendulum that he had been taken seriously ill and had died in Marseilles. Several years later, the old man learned that his son had indeed passed away in the French Mediterranean port.

Psychics require a strong focus when they are searching for missing persons. A photograph is ideal, of course, since it enables them to concentrate on an exact image and direct all their energies toward that one individual.

It was 15 years before Vo Sum took up the mantle. When he discovered he, too, had the skill, Vo Sum decided to try to find some of his compatriots who had disappeared during the Vietnamese war. He invited his kinsmen to send him photographs of their missing relatives, over which he suspended a small piece of ebonite on a string. If it turned clockwise, it indicated to him that the subject was alive; if it moved counterclockwise, it would indicate that they were dead. Vo Sum then tried to locate the individual by slowly moving the pendulum over a map. When it twirled rapidly over one spot, it told him where the subject was located.

As he continued with this work, Vo Sum found that many of his compatriots appeared to be located in six specific areas –

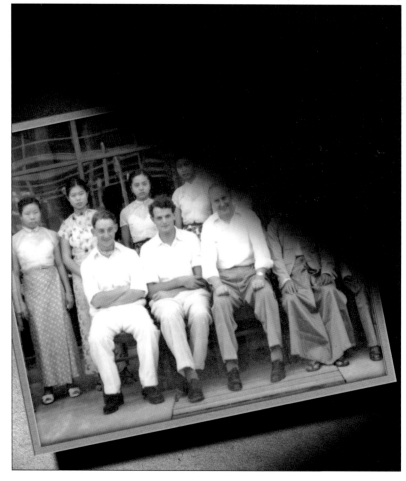

CASE FILE:

Michael Bentine: Daydream of a hostage crisis

Writer and comedian Michael Bentine had psychic experiences throughout his life. The most dramatic of these was a vision in 1980 of the raid to free American hostages in Iran. He was in the unenviable position of 'watching' as this rescue attempt went disastrously wrong.

How was a covert military operation deep in the Iranian desert 'picked up' by a comedian relaxing in Spain?

In the fall of 1980, time was running out for a group of Americans who had been kidnapped by terrorists in Iran. As the world waited to see what President Jimmy Carter would do to try to secure their release, one man, relaxing in Spain, found himself dreaming about a strange land and a terrible battle. He had just witnessed a shocking new development in the hostage crisis – one that was still top secret.

Michael Bentine is best remembered today for his wit and comic performances as a member of the famous 'Goons', but he was also a man who lived with psychic dreams and visions throughout his life. In October 1980, he was taking a break at his villa in Spain, where he was working on writing a book. Suddenly, he began to daydream and his head was filled with unexpected images.

'On my inner screen I could see a five- or six-storey building, barbed wire around the wall, helicopters hovering overhead, and I thought: *What the heck is going on?* Then I saw two single-decker buses crash into the gates of what was obviously a compound and I thought: *My God! I am picking up an attempt to rescue the hostages.*'

As Bentine pieced together the images from this strange daydream, he could see the complete plan laid out, as if he were picking it up direct from the troops then waiting to launch the assault. He could see aircraft – which he recognized as C-130 Hercules transporters – hidden in the desert and felt an overwhelming sense of doom. He knew that this brave effort was set to end in both failure and death.

Similar things had happened to him 'out of the blue' before, and Bentine had himself recognized that 'when I am in a relaxed state of mind and perhaps someone is transmitting, then I can be receiving'. Certain that he had seen the events as they were unfolding thousands of miles away, he switched on the radio, but there was no news of a rescue attempt. As the hours passed, he began to wonder how he could have had such a powerful vision without it signifying a real event. The answer was frightening. If this was a forewarning of an event that had yet to happen, Bentine knew that lives were at stake. Soldiers were about to be shot during a raid that would go dreadfully wrong. What could he do to prevent this?

'I had a couple of friends in the House of Commons', he told us. 'So I decided to ring them, and my wife said: "Don't be ridiculous. There is an English-speaking operator. This is just a tiny village. The minute you start speaking to an MP about this they'll be round here with a police car."' Balancing these reservations against his desperate need to help, Bentine instead sent a private express message to a senior government figure, hoping officials would warn the Americans. In the meantime, the raid took place, ending in tragic failure, just as foreseen in the psychic's dream.

Several days later, the MP replied to Bentine on official government notepaper and said, very circumspectly, 'My dear Michael, what a remarkable coincidence'. Bentine knew this meant that the message had got through, but this could not be openly admitted. But the minister added: 'You did not get it all right. You went wrong on the buses.' According to the news reports that had filled the media, no such vehicles had been used to break down the compound gates. Indeed, this inability was one of the reasons for the delay and failure of the mission. Unexpected problems with both the Hercules aircraft and the helicopters had thwarted the plans.

A year later, Bentine was on tour in the United States, when he was introduced to a CIA officer who was seeking a candid word. 'We are terribly interested in that business about your picking up the hostage raid', he was told, to which Bentine responding by repeating what had happened and noting his apparent inaccuracy about the buses. 'You were not wrong', the CIA man said sombrely. 'The plan was indeed for two buses to crash into the gate at the same time as the rest happened. But this never occurred because the mission went wrong. We have not publicized that fact. How did you know?'

All that Michael Bentine can say is that he did know. He saw it in his mind's eye a day before the events took place. If it had been possible to warn the White House and convince President Carter to take the advice of a psychic seriously, then lives might well have been saved.

A more successful anti-terrorist raid occurred when the SAS (the UK's Special Air Service) landed on the Iranian embassy in London and rescued hostages held inside. This event had a happy ending and provoked no known premonitions. Perhaps it was the harrowing emotions connected with the tragic attempt in Iran that spawned Bentine's psychic 'daydream'.

Such was Captain Vo Sum's reputation that the Vietnamese navy enlisted him to help find a junk believed by the authorities to be smuggling raw opium. The famous master of the pendulum tackled the problem using a photograph of a similar ship, like the one above. Under Vo Sum's direction, the junk was located and the drugs seized, completely vindicating the military's confidence in his extraordinary skills.

three of them in Cambodia and Laos. Captain Vo Sum wondered if he had found prisoner-of-war camps hitherto unknown to either the American or South Vietnamese military authorities. He wrote to the US Ambassador in Saigon offering his services, but was turned down by the Second Secretary of the US Embassy, William F. Eaton. The American authorities were not interested in employing a dowser to help them search for missing military personnel. Therefore, Vo Sum decided to concentrate on finding his own kinsmen. His talents came dramatically to the fore during a military incident in 1974.

It began when Chinese troops landed on some disputed islands to assert Peking's sovereignty, and the South Vietnamese admiralty sent a flotilla to remove them. Captain Vo Sum was part of the mission in charge of inter-ship communications. During the short battle that ensued, a Vietnamese patrol boat took a direct hit, disabling her communications equipment. It was Vo Sum's job to maintain contact, so he decided to locate her by dowsing. Using her name, *Nhat-Tao* HQ-10, he suspended his pendulum over a nautical chart and determined that the vessel was moving in a south–southwesterly direction.

As there was no other information to act upon, Admiral Tran-Van-Chon, operations chief of the task force, decided to follow up Vo Sum's findings. Twenty-four hours later, Vo Sum updated the admiral on the stricken ship's position. The search was hampered by the Chinese military, but Vo Sum kept updating his information, and two days later the men were rescued at the location he had predicted. The men reported that two crew members had drifted away on a raft, and Vo Sum commenced to dowse for them. He directed observation planes to a site, where the raft was found, but by that time the men had been lost overboard.

Vo Sum was warmly congratulated, and on June 26 he was invited to visit the office of the Assistant Chief of the Vietnamese Navy's Sea Operations Command, Captain P. M. Khue. Khue wanted his help in locating a junk, numbered 93393, which the authorities believed was carrying six tons of raw opium.

First, Vo Sum asked the pendulum if he should work on the problem. When it answered 'yes', he found a picture of a similar junk and changed the number on it to match the smuggler's vessel. Next, he determined that it was indeed carrying opium and would be seized at 6:00 a.m. on June 27. Finally, he located the position of the junk and the direction in which she was travelling. The information was relayed to the commander of a search vessel, who was regularly updated until the destroyer picked up the junk on radar and gave chase.

She was boarded almost 10 hours before Vo Sum had predicted and searched. The destroyer radioed back some hours later that there were no drugs onboard the junk. Khue told Vo Sum he had been mistaken. He dowsed again, and the pendulum still told him there was opium onboard. Vo Sum persuaded Captain Khue to order a more thorough search. This time they went to the bottom of tanks holding fish packed with ice – and found the opium. It was now 5:00 a.m.; Vo Sum had been just one hour off-target.

HOPE FOR REFUGEES AND MISSING SOLDIERS

Vo Sum founded the Vietnamese Society of Dowsers, and trained many of his compatriots in the art. As South Vietnam started to lose ground in 1975 to communist forces, the society offered its services free of charge to help find missing refugees or to determine whether they were alive or dead.

Vo Sum's naval colleague Commander Ho-Duy-Duyen wanted to know if his pregnant sister was alive. She had fallen from a crowded naval vessel, and witnesses saw her dragged out of the water, where she remained motionless. Vo Sum told the commander that not only was his sister alive, but also she had somehow managed to get all the way to safety on Phu Quoc Island. Two days later, Ho-Duy-Duyen received a call from a refugee camp at Phu Quoc to say that his sister was on a plane for Saigon.

In another instance, Chief Petty Officer Tran-Ngoc-Quang of the Naval Logistics Command came to Vo Sum with a picture of his soldier son. Tran-Ngoc-Binh had apparently been mortally wounded during an attack by a communist patrol in the Vietnamese central highlands. Vo Sum worked for several hours with the picture before advising the boy's parents that he was

After using his divining rod to identify a woman's husband as her killer, Jacques Aymar was in great demand by authorities across France to solve other crimes.

wounded, but not fatally, and that he would contact them in two or three days. Precisely, three days later, the father came to see Vo Sum with tears in his eyes. He had just received a letter from his son, telling him that he was in a military hospital and had almost recovered from his wounds. Vo Sum, who subsequently emigrated to San Diego, California, wrote: 'The tears of joy in the eyes of the 50-year-old father learning that his son was alive and would soon be home was one of the most cherished recompenses I ever had for my dowsing.'

DOWSING DETECTIVES

Centuries ago, dowsing skills such as Vo Sum's would have been more readily accepted by a considerably less sceptical society. One of the most famous dowsers of all time, Jacques Aymar, became a psychic detective quite by chance. Aymar was born in 1662 in Daphine, southern France. He was divining one day and began digging at a spot indicated by his rod. Instead of finding water, however, he uncovered the head of a murdered woman. At the woman's house, the rod reacted toward her husband, who promptly fled.

The authorities asked for Aymar's assistance in other murderous crimes. In his most celebrated case, he was asked to find the killers of a wine merchant and his wife in Lyons. Escorted by an armed guard, he began at the scene of the crime and then, guided by his divining rod, followed a trail along the bank of the River Rhone. He told his escort that the trail had been left by three murderers. Along the way, he indicated houses that had been entered by the fugitives. This was later confirmed.

The trail continued, partly on land and partly on the river, to an army barracks, but Aymar warned his

DETECTIVE FILE:
Gerard Croiset:
Exposed as a fraud?

The reputation of the man often regarded as the world's most effective psychic detective was re-examined after his death. Were his 'successes' as impressive as they seemed?

Dutch mystic Gerard Croiset was perhaps the most famous psychic detective of them all. For 40 years, he used psychometry to 'feel' images that would help to locate missing people or to identify criminals. He was regularly consulted by police officers all over the world and allegedly assisted in solving hundreds of cases.

A record of Croiset's achievements was kept at the University of Utrecht, where his greatest supporter, parapsychology professor Wilhelm Tenhaeff, had been based. After the psychic's death in July 1980, researcher Piet van Hoebens decided to make an objective study of the claims regarding Croiset's biggest successes. The results of this reappraisal greatly disturbed him.

One of Croiset's earliest triumphs was in 1953, when a man had tried to murder a Dutch policeman. The story, as popularized, was that Croiset had stunned the judge by 'seeing' a metal worker as part of the attack; this revelation led to an arrest. In fact, the records showed that the arrested man was already a suspect and that the information Croiset offered had been previously reported by the press. Furthermore, the man was later proven to be innocent.

Other case histories were also rather less than clear cut. When Croiset correctly identified a German serial arsonist as being a police officer, the remarkable vindication seemed to verify his powers. Again, however, these suspicions had been reported in the media weeks earlier, and Van Hoebens found no evidence in the tapes of the psychometry session, provided to the police by Croiset, of the spectacular insights alleged in this case.

Shortly before his death, Croiset was hired by British tabloid newspapers to help find the serial killer dubbed the 'Yorkshire Ripper'. He identified the murderer as a man from Sunderland, in the northeast of England. When the culprit was finally captured several years later, he was nothing like the man that Croiset had described, and came from the Midlands city of Bradford. Croiset's 'tip' seems to have been based on the fact that the police had received taped messages, supposedly from the killer, in which a man spoke with a pronounced Sunderland accent. Those tapes were later established as the work of either a cruel hoaxster or an accomplice, and may have cost lives as the real killer struck again.

The Dutch psychic Gerard Croiset claimed to have assisted the police in more investigations than any other paranormal sleuth. But how often were his contributions truly helpful?

CRIME FILE:

Psychic hands lead to a killer

On October 2, 1956, 18-year-old typist Myrna Aken left work in Durban, South Africa, and vanished – until a psychic murder hunt solved the mystery.

Called to investigate by Myrna's worried parents, the police quickly established a few worrying facts. Myrna's workmates noted that she had not been her usual ebullient self that day and felt sure something was amiss. They also recalled how a man some years her senior had arrived in a car, and they had argued before driving off to a hotel and bar, where they were seen in animated discussion. The Akens had no idea who this man might be. Attempts to find the car also led nowhere. After a week, there was still no trace of Myrna.

Then her brother Colin suggested a new strategy. He had a school friend whose father, Nelson Palmer, claimed to be able to find people simply by holding an item owned by them. He did not know why he could do this, but believed that somehow his mind acted like a radio, tuning into images from the ether.

Mrs Aken went to see Palmer and provided him with some of her daughter's underwear. Immediately he held this, he knew that the girl was dead. He saw her murdered, lying in a water culvert. Palmer took this news to the police and offered to guide them to the girl's body. The next day, a police sergeant, Palmer, and Colin Aken drove under the psychic's instructions to the spot, some 60 miles (97km) away, that he had seen in his mind.

Exactly as described, Myrna Aken lay at the bottom of a slope leading to a stream. She was naked and had been assaulted, shot, and then brutally mutilated. A large rock had been used to scoop out all the body parts inside her abdomen.

An autopsy clarified the meaning of this. Myrna had been pregnant, and the attack had removed all obvious trace. This pointed the finger of suspicion at whoever had fathered the child – presumably the older man who met her in his car.

Police then discovered that a shopkeeper owning a car of the same make had loaned it to his employee, a radio engineer named Clarence Van Buuren, on the day that Myrna had disappeared. Neither the car nor Van Buuren had been seen again.

When it was learned that Van Buuren had twice been at the Aken household to fix their radio, a manhunt ensued. Within a few hours, a man was reported hiding in shrubbery outside his own home. Investigators arrested the suspicious character, who proved to be Van Buuren. Before surrendering, he was spotted throwing something away – the gun used to kill Myrna Aken.

Van Buuren claimed that he and Myrna had rowed, and afterward he had found her dead in his car. Convinced he would be blamed, he drove to a remote spot and buried her. However, forensic tests on the gun proved he was the killer.

Under South African law, Nelson Palmer was not allowed to testify at Van Buuren's trial. In fact, had his bizarre role in the case been revealed, Van Buuren might well have gone free. But there is little doubt that, without his help, Myrna Aken would have been found too late to catch her killer. Van Buuren was found guilty and later hanged. Despite his part in securing justice for Myrna Akens and her family, Nelson Palmer felt weighed down by the emotional trauma of having such awful images relayed in his mind and decided to retire as a psychic detective.

companions that the men had already fled. Instead, he led them to a prison in the town of Beaucaire, 149 miles (240km) south of Lyons. There the rod picked out a man recently arrested for petty larceny. He denied all knowledge of the murders, but the psychic detective led him along the route he had followed from Lyons. The suspect was so astounded by Aymar's intimate knowledge of the crime that he confessed and was eventually executed by breaking on the wheel. Aymar continued following the trail of the other two men, but this hunt had to be abandoned when the trail crossed the French border.

During his crime detection, Aymar experienced very definite physiological effects that were not present when he dowsed for water. While following the trail left by the wine merchant murderers, he became feverish, his pulse began to race, and he felt faint when the rod became active. There were times when Aymar even spat out blood.

Still in France, but 300 years later, dowser Jean Auscher – engineer, inventor, and artist – has enjoyed much success in solving crimes. When thieves broke into the safe of the Société Technique des Sables de la Seine in Paris, manager Jean Bouvret asked him for help in recovering the missing two million francs.

Auscher employs a device incorporating a pendulum that traces patterns in Indian ink onto paper. Using the scripto-pendule, he told Bouret that there were two thieves involved who lived within an oval area traced on a map by the device. A police investigation resulted in the arrest of one suspect who lived in an apartment situated on the Rue de Poissoniers; a second man was arrested in his hangout on the Rue Poulet. The two men lived at opposite ends of Auscher's oval.

A psychometrist holds a glove to her forehead, hoping to 'sense' information about its owner. Physical contact with articles of clothing or other personal items is thought to assist in receiving psychic impressions about a particular individual.

'FEELING' THROUGH OBJECTS

One of the strangest methods used by a psychic detective is the technique known as 'psychometry'. This approach is well described by Dr John Dale, a clinical psychologist in Cheshire, England, who doubles as a psychometrist in

CRIME FILE:

Allan Showery: Getting away with murder

Can a murder victim return from the grave and possess another person's body to help unmask the killer?

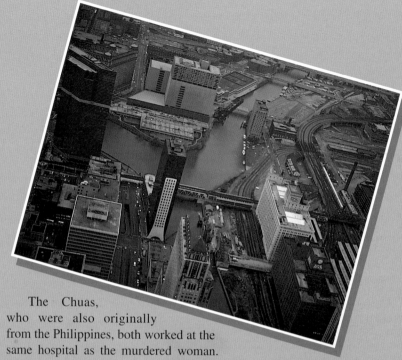

The sprawling urban landscape of Chicago, where Teresita Basa was brutally murdered by Allan Showery.

This remarkable possibility is suggested by a case from Chicago's north side in 1977. Late on February 21, 1977, Chicago PD detectives Joe Stachula and Lee Epplen were called to the scene of a homicide. A middle-aged woman had received multiple stab wounds, before being wrapped in bed linen and set on fire. It was a crude attempt to destroy evidence, and her high-rise apartment in the city revealed signs of a frenzied attack that had left little in the way of clues.

The victim was identified as 48-year-old Teresita Basa, a Philippine immigrant who had lived locally for 15 years. She worked as a therapist in a local hospital, and was well known and liked. However, the investigation into her murder was getting nowhere. Very few leads emerged, except a handwritten note in her apartment with the mysterious initials 'A. S.'.

By midsummer, Stachula and Epplen had almost given up on the case. Then they received an odd call from the police station in Evanston, north of the city, asking if the name Allan Showery had come up in the Basa murder investigation. It had not. The Evanston PD added cautiously, 'Well, in that case, you should come here and speak with Dr José Chua and his wife, Remibias, as they have quite a story to tell'.

The Chuas, who were also originally from the Philippines, both worked at the same hospital as the murdered woman. Although Remibias Chua had been in the same department as Teresita Basa, she claimed she had not known her. Not until one night in July 1977, five months after the murder, that is.

On that night, Dr Chua noticed that his wife had suddenly got up out of a chair and walked out of the room as if in a trance. He followed and found her lying on her bed talking in a strange voice that was not her own. She claimed that she was called Teresita Basa and insisted that she had been murdered by a man called Allan Showery, a colleague from the hospital.

The voice of the 'dead woman' explained that Showery had come to her apartment to steal jewellery and had then turned violent. After a detailed account of these events, Mrs Chua sat up on the bed, speaking normally, asking what had happened and complaining of a raging thirst. She could not recall a thing about what had just taken place.

Having decided not to face ridicule by reporting this bizarre experience,

Remibias Chua was 'possessed' for a second time a few days later, and the 'spirit' of Teresita Basa pleaded that they bring her killer to justice. Dr Chua explained to the voice coming from his wife's lips that the police would never believe their unsupported accusations, at which point the spirit began describing how Showery had retained the jewels and where these could be found. In particular, he had given one of Basa's stolen pearl rings to his girlfriend. Again, Mrs Chua recalled nothing after emerging from this deep trance and decided not to act on it. Only after a third 'possession' did the couple finally approach the police.

After hearing this remarkable tale, Stachula and Epplen were bemused. On questioning, it soon emerged that Mrs Chua did indeed know Basa and, more importantly, also knew the alleged murderer. This left them concerned about her story.

Yet the identity of the killer made sense. A. S. – written on the unreported note from the dead woman – could be Allan Showery. Therefore, they decided to make some enquiries.

The detectives promptly found the missing jewels in Showery's possession, exactly as predicted and discovered that he had indeed given the pearl ring to his girlfriend. He was arrested with sufficient evidence, gathered using normal police methods, to preclude the need to disclose the alleged possession. Nevertheless, without it, the authorities might never have suspected Showery.

Did the dead woman return to possess her former work colleague and point the finger at her killer? Or, did Mrs Chua recognize Basa's jewellery, which Showery foolishly gave away to female co-workers after the murder? Were her suspicions simply lying in her subconscious waiting to explode? Alternatively, perhaps fear for her own safety led her to find a way to identify the killer without having to make direct accusations in court. Whatever the truth, many close to this case believe that a dead woman actually did prevent her killer from getting away with murder.

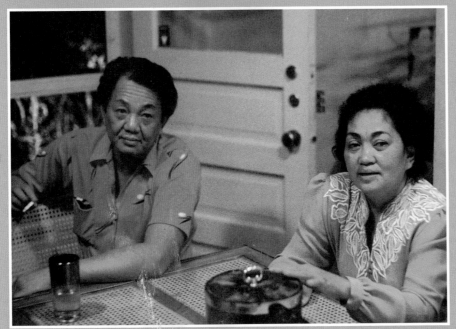

Remibias Chua and husband, José, who claims to have seen the spirit of the dead Teresita Basa take over the entranced body of his wife and commandeer her voice to name the killer.

his spare time and has worked on a number of cases.

He explains: 'What I do is simple. I take an object – any object – and hold it in my hands. I do not need to see what it is. In fact, sometimes it is better that I do not, since I then have no preconceptions. By holding this object, I focus my mind on the person to whom it belongs or the places that it has been located. I let images flood into my mind, and I describe what I see. Hopefully, these images provide clues about the events or lifetime of the person to whom this object means something.'

In a way, this method is rather like giving a bloodhound a rag to sniff. The dog then uses the smell impregnated into the cloth to hunt the landscape for similar odours and – it is hoped – find a fugitive or perhaps a well-hidden stash of drugs related to that smell.

Of course, smells are real and everybody can detect them to some degree. Dogs simply have a very well-defined olfactory sense which allows them to 'home in' on minute traces. It is less clear how psychometrists might succeed, although many believe that they function in the very same way.

As Dr Dale says: 'Everyone has this ability. We all have an innate psychic intuition, and different things can bring it to the fore. With me it is an object. By practice, I have learned to hone this skill, but that is really all that makes me unusual. In truth, anyone could do it'.

THE LOST BOY – TRAGEDY AVERTED

Those words might have rung hollow in the ears of the Tioga, New York, County Police, when, on August 4, 1982, a five-year-old boy disappeared, and no one was able to offer any clues. Tommy Kennedy had gone with his family on a Sunday morning picnic to Empire Lake. He strayed out of sight, and, before his distraught mother knew what had happened, Tommy had disappeared. After frantically rounding up others to hunt for the boy without success, the local police were called in; by mid-afternoon, Sheriff Ray Ayers was already fearing the worst.

As late afternoon approached, more than 20 officers scoured the area, while Tommy's mother tried to reassure herself with the news that her boy had left his shoes behind, suggesting that he had obviously not intended to go far. But by now, many people had been drafted in from miles around, using every initiative to find the child before nightfall. These included fire officers and scuba divers, who periodically dipped into the shallow waters of the shoreline area, as many feared that Tommy had fallen into the lake and drowned.

Since it was summer, darkness came late, yet the hunt had yielded only one 'success': a diver had found Tommy's T-shirt in a bush near the water. This seemed to confirm the ominous fears that were being spoken in hushed tones, and a sense of real foreboding struck the frustrated search party.

At 10:00 p.m., Sheriff Ayers reluctantly called off the hunt until dawn, as the thick forests and watery tributaries were becoming impossible to search in the dark. When the party regrouped to plan what to do next, the idea was put forward to call in Phil Jordan, a local psychic, who was something of a celebrity and who had reputedly helped other police departments in missing persons cases, using psychometric skills. One of the firemen, Richard Clark (in whose home Jordan was a lodger), vouched for the sincerity of the man from first-hand experience. But the sheriff was not tolerant of psychics, and it seemed unlikely that he could be persuaded to adopt this unorthodox approach.

However, Jordan did not wait for an invitation. He was already aware of the missing boy and was determined to help – particularly since the boy's father, a reporter, had spoken up for him against local bigots, who claimed that a psychic

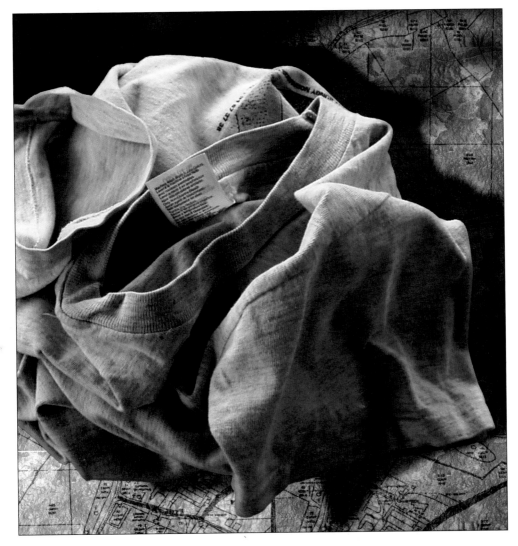

Clothing belonging to missing persons is often used by psychics to help direct search parties. In the practice of psychometry, touching an item once worn by some-one is believed to create an emotional link with that person.

must somehow be in league with the devil. During a break from the harrowing search, Clark had brought home the missing boy's T-shirt, leaving it with his wife for safe-keeping. Jordan now picked the shirt up, and he began to sink into a relaxed state as he ran the material through his fingers. As he did so, images flowed into his head.

When Clark returned home, Jordan had completed a sketch of a scene that had formed in his mind while he was holding the shirt. It depicted the lake, an area of overturned boats, a large rock, and a tree. The boy was asleep under the tree. 'He's alive', Jordan triumphantly announced, 'and that's where they will find him'.

Although Clark was convinced, persuading sheriff Ayers was a different matter. However, in the early hours that night, Don Kennedy, the boy's father, called to beg the psychic to help with the case, unaware that he had already done so. The sheriff was moved by this plea, and at first light Jordan and Clark went to join the search teams as they prepared to broaden the three-mile area they had already covered.

As the dumbfounded onlookers watched, Jordan asked the boy's mother for the shoes left by the lake. She still clutched these as a tangible link with her child. The woman handed them to the psychic and he let them settle into his palms. He seemed to drift into a state of semi-consciousness, then shook himself alert and marched off saying, 'Come on', leading the searchers into the woods.

Less than an hour later – at the spot to which Jordan led them – they found the exhausted five-year-old, under a tree in the exact location sketched by the psychic the night before. It transpired that the youngster had wandered off and become disorientated in the woods, mistakenly heading away from the picnic area, rather than toward it. The search party could not understand how they had missed finding Tommy, since they believed they had thoroughly scoured the area. If not for the psychic's tip-off, it is likely that they would not have searched that spot again until it was too late.

Sheriff Ayers was so convinced by this success that he awarded the psychometrist an honorary deputy's badge. Jordan himself said that he believed he had been guided by God, who had let him see these things in order to lead him to the missing boy.

PROVING PSYCHOMETRY

In 1985, psychometrist Dr John Dale participated in a series of trials at Manchester University in England that set out to demonstrate his claimed ability. University psychologist Dr John Shaw arranged for 17 people to put a personal item into a sealed envelope. Jenny Randles, co-author of this book, was one of the participants. Each person was to choose something special to them and to keep their selection secret. Each envelope also carried a unique number, and only Shaw knew which person was identified with which envelope (but not what was inside). These were all then handed to Dale, and his task was to use psychometry to 'read' emotions from the unseen objects within the sealed envelopes.

After Dale had offered his readings, Randles matched the envelopes with their owners and quizzed them about the accuracy of the results. Overall, about 15 percent of Dale's statements were judged correct, and some cases were remarkably apt. One woman claimed that Dale had accurately described (from her ring) many details relevant to the recent death of her husband.

In Randles's case, something curious happened. The reading given for envelope number 14 proved more relevant to her than the one offered about her own envelope (11). However, Randles had actually changed the envelope at the very last minute and had renumbered her new one to read 11A to avoid duplicating another number. This was done hastily, and so the last '1' and the 'A' ran together to look like a '4'. Dale had mentioned the name Jenny, Blackwell (the Oxford publisher for whom Randles was then writing a book), and a black cat. A black cat brooch was the item Randles had put into her envelope.

American psychic Peter Nelson uses an ancient artefact to test the power of psychometry, as performed by psychic detectives such as Dr John Dale.

Asked to comment on the statistically significant but not spectacularly high success rate, Dale noted: 'I see images and have to interpret what these mean. I can, and do, make mistakes in that process. I also sometimes see things that have not happened yet, so the owner may consider them wrong – at that moment. And I have noticed a tendency to perform less well the longer that I try. Perhaps the ability to pick up these images fades as you get bored with a monotonous task, as it would in any normal situation.'

FACT FILE:
Project: Remote View

Psychic detectives often claim that they use 'remote viewing', detaching their minds from the bonds of time and space to 'see' distant events.

Over the years, several research laboratories have conducted experiments into this phenomenon. Jenny Randles set out to test these ideas in a real-world scenario, with the co-operation of the newsstand magazine *The Unknown*, many of whose readers professed psychic abilities.

The magazine announced that, at a set date and time, a computer would randomly select a location. The readers had no idea what place would be chosen, nor what would be occurring there at that pre-selected moment. They were merely asked to enter a meditative state at the designated time and to sketch or record onto a tape any images that came into their minds. Some also recorded their dreams the night before, to test the theory that, in remote viewing, it is possible to see through the barriers of time as well as space.

On the day of the experiment, the computer randomly selected a location. Only then did Randles know she would be visiting the Irlam Locks in Lancashire on the Manchester Ship Canal. She travelled to the site and, at the appointed time, took photographs of what was happening, to compare this with the findings subsequently received from the readers.

As fate decreed, the normally quiet locks were busy on that occasion. A large oceangoing vessel was passing through,

churning up the water so that it formed a top layer of thick, white, frothy scum.

Clearly, it would have been impossible to predict such an event occurring at that precise moment – at least by 'normal' means. Yet, amazingly, several readers made significant 'hits' with their psychic visions. One reported that he had seen the letter 'A' and a triangular form – this shape is very prominent in the ship's masting. Even more remarkable is another participant's description of a piled-up plate of mashed potato – a bizarre image to conjure up, but extremely reflective of what is visible on the photograph.

Impressive as these insights may seem, no one specifically said that they could see a ship passing through lock gates – the actual event. Although some of the images proved accurate in certain ways, without hindsight it would have been virtually impossible to use them to determine precisely what it was that was being 'seen'. Like dreams, psychic images are usually symbolic or visually abstract, and rarely offer an exact reproduction of reality. Decoding what a psychic has experienced is indeed a tricky business.

A photograph taken by author Jenny Randles at Irlam Locks during her remote viewing experiment. The 'mashed potato' effect described by one of the participants, responding from 200 miles (320km) away, is very evident on the water's surface.

This November 1910 issue of the magazine La Vie Mysterieuse *relates how, while in a trance, the French clairvoyant Mme R. described a motor accident involving her cousin. Indeed, the cousin was in a car crash that same night.*

CLAIRVOYANCE

The mainstay of psychic detection is clairvoyance. It is a component of extrasensory perception (ESP), the psychic ability to see or sense what is not ordinarily detectible. This includes objects and events distantly located in time or space, apparitions, and 'presences' – in short, any awareness of things acquired without sensory means. The ability to 'hear' voices and sounds without recourse to the brain's audio sensors is called 'clairaudience'. Many mediums and psychics, such as the late Doris Stokes, have claimed they are both clairvoyant and clairaudient. It is precisely because information acquired in this way is not shared by the population at large that objective proof for the phenomenon is continually sought.

THE PROOF FOR CLAIRVOYANCE

Clairvoyance, like other aspects of ESP, is notoriously 'camera shy', and cannot be performed on demand under laboratory conditions. This lack of repeatability – the mainstay of scientific enquiry – is strong ammunition for debunkers. Most psychic events are spontaneous, and as few mediums can perform to order, some resort to cheating in order to satisfy a paying audience. Doris Stokes was one medium who publicly admitted that she had done this, while many others have been exposed over the years by investigators. This is a shame, because most of those caught 'helping things along' under pressure did appear to possess the gift.

When it comes to psychic detection, critics have often commented that it is possible to reach the same conclusions through clever guesswork and lateral thinking. That possibility can be discounted only by a scientific test for clairvoyance that rules out inference. Joseph Banks Rhine, the father of experimental psychology, developed such a test in the 1930s, while he was at Duke University in

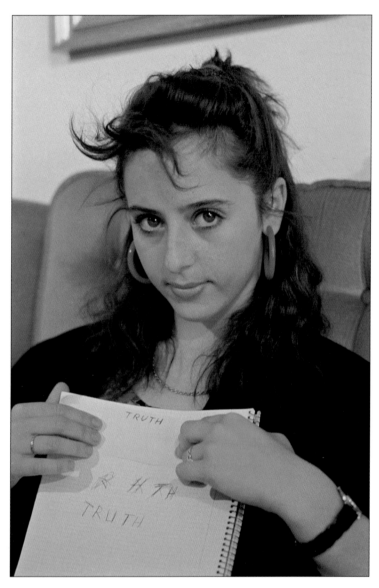

In 1989, Monica Nieto Tejada, a 15-year-old Spanish girl, proved in an experiment that she could clairvoyantly 'see' words hidden inside a sealed box. Here, she displays the target word 'truth' in her successful response.

North Carolina. For the test, five symbols were devised – a circle, a star, wavy lines, a cross, and a square – and a pack of 25 cards was created, in which each symbol was depicted on five cards. These 'Zener' cards were then thoroughly shuffled to ensure that there was only a one-in-five probability that a particular card would be produced randomly from the pack. The use of random sequences of cards eliminates inference as an explanation.

The test was for telepathy, the apparent ability to receive thoughts from someone else's mind. In many cases where individuals receive spontaneous images of a crime being committed, there seems to be a brief telepathic link with the victim.

During the experiment, the two participants, the 'receiver' and the 'sender', would sit at a table across from one another. A screen dividing the table prevented them seeing each other. At a given signal, the sender would be shown a card by the experimenter, who would then concentrate on the image. The receiver would then 'guess' the identity of the card. The card would be changed after 10 seconds for another, and the experiment proceeded in this way for four minutes and 10 seconds until the whole pack had been used.

If no ESP was taking place, the average chance of a correct guess would be one in five, or 20 percent. At the completion of the experiment, the receiver should have correctly guessed five out of the 25 cards that were presented to the sender. This is an average, and over a large number of trials the score would sometimes be slightly higher or slightly lower. The question is, in a higher-than-average score, when does this become highly significant, indicating that extra-sensory perception was at work and not pure guesswork?

The higher the score, the less likely it is that the result is due to mere luck. Statistically, if a score is rated at more than a million to one against chance – 100 correct hits out of 250 trials, for instance – then we have objective evidence for possible ESP.

'Zener' cards, with the five symbols devised in the 1930s by Dr Joseph Banks Rhine to test subjects for telepathy.

CRIME FILE:
Hit-and-run vision

Housewife Helen York of Belling, Illinois, solved a crime involving the family car even before it happened!

In early 1946, Helen was washing some dishes when she had a strange vision. That evening, her husband, Earl, and their friend Smitty, who worked for a local radio station, were at home discussing politics. The three of them were going to attend a meeting as soon as she had washed the dinner dishes in the kitchen, at the back of the house. As she finished the last pan, Helen glanced out of the window, where it was getting dark, and something very odd happened.

'The glass shivered and there on the glass, like a movie, I saw the image of our Buick, which was parked out in front of the house. Then, in the picture I saw a car, speeding from the north, sideswipe our car. The driver pulled over to the curb, and a man staggered out of his car, looked at our smashed car and started to run, with his coat tails flapping, zigzagging down the street for about two blocks'.

In the 'movie', the 'camera' followed the man into his house, where he hid behind some wooden and cardboard boxes in the basement. The scene then changed, and Helen saw the police arrive to examine the damaged car and note the registration number of the other vehicle, which was then radioed through to the main police station. Once again, the picture changed, and Helen watched as the driver was taken inside the station to the desk sergeant, who booked him for drunken driving and leaving the scene of an accident.

The glass seemed to shiver a few times, and then returned to normal. It was not the first time Helen had experienced clairvoyant visions, and she wondered how far into the future she had seen.

As they left the house that night, Helen did not mention what she had 'seen' because of her husband's scepticism in the past. The political meeting was a regular event, and it was their turn to drive, but Smitty insisted on using his car. Helen suggested that their car would be better in the garage, but Earl decided to leave it parked on the road until later.

They arrived home late feeling quite tired. Helen walked indoors, leaving her husband to move their car into the garage. He and their friend followed her inside a few moments later, yelling that someone had smashed into the side of the Buick. The two men said that she should call the police right away while they inspected the damage. Helen could not help but reply: 'Why phone the police? I'm tired and I want to go to bed. Do it yourself. Besides, they know all about it anyway. In fact, they've even got the man who did it.'

Smitty wondered how she knew and asked sarcastically if she had been looking into her crystal ball. He laughed, and Helen then began to tell them about her experience, but she cut it short. They were always making fun of her. Earl came to her defence and said he believed her, but she decided to call the police to put an end to the discussion.

The desk sergeant told her that their neighbour had seen the collision and had called the police. Officers had gone to the suspect's home where he had fled on foot, and they found him hiding in the basement behind some cardboard and wooden boxes. The man was now being held for drunken driving and leaving the scene of an accident.

PAVEL STEPANEK'S AMAZING ESP

The former Soviet Union had a keen interest in clairvoyance for military purposes and actively encouraged research. The Russians knew that hypnosis was an effective tool for improving ESP. Indeed, mediums often drift into a state of altered consciousness, or self-hypnosis, before making contact with their spirit guides or receiving psychic information. Czech parapsychologist Milan Ryzl experimented extensively with hypnosis, asking his subjects to detect objects in sealed boxes while in a deep trance. One of Ryzl's psychic stars was a bank clerk called Pavel Stepanek, with whom he worked in the 1960s.

Stepanek, a quiet and unassuming man, proved a poor hypnotic subject, so Ryzl moved on to more formal experiments with him, and these were more successful. Ryzl produced a number of cards that were white on one side and black on the other. Stepanek was asked to 'guess' which colour was uppermost when the cards were placed in individual envelopes. By chance alone, he should have got 50 percent correct, yet in one experiment involving 2,000 guesses, he answered correctly 1,140 times – a success rate of 57 percent.

This 1891 illustration shows Mr C. N. Barham hypnotizing one of his servants, who in that condition manifested clairvoyant powers. Most psychics work while in an altered state of consciousness, but Pavel Stepanek was an exception.

This was well above chance, but Ryzl was puzzled: if the high score was due to ESP, why was Stepanek not right on every occasion? He reasoned that the ESP was intermittent and only worked every seventh guess or so, and that the other six were down to chance.

Ryzl modified the experiment so that Stepanek made not just one guess at each card, but a number of guesses. The guesses for 'black' or 'white' were added up for each card, and whichever was in the majority was accepted as Stepanek's definitive 'guess'. Later on, a new set of 100 cards was made, with each card placed inside a double layer of

Mr and Mrs James Coates conducting a trial of clairvoyancy. She is attempting to read the contents of an envelope through extrasensory perception. Sceptics often dismiss such experiments, citing stage magicians who can produce similar results using trickery. They assume that all 'psychics' are either self-deluded or frauds.

opaque packaging. The psychic was allowed 10 guesses for each card, and as before the majority results were collated. Out of 93 'guesses' (for seven cards, guesses were split equally between black and white), 71 percent were correct – clearly a significant result.

In 1962, Western scientists became interested in Ryzl's work with Stepanek. Gaither Pratt of the Parapsychology Department of Duke University in North Carolina became actively involved in subsequent experiments. In one test, it was discovered that there were 15 cards in the pack of 100 that Stepanek repeatedly got right. Ryzl presented just these cards to the psychic hundreds of times, and Stepanek 'guessed' every one accurately. The mild-mannered bank clerk seemed to have generated a relationship with these particular cards.

It was also noted that Stepanek made particular guesses when certain envelopes were presented to him. Ryzl wondered if small scratch marks on them might be distracting him, so the envelopes were placed in opaque covers to hide them from view. However, Stepanek continued to make the same guesses when these envelopes were presented to him, even though he could no longer see them. The researchers concluded that Stepanek was unconsciously using ESP to detect the envelopes, not the cards that they contained. When the envelopes were put into different covers, the results were unaltered. The psychic still thought that he was sensing the cards, but it was the envelopes to which he was responding.

Gaither Pratt, together with Dutch scientist J. G. Blom, then conducted an experiment that, in the American's words, was to 'provide conclusive evidence that Stepanek was demonstrating ESP'. The two researchers prepared 40 cards, 20 green and 20 white, and placed these in envelopes in such a way that neither man could have known which target colour was contained in each envelope. Pratt shuffled the envelopes and presented them, in Blom's presence, eight at a time, each concealed in an outer cover. Over a four-day period, 4,000 guesses were made, with 2,154 correct 'hits' – odds of around half a million to one! This time, the researchers found that Stepanek was detecting the cards.

Over the next few years, Pavel Stepanek demonstrated his ESP ability to a large number of scientists around the world. This sort of repeatability is rare and therefore remarkable. Amazingly, his ESP detached itself from the cards to focus first completely on the envelopes, and then on the outer sleeves. In the end, the sleeves had to be concealed inside padded jackets. Stepanek visited the University of Virginia to work with Pratt, Dr Ian Stevenson, and also Dr Jurgen Keil from Tasmania, Australia. In February 1968, he was consistently accurate during numerous experiments, but, as with many psychics, his abilities later began to desert him.

THE ENDURING GIFTS OF URI GELLER

One renowned psychic whose powers have not waned is the controversial Israeli superstar Uri Geller. Famous for his metal-bending stunts, Geller has also used his talents in the detection of precious minerals for mining companies. Despite endless challenges to his authenticity by disgruntled stage magicians and paranormal debunkers, no one has demonstrated that Geller is a fraud – in fact, quite the contrary. Even sceptics have been impressed by his apparent psychic abilities.

His mother recalls that she watched a soup spoon resting in her four-year-old son's hand first bend and then break apart. There were times, she recollected, when he seemed to be able to read her mind. The boy's first public performance was in a school in 1969, yet just one year later the knives were out for him and he was branded a cheat. The controversy attracted American scientist Dr Andrija Puharich, who was impressed enough to arrange for the young Israeli to visit Europe and North America for a series of experiments.

Most of these tests took place at Stanford Research Institute in California, under the control of physicists Dr Harold Puthoff and Russell Targ. There Geller successfully dowsed for objects in sealed canisters, deflected the needle of a magnetometer, affected the screen of an ultrasonic scanner, and interfered with computer tapes.

In one experiment, he was put in an electrically sealed room about 164ft (50 metres) from the computer department. Targ then created a simple picture of a kite on a computer screen, and Geller was asked to draw the image using ESP. Although the subject did not 'receive' the image of the kite, he was moved to draw a square with intersecting lines inside of it, which looked very much like the original picture. In London, Professor John B. Hasted, retired head of Experimental Physics at Birkbeck College, tested Geller's metal-bending feats with positive results. He attached strain gauges to the metal objects and fitted mirrors that reflected laser beams, to give an accurate measurement of any movement. Professor Hasted commented about the initial experiments: 'Keys and other objects were bent without the application of the necessary force, and pulses of electromotive force were produced by Mr Geller. No physical or chemical explanation of these phenomena is apparent.'

Hasted next carried out a series of experiments where Geller was not even allowed to touch the metal objects. These were placed at increasing distances from the subject, to test how far his 'power' extended. The scientist concluded that an energy field extended vertically from Geller, and when this electrical field reached the metal, it would bend it.

Uri Geller is a real showman, and his public demonstrations seem on the surface no different to the tricks carried out by conjurers. This has drawn the wrath of stage magicians, who dispute that Geller has paranormal powers. The most vociferous of his critics has been the American conjurer James Randi; this feud culminated in a series of acrimonious lawsuits in which

Uri Geller has confounded his critics. Unlike most other psychics, he can perform to order, convincing many that he is simply an adept conjurer. However, despite concentrated efforts to expose him as a fake, no one has presented unambiguous proof of any alleged deception. When studied under controlled conditions, Geller's metal-bending efforts have defied explanation.

DETECTIVE FILE:

Geller power: story of a psychic superstar

Perhaps the most famous personality in the paranormal field, Uri Geller has achieved unique celebrity status. Never discredited by sceptics, his inexplicable skills have been hailed by scientists and heads of state.

In an interview published in 1996, Uri Geller reflected on his life and how his 'psychic powers' came about:

'When I was six years old, living in Tel Aviv, bullets were fired into our window by a soldier. The window would have shattered on me, but a teddy bear somehow moved across my face, shielding me. Another time I was playing in a garden when I heard a strange noise in the sky. When I looked up, a light hit me and I passed out. I often wonder if this light came from a higher intelligence.

'I became a model after being injured in the Six Day War. One day, I bent a key for a photographer and he invited me to a party. The parties became more prestigious and suddenly there was Prime Minister Golda Meir. She saw something in me, and when she was being interviewed and asked what she predicted for the future of Israel, she said: "Don't ask me, ask Uri Geller." It was the biggest plug of my life!

'I went to the States and was tested at SRI [Stanford Research Institute] in the early 1970s. They validated my powers. It was written up in *Nature*. Then the attacks started. At first I turned my back on the attacks and never sued. But when my children were born, I thought, wait a minute, that's enough. I'm not going to let people lie about me any more, and I took people to court.

'I quit the limelight and went to work for oil companies, using my abilities to prospect for minerals. I became very independent and wealthy from it. But money is not the most important thing for me – health is more important. I was also recharging myself spiritually. I went to Japan, under Mount Fuji, a very spiritual place, and lived there for awhile.

'Now I'm doing confidential, but positive, work for scientists. They're not investigating me anymore. Recently I met the Nobel Prize winner Brian Johnson. He's one of the most important physicists in the UK, and he was really impressed with my abilities.

'I started something in 1969, and it still hasn't stopped'.

Geller during his famous 'blindfold driving' experiment in Tel Aviv. He is continually finding new ways to stretch his talents – or are these simply means of gaining publicity?

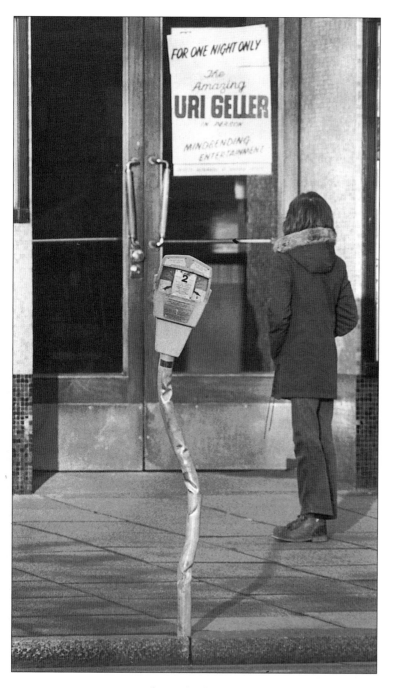

*Mind over meter?
A 1973 performance
by Geller is promoted
using comic
'evidence' of his
paranormal powers.*

Geller sued for libel. The legal battle was fought on several continents until the two men decided to call a truce.

Opinion is still divided over whether Uri Geller really does use psychic powers or is simply the most skillful magician in the world. While his feats can be duplicated through trickery, Geller always seems to have the edge over his opponents. In one of his typical demonstrations, he claims to use telepathy to duplicate an image that someone has drawn on a piece of paper. This is a standard conjuring trick, in which a stage magician asks a member of the audience to draw a picture and then uses a skill called 'pencil reading', where he copies the movement of the pencil, to make his own 'psychic' duplicate. Another method is for the magician to pretend to draw something, while asking the assistant to show everyone what they have done first. As this is happening, the magician sneaks a peek and makes a quick sketch using a piece of lead pencil attached to his thumb. Another method is to ask the assistant to concentrate on the image he has just drawn. While he is doing this, the magician watches the assistant's eyes and nose as they redraw the image in their mind, hoping for tiny movements to give clues to its shape.

When Uri Geller does this 'trick', such methods can be ruled out. A journalist from *The X Factor* magazine drew a five-pointed star in his notebook, out of sight of Geller, and when asked to concentrate on the image stared fixedly into space. Geller still produced an almost identical star, exactly the same size as the original. When performing such a feat, Geller is also quite willing to show his drawing before the assistant reveals theirs.

Objective testing of the techniques of psychic detectives has yielded some empirical evidence for their veracity. Yet the failure of methods such as dowsing to produce consistently good results in a laboratory has made the scientific establishment reluctant to endorse the validity of psychic phenomena. The controversy surrounding Uri Geller typifies this dilemma. As researcher Guy Lyon Playfair puts it: 'The case for Geller is just as reasonable as the case against him.' He believes that, because of this, people will continue to champion one side of the argument or another, regardless of any 'evidence' or 'counter-evidence'.

According to Playfair, we all have varying levels of psychic abilities, and people who have risen to the top in their professions may well have done so with the help of inherent ESP. His view is supported by the results of a study conducted in 1974 by Douglas Dean and John Mihalask of the Industrial and Management Engineering Department of Newark College of Engineering in New Jersey. Statistical analysis of the experiment's findings strongly suggested that company presidents scored highly in precognition tests.

Psychic researcher Dr Elmar R. Gruber (second left) looks on as Uri Geller takes part in a telepathy experiment on a Luxembourg television show in 1988. Are the Israeli's apparent psychic abilities genuine, or is he simply a very skilled magician? Perhaps the truth lies somewhere in between.

Supernatural Crime-Busting

AS WE HAVE SEEN, INDIVIDUALS who appear to have paranormal abilities can play a valuable role in crime investigations. Their unique insights are sometimes critical in yielding information that could not be obtained through conventional police methods. Psychics are frequently asked to help provide leads on serious crimes such as murder cases. However, their skills can take many forms, and they may prove useful in tackling a variety of other crimes, including thefts and missing persons. In fact, psychic detectives have allegedly had a hand in solving some very curious cases indeed.

As a woman of Romany descent, Nella Jones had always been aware of the supernatural world. In describing the visions that had occurred throughout her life, she said: 'I see lots of things, and hear and smell things, too.' From time to time she felt that she 'knew' things that clearly related to criminal acts. She would duly pass this information on to the police and was eventually accepted as a recognized informant. But it was a slow process. One day, in February 1974, Nella was doing the ironing during a break from running a busy cleaning company. The television news was on in the background, but she was not paying particular attention to it. Then suddenly some words leapt out at her from the screen, as if someone, or something, was drawing her to them.

She turned to watch the report and learned that thieves had stolen a painting valued at £2 million from historic Kenwood House in north London. Detectives explained that they had no clues. As soon as she heard these words, Nella suddenly experienced a vision, in which she saw a lawn in front of a big house.

Nella Jones, whose clairvoyant visions have aided the police forces of southern England on many occasions.

Immediately, she muttered: 'They've got the wrong place.'

Snatching a piece of paper, she quickly drew a map, without consciously thinking of what she was doing. As she emerged from this strange state of reverie, she saw that there were two crosses marked on the map – almost as if they signified hidden treasure. Nella immediately picked up the phone and dialled the number of Scotland Yard.

Her call was routed through to the local police handling the investigation. They confirmed that a 200-year-old painting, *The Guitar Player* by the Dutch artist Vermeer, had been stolen in a lightning raid by thieves armed with sledgehammers. They were in and out in just seconds. Owing to the artwork's fame, it seemed unlikely that the gang was intending to sell it. But police as yet had no idea who the robbers were.

Nella told the authorities of her vision and the map she had drawn. She also described how she had 'seen' the robbers dump the heavy frame as they fled the large house. But the detective simply replied in polite tones, and Nella knew what that meant. 'They thought I was a nutcase!' she says bluntly.

AN INSPIRED DISCOVERY

A few hours later, the position had changed. With nothing to lose, the detective who took the call ordered a search of the location Nella had earmarked. There – just where she had said – was the frame of the Vermeer. Now the police insisted she come to the station, ostensibly to help with their enquiries. Nella was delighted, believing that they were taking her powers seriously. In fact, they were wondering if she was one of the armed gang!

Detective Inspector Jim Bayes took her to the site of the robbery. Although Nella had never visited Kenwood House before, she looked at her scribbled map and, without hesitation, headed straight for a small pond, pointing excitedly. 'There!' Nella cried, taking off her shoes, pulling up her skirt, and wading straight into the muddy water. Bayes stared open-mouthed as the middle-aged woman 'bent down and came up with something. It was under a couple of feet of water'.

In fact, Nella had found part of the metal alarm that had been attached to the stolen painting. It had obviously been discarded by the thieves as they fled. Intensive police searches had not uncovered this evidence, yet the psychic had walked right up to it. Now she had to be considered as a prime suspect, since, as Bayes's commanding officer put it: 'How else could she have known?'

However, it took only a short time to establish that Nella had an impeccable reputation, not to mention a watertight alibi for the time of the theft. Could her unlikely story be true? Nella told

When a priceless painting was stolen by audacious thieves, police were left with virtually no clues.

The magnificent grounds of London's Kenwood House, where Nella Jones stunned detectives with her uncanny ability to lead them straight to vital evidence. Her performance was so startling that at first police suspected she might be one of the armed gang herself.

police that the painting was stolen as part of a ransom strategy and that the thieves would demand money for its return. Indeed, the theft proved to be a fund-raising exercise by the IRA, and several ransom demand letters were sent, threatening to destroy the painting on St Patrick's Day unless a large sum was handed over. Nella assured the authorities that this was a bluff; she was certain that publicity was the real aim and that the painting would be returned. She even predicted that it would be found in a cavernous area within a cemetery, saying that she had seen the police finding it.

A covert nocturnal search at nearby Highgate Cemetery was organized, but nothing was found. It seemed that Nella's powers had failed

FACT FILE:
Altered states

What triggers spontaneous psychic visions, where the mind suddenly shifts from the everyday world to enter another realm?

Scientists researching the nature of ESP and visionary experiences have found impressive evidence that such phenomena occur during altered states of consciousness. In separate experiments conducted at Stanford in California and Cambridge in England, psychologists such as Dr Harold Puthoff have found consistent results. In studies designed to identify psychic abilities, subjects who had their external senses blocked by being put into a darkened room while wearing headphones issuing a continuous 'white noise' actually scored better than unrestricted subjects. In one test, a computer made a random selection from a sample of paintings designed to convey particular emotions, and the experimenter then sought to suggest this mood by ESP. On the basis of this mental concentration alone, many of the test subjects correctly identified the painting.

Dr Michael Persinger, at Laurentian University in Sudbury, Ontario, Canada, also found that visionary experiences were more common if the brain state of subjects was altered by subjecting them to an electromagnetic field.

These findings match the evidence from spontaneous reports by psychics such as Nella Jones, who experienced sudden visions as her mind 'idled' while she was doing the ironing. Analysis of 200 psychic claims by the authors of this book showed that more than 40 percent of reported ESP visions during waking hours occurred during similar states of reverie – such as when driving alone late at night or washing the dishes. During these situations, the conscious mind is engaged in a routine operation that can be continued without effort, freeing us to heed flashes of insight that well up from the subconscious. It may be that such brief visions occur all the time, but are swamped by the moment-to-moment requirements of conscious thought during daily life. Thus they go unrecognized – except during sleep, when they may intrude into our dreams. Although ESP during 'reverie' is the most common basis for spontaneous waking visions, more than 60 percent of all reported psychic phenomena occur through dream images.

ESP operates best during altered states of consciousness, as laboratory experiments have demonstrated. But how is it possible for anyone to have a sudden psychic 'flash'? Paranormal visions often occur out of the blue, when the conscious mind is lulled into 'automatic pilot' by repetitive actions such as driving alone at night.

her at the last. But they had not. A few days later, acting on a tip-off, police found the painting near a crypt at another cemetery five miles (8km) away.

There are many strange cases involving the psychic discovery of hidden treasure, and one of the oddest is recounted by Lancaster, California, resident Audrey Leabo. It concerns her mother, Helen Baulch, who in 1910 was 10 years old and staying with her family in an old house in Oxfordshire, England. The first night she heard an unusual sound and went to the bedroom window, where she saw a man digging by the garden wall. When she told her parents in the morning, they just smiled at her childish imagination.

The same thing happened the following night, and her family told Helen to stop making up stories, as she could see for herself that the ground was undisturbed. Each night the same thing happened, and Helen became almost hysterical at the disbelief of her family. To calm the child down and convince her that it was just a dream, her grandmother instructed the spot to be dug up. There they found a pot of coins dating back to 1665, the time of the Great Plague. Had the owner perhaps, before fleeing to escape the Black Death, buried his money and then succumbed to the disease? In any case, the ghostly apparition of this man had clearly led young Helen Baulch to uncover his centuries-old secret.

When trying to locate objects, psychics often employ an item such as a bent coat hanger, pendulum, or compass, which they believe will point or swing to indicate the spot. However, there are less conventional methods of dowsing. Uri Geller runs the flat of his hand over an area and allegedly feels a pressure when it passes over gold or oil.

URI GELLER'S POT OF GOLD

Psychics have employed their talents to search for valuable minerals and precious stones, with some success. Uri Geller seemed to disappear from the public eye in the 1980s, only to suddenly re-emerge as a multi-millionaire living in a London mansion. Where had his fortune

Uri Geller demonstrating his hand dowsing technique to psychic investigator Colin Wilson. Geller dates his 'powers' to the age of three, when he received an electric shock from his mother's sewing machine.

come from? The Israeli mystic's explanation was as intriguing as it was controversial. He had earned his millions, he explained, by locating gold and oil for large international companies.

Apparently, he had learned in 1973 that he had an ability to find objects when wealthy industrialist Sir Val Duncan asked him to locate various things that he had hidden around his house. Geller proceeded to dowse for them, in his own idiosyncratic way. He did not need any of the usual props, such as a forked twig or a pendulum, since he discovered that by searching with the palm of his hand faced downward he felt a pressure against it when nearing a hidden object.

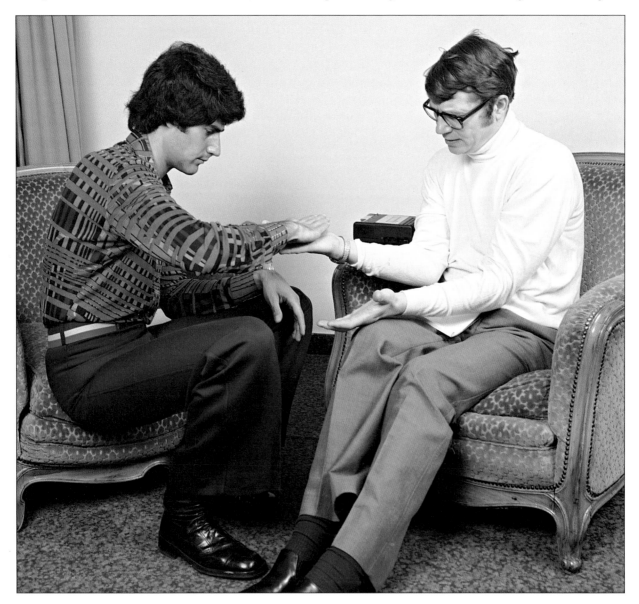

After dabbling for some time for no financial gain searching for oil in Mexico, and in the coalfields of South Africa, where he identified a valuable source of coal, Geller decided to try to earn a living from dowsing instead of performing as a mere diversion. This began in 1982 when a Japanese businessman hired him to search for gold in Brazil. He agreed to pay the psychic two million dollars if he could successfully pinpoint places where he should test-drill.

Geller calls his particular method of dowsing 'remote sensing'. Before visiting the target area, he spends several hours a day studying maps of the location. He memorizes the details and then runs his hand over the maps until he feels 'magnetic sensations' on his fingertips. At those points, he makes pencil marks on the map. He repeats this for several days or sometimes weeks, to ensure that the sensations remain consistent. The next step is to fly over the places marked on the map for some 'hand-dowsing'. If these findings remain positive, then Geller tramps over the spots for some fine-tuning.

In 1985, he was contacted by Australian Peter Sterling, whose company Zanex Limited had secured mining rights in the Solomon Islands. Zanex was extending its search for diamonds to an unexplored island, which Geller was recruited to scout. He carried out some remote sensing, and at one of the sites he indicated, kimberlitic rocks were extracted and analyzed at Melbourne University. Scientists reported: 'The sample indicates a high prospectivity of the rocks from that area for diamond-bearing host rocks.' This was confirmed in an interview with Sterling for the *Financial Times*, in which he stated that he was 'well pleased' with his investment in Geller. Sterling provided Geller with a testimonial letter that stated: 'I confirm that Zanex is about to commence exploration in areas identified by you in Solomon Islands. The most interesting area identified to date is on Malaita Island, where upon your instructions we are about to commence a search for gold and diamonds. We have already confirmed the presence of kimberlite which could be diamondiferous in this area. Other areas will be investigated in due course.'

THE BARE-FOOTED FORTUNE HUNTER

Uri Geller is not the only one to claim that they can find 'treasure' using psychic means. Kathryn Hilton was so good at finding things that as a child she was nicknamed 'Lucky'. She was about eight when she began deliberately using her talent – she set out to find a nickel in the schoolyard and found one. After that Kathryn was always finding lost money and, in the process, discovered a curious thing. She hated wearing shoes, and it was when she went barefoot that she found the coins. With her shoes on, she could not find a thing.

On one occasion, when she was walking home through deep grass alongside a ditch, she had a mental flash of vivid green and a feeling that there was something at the edge of the ditch. She looked down and detected something half hidden in the grass that was not quite the same shade. It was a $10 bill. Many years later, this skill of 'sensing' things was to take a different turn.

Years later, in the winter of 1965, Kathryn Hilton was living in San Fernando, California, when a terrible storm blew up one day. She was at work, and as the wind grew stronger she began to worry about her almost-blind collie dog, which was in the fenced back yard. Even though the animal had the garage for shelter, her worries increased as the day wore on and the weather became more threatening. When she arrived home, Kathryn discovered to her horror that the fence had blown down and the dog was gone.

As she stood in the dark street looking up and down, she suddenly received a strong mental impression of a large parking lot full of vehicles and of a dog wandering among them. She climbed into her car and started driving until a small inner voice said: 'Stop.' She had stopped next to an alley behind a shopping centre; the dog was nowhere in sight. A picture of the parking lot at the end of the alley suddenly flashed into her mind, along with an image of the dog

As a violent storm brewed while she was at work, Kathryn Hilton became certain that her dog had escaped from home. She 'tuned in' her mind and followed an intuitive trail that led straight to her missing pet.

walking toward the exit. She drove down the alley, but before she reached the parking lot, her headlights picked out the dog coming toward her.

Kathryn Hilton developed a reputation for finding lost things, and in the autumn of 1974, Don Shaw of North Hollywood called at her home to ask for help in finding his lost Shetland sheepdog. Shaw professed that he was psychic, too, but had failed to find the dog on his own. It had been left with friends three days ago while he went on a business trip and had run away almost immediately.

They drove to an area where Shaw had not searched and followed a couple of his hunches – to no avail. Then Kathryn received 'a shadowy mental flash' of a dog curled up under a bush. She turned into a street and had the same flash

CASE FILE:
Mermet: King of the pendulum

When challenged to find gold, the French monk Mermet duly uncovered it – in the most unlikely of places.

There is an interesting story associated with the French abbé, Mermet. Mermet was famous across the European continent during the early part of the twentieth century as a successful dowser. Using a pendulum, he searched for missing people, water, and precious minerals, and was dubbed 'King of the Pendulumists'. Mermet was even consulted by the Vatican over some archaeological finds that were baffling its experts.

On this occasion, he was in the Swiss village of Sedeilles dowsing for a water supply. After hours of fruitless searching, he exclaimed to the head of the town council that it would be easier to find gold than water. The senior councillor asked him, if that was the case, to show him some gold. Not far away, two harvesters were working, and the abbé suggested that it resided with one of them. They went over to the men, and, using his pendulum, Mermet pointed to one. The man laughed and wondered how the dowser could think he had any gold considering the poor clothes he wore.

A crowd had gathered and demanded that the harvester prove he did not have any gold. He stripped to his trousers and Mermet still insisted there was gold on him, although the harvester continued to deny it. By this time, he wanted to get back to work and was tired of the monk's foolishness, so he demanded that, if he knew where the gold was, he should take it. Mermet took hold of the man's belt and said, 'Isn't this gold?'

At this, the harvester remembered something that he had long forgotten. Years ago, in August, 1914, when he was called up for war, his mother had sewn a gold coin into his belt for use in emergencies. After the war, he had completely forgotten about it – until this bizarre encounter with Mermet.

The pendulum was a favourite tool of French priests who dowsed. They often improvised with a simple ball and string, or a dangling crucifix. Father Jurion used a crystal on a chain to diagnose and treat cancer. Abbé Gabriel Lambert successfully dowsed in Kensington Gardens, London, using a brightly coloured pear-shaped bobbin hanging from a silk thread.

again, this time sharper and clearer. About halfway down the road, she stopped the car and 'saw' a small house among some trees with a fenced yard and shrubs. She told Shaw that she felt the dog had been in the street and was now at someone's house. Yet the road they were on now seemed devoid of houses.

Nevertheless, Kathryn decided to drive on, and there, off to one side and hidden in the trees, was a house. Don Shaw shouted, 'He's here!', then leapt out of the car and ran toward the house. As he approached the front door, the dog raced around from the back of the house. After Shaw thanked the house owner for looking after the dog, Kathryn asked him how he had known it was there.

He replied, 'It was the strangest thing. I've never had anything like that happen before. As you were stopping the car, I just knew he was there. As I ran toward the house, I saw right through it into the back yard and there he was. It was as if the house had no walls'.

Psychometry to the Rescue

Kathryn's services were called upon again in the summer of 1977, when she received a call from a woman who had lost a diamond earring in the kitchen of her apartment. Kathryn said that she would try to find it by means of psychometry using the companion earring, which the woman still had.

The woman explained how she had moved the earring to a more comfortable position at the breakfast bar; then, as she walked across the kitchen, she unconsciously went to touch the earring and found that it was gone. Kathryn imitated her movements, then walked abruptly to the refrigerator and stood there – but the woman was adamant that she had been nowhere near it. Kathryn was certain that this was where the earring was. She meditated for a moment holding the other earring. Then, something made her look down, and she saw something glittering in a shadowed area next to the refrigerator. Kathryn reached down and picked up the missing earring. The amazed woman could not believe that it had taken the psychic just 10 minutes to find something that she had searched for desperately for several days.

When Kathryn Hilton moved to central South Carolina in the spring of 1983, her talents proved useful there, too. One day that summer, she stopped at the local post office for some stamps and found Mrs Truesdale, the postmistress, looking very worried. Two weeks ago, she had lost a computer printout containing some personal information, and she now found it was going to be very difficult to obtain a fresh copy. Apparently, she had lost it on the short journey from her car to the post office on a very windy day.

Kathryn told Mrs Truesdale that she had a special talent for finding things and said she would go outside and look for it. The postmistress was very sceptical, as she and her husband had already made a thorough search of the area. Determined to give it a try, Kathryn went outside. She returned a mere eight minutes later with the missing piece of paper, albeit slightly torn and wrinkled.

Kathryn Hilton realized that her talents had to be nurtured in order to develop. She believes that psychic abilities reside dormant in all of us and are stifled during childhood, when we are socialized into a belief system that includes strict no-nonsense rules of what is 'possible' and what is 'impossible'. Kathryn has some personal views on how the psychic process works.

Information is often presented to psychics through images. Such visions must be recorded and carefully interpreted to find their meaning. Accurate decoding of psychic impressions is a common problem.

Clairvoyance, Hilton believes, works when information-carrying vibrations enter the brain, which then decodes them into visual images. The accuracy and clearness of the images are dependent on many factors, including the ability of the brain to correctly decode the vibrations. Many other psychics blame faulty decoding as the reason that they get things wrong.

She goes on to note: 'Psychometry was used to find the diamond earring; I had the other one to hold and depended upon the natural law of attraction to lead me to the lost one. Sensitive fingers have to be developed the same way calluses are developed when playing a guitar. Vibrations are still vibrations, whether they enter your body through your eyes or your fingertips. The ability to convert them into mental images is always there. To find the lost document was an experiment in telepathy. I didn't really search; I was made mentally aware of where it was.'

BOB CRACKNELL AND THE CHURCH FRAUDSTERS

It is hard to imagine anyone less like a psychic detective than Bob Cracknell. This burly, bearded Londoner has an intense stare and resembles an American

Peter Hurkos: The power of psychometry

Having discovered his psychic gifts literally by accident, Peter Hurkos found fame as a supernatural sleuth.

Psychic detectives use a variety of techniques when visiting a crime scene to try to discover what took place. Psychometry is a common method, in which an object involved in the crime or belonging to a victim is held to elicit a psychic impression. Generally, it is not the object itself – which may be anything from the murder weapon to a scrap of clothing – that seems to be the key. This simply acts as a focus for the innate visionary skills of the psychic. Touching the associated item unleashes images from within the holder's subconscious mind which are linked to the crime – visions that otherwise cannot be so readily conjured up when needed during an urgent police enquiry.

The second most famous psychic detective to come from the Netherlands, Peter Hurkos, often used psychometry. Along with fellow Dutchman Gerard Croiset, his celebrity was such that he was consulted by movie stars and police forces alike, all around the world. However, his career was not without controversy. Hurkos was born as Pieter van der Hurk, but anglicized his name after he settled in the United States,

Peter Hurkos surveys the scene in the living room of the house where actress Sharon Tate and others were murdered in 1969. Hurkos correctly 'sensed' that there had been several culprits in the apparently ritualistic slayings.

where much of his investigative work was carried out.

According to his biographer, Norma Lee Browning, Hurkos has an astonishing success rate of more than 90 percent. Yet, unlike most psychic detectives, he has not had strange experiences throughout his life. In fact, he claims that he was not born with special powers, but developed them in 1943 when he fell off a ladder while painting an army barracks. He recovered in hospital to find that he was now plagued by visions of people and places distant in time and space.

Various accounts of Hurkos's psychic career describe one of his first experiences, which involved a fellow patient – a man who Hurkos 'knew' was a British agent and whose life was in imminent danger. Hurkos tried to warn the hospital authorities of this, but they assumed he was hallucinating since he was under medication after his head injury. However, it transpired that the other patient was indeed a spy and was later shot – just as Hurkos predicted – when caught by the Nazis in a crowded city street.

This version of events has been challenged by Dutch researcher Piet Hoebens, who investigated for the journal *Zetetic Scholar*. He checked all war records for the appropriate dates and was unable to find any reference to a British spy being shot by the Nazis in public. Of course, wartime information is often incomplete and there may have been reasons to hide such an incident. Nevertheless, the case has not been formally documented.

Hurkos's lively career inevitably attracted media attention. When he visited Britain after the December 1950 theft of the Scottish coronation treasure, the Stone of Scone, the press was fascinated. Hurkos offered many 'impressions' regarding its location, and these later proved accurate – at least as to the nature of the theft, which had been the work of fervent nationalists aiming to repatriate the stone from London. (Although it could perhaps be argued that one hardly needed to be psychic to work out the likely culprits in this case.) The police later said that the insights provided by several psychics had played no part in their attempt to recover the missing stone.

Nevertheless, when Peter Hurkos returned to the Netherlands, the Dutch newspapers had a field day with stories about the psychic suffering 'unforeseen' consequences when he was stopped by customs and his luggage searched for contraband! Hurkos later claimed that he could never successfully use his powers for his own benefit.

Hurkos again hit the headlines in 1969 when the movie star Sharon Tate was found brutally murdered along with several of her friends. The media followed the psychic as he visited the murder site in an attempt to gain impressions from the scene and the victims' personal effects. Hurkos duly informed the authorities that he believed several people had been involved in the murders. This proved to be correct – although not three men, as the psychic had 'seen'. In fact, three women and one man were implicated in the final court case, which saw cult leader Charles Manson convicted of the crimes.

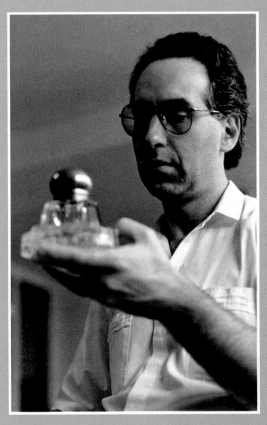

Here, US psychic Peter Nelson demonstrates psychometry, as he holds an object and attempts to obtain information about its owner. This was a controlled experiment conducted to test Nelson's alleged ability.

linebacker more than a man who has assisted the police in solving crimes. In exercising his supernatural sleuthing skills, he has frequently put his own safety on the line when confronting dangerous criminals.

His first case was unusual and came about virtually by accident. A friend of his was talking casually to a London *Daily Express* reporter in a pub. The reporter had spent several months in 1975 chasing two swindlers who had defrauded the church in a crime said to total £3 million, but police had lost their trail. What was needed was a clairvoyant to find them, the reporter jested – unaware that his companion knew just the man!

The two suspects had created a charitable organization as a front for swindling the clergy, who signed bogus hire purchase agreements to buy church organs. After accumulating a great deal of money and fooling many, including their staff, the conmen allegedly left for France in a private plane to take a 'holiday'. They sent a postcard saying that they had arrived safely, then disappeared. By the time the police closed in on them, the exposed fraudsters had fled the country.

Cracknell, knowing little of this story, agreed to meet the reporter and study his photographs of the missing men. As soon as he began handling the pictures, his head filled with images, and he was able to convey accurate character portraits of both culprits. He also revealed details not made public, including the fact that a bishop was being black-mailed. This convinced the journalist to take Cracknell's comments seriously.

The psychic was convinced that the two men had not really travelled to France and that the postcard was a ruse. In fact, they had gone there for a day before returning to the United Kingdom. The police, meanwhile, were working with Interpol, following up a sighting of the pair in Barbados. Six months had passed since they had left for France, and detectives were sure that, had they returned to the United Kingdom, they would by

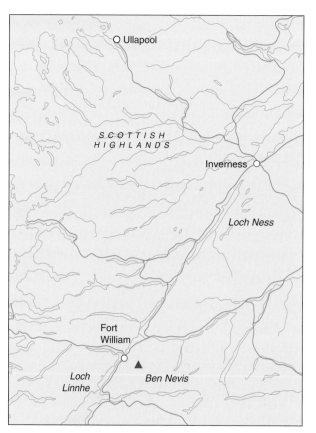

Psychic Bob Cracknell embarked on a private quest to the Scottish Highlands in search of a gang that had carried out a multi-million pound fraud. Convinced that the conmen had fled to the small town of Ullapool, Cracknell was forced to track them down himself after police failed to heed his supernatural information.

now have been traced. But Cracknell was utterly convinced he was right.

Despite police scepticism, Cracknell went to Sussex, the scene of the crime, and met with close friends of the missing men. After handling the fraudsters' clothes and other personal belongings, he issued a new flood of information. Not only was he certain that they were still in Britain, but he also saw them as living a monastic lifestyle in western Scotland. Their startled former friends confirmed that the two men had talked about this kind of existence and loved the small western Scottish town of Ullapool. As soon as the name was uttered, Cracknell knew this was where they were. He says, 'The whole of my body started to vibrate'.

His optimism was dashed when the reporter advised him that police had already had the same suspicions and been to Ullapool. After scouring the area with hundreds of men, they found nothing. The newspaper would not put fresh resources into rechecking this lead on the whim of a psychic, and, despite Cracknell's suspicions that one of the men's friends was implicated, the police required evidence to change the course of their investigation.

ON THE TRAIL OF THE CONMEN

Cracknell, however, was not constrained by the need for proof that would stand up in court. He knew that he was right and decided to set off for Scotland all on his own to hunt down the crooks. In an amazing combination of private detective work and psychic intuition, he traced the men's movements. First, he managed to find a ferry operator who recalled one of them. Then came a remarkable 'coincidence'. While driving to check out a monastery near Fort William, Cracknell stopped to pick up a young couple hitchhiking and felt the urge to show them the photographs. The woman immediately identified one man, saying that she had served him a meal at the restaurant where she had worked. It was the Royal Hotel in Ullapool.

Aware that now was the time to call in the authorities, Bob Cracknell tried to persuade the reporter to act, but to no avail. A year had passed since the crime. When Cracknell approached the police directly, they simply listened politely, allegedly telling one of the case witnesses that they dealt in facts and would not respond to the word of a 'crank'. Cracknell was so infuriated at this derision that he lodged an official complaint and eventually received an apology about the ill-chosen comments of a junior officer. He was also properly interviewed by senior detectives; in his statement, he identified an accomplice – one of the missing men's friends – whom he claimed had met the two suspects on their return to the United Kingdom and driven them to Ullapool.

Three days later, the two men were arrested. They had been found living in a cave on Priest Island, an old monastic settlement in western Scotland, having gone there from their base in nearby Ullapool. The man that Cracknell had identified to police admitted driving them north on the day after their flight to France.

Tragic schoolboy Graeme Thorne was kidnapped on his way home from school in Sydney, Australia, by vicious criminals attracted by his family's lottery win. A psychic was enlisted to help find the boy, but sadly it was too late to save his life.

When the case came to trial and the men were found guilty, there was no reference to Cracknell's role in its resolution. Police confirmed what he had told them, but insisted that they had solved the long-running matter by normal police methods and a tip-off from an informant. They did not admit that this informant (the man who had driven the fugitives to Scotland) had confessed soon after Cracknell had confronted him at his home.

THE KIDNAPPING OF GRAEME THORNE

Lives can turn on the strangest of things, and so they did in July 1960 for Basil and Freda Thorne in the Sydney, Australia, suburb of Coogee, near the famed resort of Bondi Beach. What began as a piece of fantastic luck – winning the jackpot in a lottery – rapidly turned into a nightmare when criminals homed in on their fortune. On July 7, their eight-year-old son Graeme was kidnapped on his way home from school and, in a phone call hours later, a huge AUS$50,000 (US$40,000) – worth about 10 times that sum today – was demanded as ransom. Although Basil Thorne did not hesitate to draw out the money, there was then ominous silence from the kidnappers.

As chance would have it, a police constable who had been standing by the phone in the Thorne house had taken the call and pretended to be the missing boy's father. A nationwide manhunt was immediately launched. This heavily publicized dragnet had apparently terrified the kidnappers, who had hoped that the Thornes would pay up without alerting the authorities.

The search for young Graeme yielded nothing, as the kidnappers remained in hiding. Massive rewards were offered by both the New South Wales government and various newspapers for the child's safe return – these sums eventually totalled the same amount demanded by the kidnappers. As Basil Thorne appeared on television to offer his full lottery win in exchange for the return of his son, the frustrated Sydney police decided upon a new, and most unusual, strategy – to turn to psychics for help. Gerard Croiset, who had been consulted on several criminal cases, was flown in from the Netherlands, but his map dowsing failed to locate the boy. A seance was even held covertly in a police station at Bondi; this, too, brought no leads.

It was then that children's radio presenter Keith Smith, who had some experience of working with a psychic from New Zealand, was contacted by Sir Frank Packer, the millionaire owner of one of the newspapers offering a reward. Smith and his psychic assistant agreed to help find the child, provided that they would not be named and would not receive any reward money. A photograph of the missing boy and personal items, including a lock of hair, were forwarded to New Zealand. Tragically, just as the psychic was using these to gain his impressions, the body of the youngster was found. The remains were located in an area that had been described by the psychic, although he had not yet had time to pinpoint an exact site.

Basil Thorne, father of the missing eight-year-old, made an anguished television appeal in 1960 offering his full lottery winnings in exchange for his son's safe return. Sadly, it was in vain.

A man was later convicted of the kidnapping and murder; he apparently strangled the child as soon as it was clear that he would not receive the ransom money in secret. By the time psychics were consulted, Graeme Thorne was already dead. However, even if the boy had still been alive, precise information from New Zealand may have come too late to save him. When a life is literally on the line, a psychic detective has to be both swift and explicit in directing the authorities where to look.

PIPE DREAM

In the hunt for missing people, psychic Dorothy Allison has encountered similar problems. Having inherited from her mother the gift of dreaming things that came true, she had long helped out family and friends by sharing her insights.

But she was in her mid-40s before one such incident brought her into the realms of psychic detection.

On December 3, 1967, Allison had a disturbing dream in which a little boy was stuck inside a pipe somewhere in a park. She 'saw' the dilemma unfold and knew that it was near her home in New Jersey. The image remained in her mind through the following weeks, and the memory became increasingly distressing, since it was so vivid and realistic that she expected it to happen in real life.

After worrying all through the Christmas holidays, on January 3, Allison approached the local police chief, Francis Buel, who was to become a long-standing ally. He was surprisingly sympathetic and listened intently. This was because he recognized her description of the child in her dream – this matched that of a missing child, Michael Kurcsicks, who had vanished while out playing some weeks before. At the time that Allison had had her dream, the boy was already being searched for, with increasing pessimism.

Allison related as much information as she could to try to define precisely where the young boy was, but feared that it was a lost cause. In the bitter northern winter, no one could survive out in the open for much more than a day, let alone weeks. Unfortunately, since she could not specify the location of the pipe in her dream, there was little prospect of the police finding Michael.

In fact, it was February 7 before the terrible reality of Allison's nightmare was revealed. The weather was

Dorothy Allison's harrowing dream of a child trapped in a pipe proved to be a vision of a real-life tragedy, in which a young boy drowned while playing. This psychic experience, despite its grim outcome, marked the beginning of Allison's work as a recognized supernatural detective.

unusually warm, and rivers that had frozen solid now began to melt. The body of Michael Kurcsicks simply slid from a water pipe and was found. He had drowned while playing, and his body was swept into the pipe, where it became trapped as colder weather turned the water to ice.

Investigating officer Sergeant Don Vicaro was so impressed that he recruited Dorothy Allison on many future cases. She has always declined to take money for her services, accepting just a few souvenirs, such as police badges for her wall. Indeed, she considers it a privilege to use her 'intuition' in an effort to help others. She always insists upon getting proper authorization, in the form of a

written request from the police to help in the search, before agreeing to start work. As far as she is concerned, her assistance has to be treated as a professional act and not something for the media to exploit.

The hunt for a missing person can be an intensely painful experience. A tragic outcome brings the immense disappointment of wondering if one could have prevented it by being just a little more exact or acting a fraction quicker. Although with Michael Kurcsicks, nothing Allison could have done would have made a difference, she realizes that the police '... need specific details. If you cannot give that, then how can you say that you are a psychic?'

Unfortunately, dreams and visions are not always specific and cannot be conjured up to order. It is necessary to work with what you get. Sadly, that is sometimes simply not enough.

DETECTIVE FILE:

Dorothy Allison: Psychic extraordinaire

Her insights on cases such as the 'Son of Sam' murders made Dorothy Allison the greatest paranormal crime-buster of modern times.

An ordinary housewife and grandmother, Dorothy Allison (1925–1999) was also the world's most prolific psychic detective. Her astonishingly accurate perceptions helped to solve an unprecedented number of crimes.

Dorothy Allison may well go down as the twentieth century's most extraordinary psychic detective. Even her death, just four weeks short of the start of the new millennium, had a supernatural twist.

Born in 1925 in northern New Jersey to a Catholic mother who had also had many psychic experiences, young Dorothy correctly predicted the sudden death of her father. As a 14-year-old, she saw him struck down by pneumonia, having been in perfect health.

Warned by her mother never to try to use her powers for personal gain, Allison settled down as a housewife and mother. It was many years – and several grandchildren – later that she began her long career aiding police in the north-eastern United States and southern Canada. This role commenced in early 1968, when astounded police discovered the body of a six-year-old boy who had drowned and become trapped, frozen in a pipe – just as Allison had foreseen in a disturbing dream reported weeks earlier.

After that first incident, she tackled more than 5,000 cases – never taking any payment, despite the authorities crediting her with solving at least a dozen murders and helping police to locate more than 50 missing children.

Dorothy Allison's visions were amazingly precise. In 1976, Allison reported seeing the word 'Mar', the number 222, and oil connected to the whereabouts of a missing teenage girl. At the time, New York police could not understand these clues, but they proved remarkably accurate when, two years later, the girl's body was found at a remote coastal spot on Staten Island. She had been left inside an oil drum with the number 222 on it and next to a rock on which somebody had written the word 'Mar'.

In 1974, Allison gave precise details of the locations in Pennsylvania and New York where kidnapped newspaper empire heiress Patty Hearst was being held captive. She also correctly predicted to authorities that the young woman would bond with her kidnappers and assist them in a bank robbery.

Three years later, the psychic was consulted over the serial killer known as 'Son of Sam', who was targeting young

On August 6, 1977, with the serial killer 'Son of Sam' still at large, New York police are given a videotape briefing on the murderer. Officers were instructed to warn couples away from secluded lovers' lanes, where many victims had met their deaths.

couples in New York. Dorothy Allison told police that the mass murderer would eventually be snared by a parking ticket. That turned out to be exactly how David Berkowitz was brought to justice.

One of the police officers with whom Allison often worked – Detective Chief Robert DeLitta of Nutley, New Jersey – admitted that he had initially been sceptical of using psychics, but had changed his opinion, saying: 'There are certain people who have that ability and I honestly believe that Dorothy Allison was one.' Nevertheless, he conceded that, 'for obvious reasons', the success of any psychic was rarely recorded in official police reports. The authorities preferred not to complicate the legal process with

talk of the paranormal.

In 1990, Dorothy Allison advised her family that she knew when she was going to die – just before her 75th birthday. In fact, her death, on December 1, 1999, was a month short of that date. Right to the very end, her uncanny 'impressions' had proved exactly right.

David Berkowitz, of Yonkers, New York, is finally placed under arrest at Brooklyn's 84th precinct on August 11, 1977. The 'Son of Sam' killer was caught out by a seemingly trivial detail – a parking ticket – exactly as psychic Dorothy Allison had predicted to investigators.

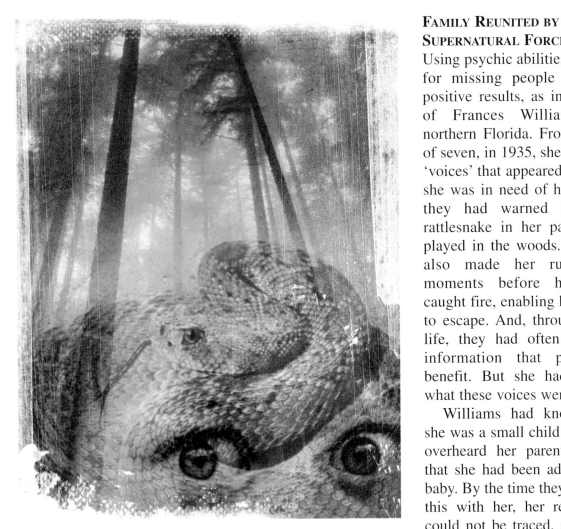

FAMILY REUNITED BY SUPERNATURAL FORCES

Using psychic abilities to search for missing people can have positive results, as in the story of Frances Williams from northern Florida. From the age of seven, in 1935, she had heard 'voices' that appeared whenever she was in need of help. Once, they had warned her of a rattlesnake in her path as she played in the woods. They had also made her rush home moments before her house caught fire, enabling her mother to escape. And, throughout her life, they had often conveyed information that proved of benefit. But she had no idea what these voices were.

Williams had known since she was a small child (when she overheard her parents talking) that she had been adopted as a baby. By the time they discussed this with her, her real mother could not be traced, so it could not be discovered if she had any siblings. Then, in 1967, the voices appeared again, saying that they would help her to find her real family. They told her to place a letter in a newspaper in Tampa Bay, Florida, some miles from where Williams lived, and from the children's home in Jacksonville where she had stayed as an infant. Amazingly, three long-lost sisters and one brother spotted the newspaper announcement and contacted Williams. All had been separated from each other for many years, and all 'chanced' to live in the catchment area of the *Tampa Tribune*.

Within days of this remarkable success, intuition led Williams to contact the governor of Florida for help. He was so moved by her story that he ordered the director of the children's home to open up the dusty reams of sealed files and provide the final clue that led to the discovery of one remaining sister who had never been in contact with the others.

From a young age, Frances Williams was warned by 'voices' whenever danger lurked. On one such occasion, her invisible protectors prevented her from encountering a rattlesnake. By learning to trust in these mysterious voices, she was eventually reunited with her long-lost family.

Within just three months, all six children, who had been parted some 40 years before, were at last reunited – sadly, only just in time. The eldest, Frances Williams's only brother, died from a massive heart attack within days of the last sibling being traced. As the five sisters met at his graveside to gain strength from their new-found unity, Williams says that she realized for the first time the origin of the voices that had guided her. They were the parents that she had known for just a few weeks as a baby and whose sudden death had led to the children being taken into care. Tragedy had driven them apart. But fate, fortune, and psychic detection had brought them back together.

PREMONITIONS OF DISASTER

Alan Vaughn is an American psychic who is never afraid to talk about his experiences and is always willing to put on record what he believes. In the interest of saving lives, he feels that it is best to share his visions immediately, at the risk of looking foolish if they prove incorrect. Hesitating to act, on the other hand, would bring a sense of responsibility for any ensuing tragedy.

Vaughan was a mainstay of the Premonition Bureau set up by London science journalist Peter Fairley. Fairley established the bureau after collecting statements from people who believed that they had foreseen disaster in the small Welsh mining town of Aberfan in October 1966, when a rain-sodden slag

In October 1966, a mountainous pile of coal slurry collapsed onto the village of Aberfan, Glamorgan, in Wales, engulfing the primary school and surrounding houses – killing 116 children and 28 adults. This horrifying tragedy had provoked a global wave of premonitions and led to the creation of the world's first bureau dedicated to the official recording of psychic visions.

CASE FILE:
Ted Kaufmann: Mystery crash

When two men disappeared without trace in the dead of winter, no one believed the bizarre explanation given by a local dowser – until spring came.

In 1982, northern New York state suffered a very harsh winter. Therefore, police sources feared the worst when Canadian woodsmen John Montgomery and Thomas Parks, who were living locally while working for a paper mill, vanished on the night of February 2. They had gone to a nearby store late one night to buy some milk and should have been back home safe and sound in just a few minutes. Instead, they never returned.

Local police chief Ed Litwa was baffled. After weeks of searching, and despite enlisting the help of the state police, they had found no trace of the two men – although their cherry-red pick-up truck with Canadian licence plates should have been difficult to miss. The missing men were not back in Canada and had clearly intended to return from their trip that night, since all their property was still at their temporary residence in Lake George.

The theory that was considered most viable was that the men had rather foolishly attempted to drive across the frozen lake surface and had crashed through the ice into the water. Although extensive efforts were made to find any evidence for this, the persistent, rapidly compacting snow obscured any tire tracks or breaks in the ice within hours.

Bob Bryan, a detective drafted from the state police, was first to suggest the use of psychics in the hunt. Two female psychometrists, who had aided Bryan before, pored over the map, but failed to turn up any clues. Despite this, Litwa considered enlisting a third psychic, Ted Kaufmann. Kaufmann was a former New York City insurance broker now retired to a small community in the adjacent Adirondack Mountains. His method of investigation was by asking questions using a pendulum and a map; the pendulum was believed to swing in response to psychic intuition.

There was general reluctance to giving supernatural methods another

Map dowsing is a common method used to locate missing persons. The dowser pinpoints locations as the pendulum swings in response to queries.

Map depicting the area around Lake George, in upstate New York, scene of the widespread police search for two missing woodsmen, whose baffling disappearance was correctly explained by pendulum dowser Ted Kaufmann.

chance, but Litwa eventually decided that they had nothing to lose by inviting Kaufmann to try to locate the men. By now, they had been missing for a month. So the dowser arrived in Lake George and started his experiments using a large-scale map.

After posing a series of questions regarding various possible solutions to the mysterious disappearance, Kaufmann announced that the men were in the lake. Moments later he identified the precise spot where he said the pick-up truck had fallen into the water.

Despite the psychic's certainty, the police were not impressed. They knew the way in which the lake froze, and this spot was completely improbable for a number of reasons. For one, the ice here was thicker than in most parts, and if there was a danger of the truck falling through into the water, then it would have done so well before reaching this point. So Kaufmann was sent home, and the police more or less wound up their search.

Almost two months after Montgomery and Parks had disappeared, the case was finally resolved. On March 29, hours after the spring thaw had set in, John Montgomery's body was found floating within the crumbling ice pack. Divers were sent down and immediately located the pick-up and the body of Thomas Parks on the lake bottom just beneath. The milk carton was still lying on the seat next to him.

The Lake George police were stunned by this unexpected turn of events, because the bodies and the truck were

located at Orchid Point – the precise spot to which Kaufmann had directed them. For the first time in living memory, this area had been the first part of the ice-bound lake to thaw. It took a close search by the divers to explain why. Unexpected faults had appeared in the rock on the lake bed. These had allowed warm spring water to seep through, meaning that the ice in just this one spot never froze properly. That, of course, meant that anybody daring to drive across the lake would have met disaster in this totally unlikely location. Montgomery and Parks had been the unlucky ones.

The question that the authorities could not satisfactorily answer was: Just how had Ted Kaufmann discovered this completely unpredictable fact simply by dowsing a map and posing a few questions into the ether?

As the milder spring weather approached in March 1982, the frozen waters of Orchid Point, at New York's Lake George, melted to reveal their deadly secret.

CASE CLOSED

CRIME FILE:
Riddle of the missing hitchhiker

In the search for a missing teenager, a long-distance vision proved eerily accurate – but for the wrong case.

When 17-year-old Pat McAdam disappeared from Dumfries and Galloway, Scotland, on February 19, 1967, her fate proved a total mystery. She had spent two days with her friend, Hazel, on a weekend shopping trip to Glasgow and, tired but happy, they were given a lift home by a truck driver. Hazel was dropped off by this man in Annan. When he was traced, he claimed that he had then driven on with Pat and taken her to a point near her home in Dumfries. He said that she had walked onward from there. However, locals recalled seeing this truck taking various back roads into a wooded area near the Water of Milk and remembered it because of the traffic chaos created. This route is north of the obvious road from Annan to Dumfries.

After three years of fruitless searching, with no leads to point to Pat McAdam's whereabouts, local journalist Frank Ryan went to Utrecht in the Netherlands to meet with Gerard Croiset, the famed psychic. In a series of long-range sessions and one subsequent trip by Croiset to southwest Scotland, the Dutchman offered an astonishing series of images, which appeared to him either as spontaneous visions or after looking at the map.

Among the details supplied by Croiset was a description of a specific type of bridge, some clothing trapped in indeterminate tree roots on a steep bank, and a derelict car located in the garden of a cottage with an old wheelbarrow propped against it. These were not vague images, and when they exactly matched a rural area surrounding a bridge over the Water of Milk at Middleshaw, it looked as if Pat's body (Croiset was sure she was dead) would be found there – for this was also where the truck had been spotted.

When a body was later found near Middleshaw, it looked as if Croiset had scored an amazing success. But, in truth, he had not. This body was of a middle-aged woman who had disappeared more than a year after Pat McAdam and who had drowned in a pond. At the site so precisely described by the psychic, even while he was in another country, nothing was ever found that could be clearly linked to the missing teenager.

Croiset insisted that he did identify where the girl's body had been dumped, but that it had probably been washed out to sea and lost forever before he was asked to assist in the case. The truck driver continued to deny any involvement in Pat McAdam's disappearance, but was later imprisoned for another murder.

The Dutch psychic detective Gerard Croiset working at his home in Utrecht. Croiset's personal papers, reporting a lifetime of supernatural investigations – including the Pat McAdam case – are held in trust by the local university. The disappearance of the young hitchhiker remained a mystery, despite Croiset's assistance.

heap engulfed a local school, killing dozens of young children. By creating a bureau to record people's premonitions in advance, it was hoped that lives might be saved in the future.

In the late 1960s, a number of accurate predictive dreams were lodged with the bureau by Alan Vaughn from his California home, thousands of miles away. He also regularly passed on his visions to police forces all over the United States, ever since he had been consulted by a state's attorney from Lancaster, Pennsylvania, who was looking for a missing 14-year-old girl. Vaughan correctly foresaw the arrest of a teacher as her murderer, even noting the make of car that he drove.

Vaughn's biggest opportunity came with the chance to prevent the assassination of Robert Kennedy. This began when he received a series of dream warnings starting on April 6, 1968. These took a very symbolic form in which he saw Kennedy as a Greek mythic hero who was heading for self-sacrifice. The images were extremely jumbled and difficult to interpret, but he began to get a sense that the deaths of John F. Kennedy, Martin Luther King Jr., and perhaps now Bobby Kennedy were somehow related and that racist issues

Members of the white supremacist group the Ku Klux Klan pose in their trademark pointed hoods. Alan Vaughn's dream premonitions surrounding the deaths of Martin Luther King Jr. and the Kennedy brothers (symbolically represented by the initials K K K) seemed to suggest a link with racial issues.

The world's first premonition bureau had one star psychic – Californian Alan Vaughn. Vaughn correctly foresaw many tragic events, including the murder of Senator Robert Kennedy on June 5, 1968. Here, he lies on the floor of the Ambassador Hotel in Los Angeles moments after being shot.

The team from the Maimonides Dream Laboratory in Brooklyn, New York, where experiments in dream telepathy were conducted in the 1960s and 1970s. Just a week before Robert Kennedy's assassination, Vaughn had written a cryptic warning, based on his visions, to Professor Stanley Krippner (pictured left), urging the researcher to warn Kennedy that his life was in peril.

were associated with them all. Indeed, the symbology of the three men's initials – K K K – tied in with the infamous Ku Klux Klan, then active in violent race protests in America's Deep South.

Although unable to make specific predictions from this mix of dream images, Vaughn was sufficiently sure that something was going to happen that he sent a warning to the London *Evening Standard* on May 20. At that time, the newspaper was administering Fairley's Premonition Bureau and logging information as it came in. This message from Vaughn stated that Kennedy could be shot within the next two months.

A further vivid dream woke Vaughn on May 25 and added new details to the scenario. He could now see Kennedy in a room filled with people and moving toward another room as a man shot him. But where was this room and when was the event to happen?

The psychic worried for three days about what he should do. He realized that, if he simply offered up his vague concerns to the authorities, nobody would take him seriously. Kennedy was not going to cancel all engagements on the whim of a stranger professing weird visions about Greek mythological heroes. So Vaughn decided to write a letter to Professor Stanley Krippner, urging him to act on his behalf. Krippner was a respected psychologist who ran a dream laboratory in Brooklyn, New York, and whose work was highly regarded. Krippner had already done some research with Vaughn and was aware of his success rate. So, when he received his letter, dated May 28, the scientist certainly took the matter seriously.

Vaughn was asking the doctor to 'think of any way of drawing [Kennedy's] attention to such a threat …'. He was desperately hoping that someone could get a message to the politician and warn him of the danger he was in. But Krippner was not convinced that Kennedy would listen even to him, and in any case he had no obvious way of getting in touch with such a powerful man.

A week later, Robert Kennedy was assassinated at a rally in a hotel in Los Angeles. The scenes shown around the world on television stunned Vaughn, as they matched so many features of his dreams. Sadly, it had simply not been possible to unravel in advance the full meaning of his symbolic visions. As a result, a good man died.

RELIVING A MURDER

When, in the autumn of 1994, three-year-old Tabatha Horn went missing from her home in a small Michigan town, the case proved an emotive one. Her mother's boyfriend, a prison warden, claimed he had taken her for a short car ride, but that she had vanished from the car when he left her for just a few moments to go into a grocery store. No amount of searching led to her discovery.

Elizabeth Mahan was one of many people who read about the family's plight and empathized with it. Yet Mahan was different; she was psychic and immediately began to experience horrific sensations that seemed to be connected with the missing girl. These started with violent migraines alerting her to the need to 'act'. Since the headaches occurred when she was reading about the case, she felt that someone was trying to get a message to her about the matter. Intuitively, she knew that it was Tabatha. The little girl was dead and was trying to help her parents find her body. But all that the psychic could pick up were the words 'Bad Man!'

The next day, she started to get a sensation of being pushed into the ground and then saw images that shocked her. In these visions, she saw the child being buried beneath something green, not far from a wishing well. Sure that these scraps of information were sufficiently useful to help detectives, Elizabeth contacted the police and spoke with investigating officer Matthew Eckerman.

Eckerman would not normally have listened to a psychic, but this woman's words struck a chord. He immediately remembered that, while looking for the girl, they had searched a wishing well on the grounds of a house – there was no way this woman could have known that. So he despatched a local officer to have a closer look. Tragically, little Tabatha's body was found in a shallow grave close to the well. She had been buried under a green child's car-travel seat. The officer who made the shocking discovery, Sergeant Barry Trombly, confirmed, 'She led us right to the body'. Soon afterward, a man was arrested and charged with the murder of the little girl.

Elizabeth Mahan seemed to establish some sort of telepathic link with the spirit of the missing girl, who had been murdered and was anxious to have her burial site discovered.

CASE FILE:
Abraham the prophet

American president Abraham Lincoln had several precognitive dreams – one about his own death.

During the Civil War, Lincoln experienced a recurring dream in which a damaged ship was being chased by a Union vessel. On every occasion, it prophesied a coming Union victory. However, his most chilling dream occurred one night in 1865.

Lincoln was sleeping in the White House when he dreamt he was awoken by a frightful sobbing. In the dream, he arose from his bed and went to see what was wrong. There, in the East Room, he found soldiers guarding a body lying in state. People were filing past the body, so Lincoln could not see the face of the dead person. He turned to one of the soldiers and asked him who it was. The man looked at him and said: 'It's the President; he was killed by an assassin.' At this point, the mourners let out such a loud cry of grief that Lincoln woke.

The president told his wife, Mary, and several close friends about the dream. Just a few days later, on 14 April, Lincoln was in Ford's Theatre, in Washington, when he was shot by actor John Wilkes Booth. He died the following day.

Lincoln confers with McClennan at Harpers Ferry after a Civil War battle. The president often had dreams that symbolically pre-saged forthcoming Union victories.

WITNESS TO A 200-YEAR-OLD MURDER

Canadian history teacher Ervin Bonkalo and his wife, Marie-Luise, became embroiled in a murder two centuries old when they visited the United States in the summer of 1979. They arrived at their Gettysburg, Pennsylvania, motel on July 5 to discover that the room they had booked had been let. Instead, they were given a room in the oldest part of the building, dating from the eighteenth century and built of solid grey stone.

The couple left their toy poodle in the room and went out to dinner. When they returned, the dog was not in its basket, but huddled in a corner, shaking. This was unusual, as the animal regularly travelled with them and had no trouble at all in hotel rooms. The Bonkalos prepared for bed, and since the room had no air conditioning, Ervin left ajar a window that looked out onto a courtyard. He took the poodle out for a short walk, and when the dog refused to re-enter the building, he carried it

CASE FILE:
Death foreseen

When a young boy was killed in a road accident, his mother discovered to her horror that he had actually recorded an account of his own death.

It was only after 12-year-old Richard Meese had been killed that his mother discovered that the schoolboy had left a detailed record of his own death. Richard, of Wordsley, in England's West Midlands, was killed in October 1993 when he was crossing the road. He was struck by a fast-moving car driven by a 21-year-old woman who had sped through a red light.

When looking through her dead son's effects, Linda Meese discovered an audio cassette which he had hidden. He had loved pretending that he was a DJ and reviewed television shows, recording his efforts onto a tape recorder. The macabre commentary she now found must have been recorded shortly before the tragedy and to her ears seemed totally out of character with the boy's normally upbeat material.

Richard described crossing the road on his way to school when he saw a car coming toward him with a woman behind the wheel. He then spoke of being taken after the impact into a large building and of being unable to open his eyes. One of his arms hurt, he said, but his legs were uninjured. The recording ends with the words, 'They put me in a wooden box. They stripped me naked … goodbye'.

Richard died as a result of head injuries, and, although one of his arms was bruised, his legs were not injured, despite the massive impact that he suffered. When his mother saw him in hospital, he was undressed.

Linda commented: 'It is uncanny what he said. I don't know if he believed what he was saying, but it is almost like he had a premonition of his own death.'

Did schoolboy Richard Meese have a vision that he would die after being hit by a car? His accurate pre-recorded description of the event provides chilling evidence to suggest the role of psychic phenomena.

up to the room. Eventually, they all settled down to sleep. Some time later, Ervin was awoken by his wife's screams. She was sitting up staring at the open courtyard window and trembling. Ervin asked her what was wrong, and Maria-Luise described how she had seen a half-naked black man, with a knife clenched in his teeth, jump into the room through the window. 'He wanted to kill me … ' she said.

Ervin replied that it must have been a nightmare, but his wife insisted she had been awake – the noise of someone trying to remove the fly screen had woken her up. As if to reinforce what she had said, the dog was sitting in a corner, quivering and whimpering. They left the light on for the remainder of the night, and Ervin kept vigil.

HISTORY REPEATS ITSELF

In the morning, he went to the manager's office and, without giving any details, told him that some-thing 'interesting' had happened during the night. Ervin had made a careful study of the exterior of the building, and a strange scenario had somehow crept into his mind that he now wanted to present to the manager.

He related: 'Before the motel was built – about 200 years before – a rich farmer lived in the stone house in the middle. The room where we slept is in a little house that was the quarters for the female slaves. The slave owner, or his son, ordered a black servant girl to sleep with him. She reluctantly agreed, to avoid being severely punished or sold if she refused. However, the girl already had a lover, one of the black male servants. The jealous lover went to the female slave house, entered through the window, and killed the girl with a knife. My wife saw this scene in a nightmare.'

The manager was amazed and asked Ervin if he had studied the history of the area. When he said he had not, the manager went to the bookcase and removed a slim paperback entitled *The History of the Bucknell Plantation*. The book had been written by the manager's grandfather, who had bought the estate from the Bucknell family's last descendant. In it was a record of the murder, which had happened just as Ervin had described it, and a date – July 5, 1779 – exactly 200 years ago.

After his wife had a terrifying vision of a knife-wielding black slave entering their motel room, Ervin Bonkalo received inexplicable impressions about a murder that seemed to have occurred some two centuries earlier. Amazingly, historical records proved it to be true.

HARNESSING CLAIRVOYANCE

While some people experience spontaneous visions, professional psychics seem able to use their 'powers' at will. When seven-year-old Carl Carter disappeared one day in late October 1978 from his Los Angeles home, police were baffled. They did not know whether he had simply wandered off and become lost, or had been abducted. It was a retired police officer who suggested that they enlist the help of a local psychic, known only as 'Joan'.

Just hours after her involvement, the missing person case had changed to a murder enquiry. Joan told the police that the boy was dead, and she described the man that she thought was responsible for the murder. A police artist produced a sketch based on Joan's description. This was shown to Carl's parents, and his father said, 'That looks like Butch'. Within an hour, local man Harold Ray 'Butch' Memro was arrested. He confessed to strangling the youngster and also admitted killing two other boys two years earlier.

The practice of foretelling the future is global, and a belief in divination is intrinsic to many cultures. Here, a Chinese clairvoyant and palmist consults with a European client in Temple Street, Kowloon.

CASE FILE:
The phenomenon of second sight

Clairvoyant experiences are nothing new and have been reported over many centuries.

The ability of some individuals to perceive events without recourse to the usual five senses has been well documented over the years. Emanuel Swedenborg, the eighteenth-century Swedish scientist, philosopher, and theologian, had a vivid experience which was recorded and investigated by the German philosopher Immanuel Kant.

Swedenborg had arrived in Gothenburg from England on a Saturday at about 4:00 p.m. While he was talking with some friends, something suddenly took hold of him and he broke away to go for a walk outside. Upon returning, he described a terrible vision that had overtaken him.

In the vision, he had seen a fire break out just three doors down from where he lived, 300 miles (483km) away. A fierce blaze was still raging, he said, and Swedenborg continued to be agitated until 8 o'clock that night, when he proclaimed that it had finally been extinguished.

News of Swedenborg's strange experience spread across the city, and he was asked to give a first-hand account to the governor of Gothenburg. It was not until Monday when a royal messenger arrived in the city that Swedenborg's clairvoyant vision was confirmed to be accurate.

Swedish philosopher, scientist, and clairvoyant visionary Emanuel Swedenborg claimed to be in touch with the dead and beings on higher planes. He recorded his experiences in several weighty volumes.

CLUES FROM BEYOND THE GRAVE

Jane Neumann died on November 22, 1993, exactly 30 years after the assassination of John F. Kennedy. Her body was apparently discovered by her husband, Jim, who initially claimed that there had been a break-in and she had been shot. Later, he changed his story and claimed that Jane had shot herself and left a suicide note, which he had burned to save her family embarrassment. He had thrown the shotgun into a river. Yet the manner of her 'suicide' was bizarre, to say the least.

According to her husband, Jane had rigged the shotgun so that it would fire through a hole in the wall when she pulled a string. Her sister, Kate, thought that the angle of Jane's head was unnatural for someone who had shot herself. The gun barrel was too high for her mouth, and the gun would need to have been rigged with a 30lb (13.7kg) line, according to a ballistics expert. Kate said that her sister did not own a gun and was inexperienced in the use of one.

Although they had their doubts, Jane's family liked Jim and did not want him falsely accused of murder. Kate thought of him as a brother, and they walked hand in hand at Jane's funeral. The couple had come to Kate's every Sunday for lunch with their son, Robert. Despite all this, there was a negative side to Jim Neumann that had not escaped Kate.

HUSBAND A SUSPECT?

While Jim was charming, handsome, and harmless-looking, Kate claimed that he was very controlling and manipulative of her sister, taking charge of her money even when they were simply dating. The investigation uncovered other unsavoury details, including the fact that, shortly before Jane's death, Jim had got rid of their dog because, he said, it kept urinating on the new carpet. He told his wife that she could go and see it whenever she liked, then said that he had given it to a stranger in a supermarket parking lot. He subsequently claimed that it was with someone who lived on a farm, before finally 'admitting' that he had handed it to an animal adoption agency in St Paul, Minnesota. The police discovered that he had in fact given it to an animal centre in St Croix, Wisconsin. While he had given the centre his real name, the address was an old one, and, chillingly, he had said the reason for giving up the dog was because the owner was dead.

The family found a newspaper in the house, apparently kept because it carried the announcement of Kennedy's death. Significantly, perhaps, it also contained the story of a murder that had certain parallels with the death of Jane Neumann. The victim, Carol Thomson, had been murdered by a hitman hired by her husband. Had the story inspired Jim Neumann, and did he have his wife killed on the 30th anniversary of Kennedy's death because it gave him some kind of sick satisfaction?

As further doubts crept into her mind, Kate found that she was dreaming about her dead sister. Jane had seemed happier than ever in the weeks leading up to her death; suicide did not make any sense. In her dreams, Kate talked to Jane and pleaded with her to tell the truth of what happened. Eighteen months after the grisly tragedy, Kate made psychic contact with Jane.

Marcy was a friend of Kate's, but she knew very little about her family or the sad event that had befallen them. The two women were talking in Marcy's studio apartment, when Marcy suddenly said that she had something to tell Kate. She feared it might damage their friendship; but nevertheless, she felt it had to be said. The 'something' was that a young woman was standing next to Kate, one hand on her shoulder, trying very hard to speak to her. 'You can't hear her', Marcy said, 'and she is very frustrated and upset'. To Kate's amazement,

In her dreams, Kate talked to her dead sister, Jane Neumann, begging her to tell the truth about whether she really had committed suicide or had in fact been murdered.

Marcy then went on to correctly describe Jane, even though she had never met her or even seen her in a photograph.

Marcy confessed that she had discovered an ability to channel spirits after her brother's accidental death from a gunshot wound. During channelling, the spirit temporarily takes over the body of the medium, and that had happened spontaneously with her brother. Now she volunteered to try to help Kate by deliberately channelling the spirit of her sister – something she had never attempted before. 'Jane will be there', Marcy said, even though Kate had never mentioned her sister's name.

Marcy's father was present during the first session. While she was meditating, Kate and Marcy's father said prayers. Then Marcy's brother came through and gave them a hug. After a further period of meditation, the spirit of Jane took control of Marcy's body, as Kate explains: 'I knew it was Jane. Marcy is five foot five and Jane barely breaks five feet. She carried herself as if she were shorter, and she had Jane's inflection and vocabulary.'

The possessed Marcy grabbed Kate's arm and asked, 'How could you think I committed suicide?' Speaking through Marcy, 'Jane' then went on to recount the events of that afternoon. She claimed that she had arrived home to find a stranger waiting. Already in terror, she was then injected

Channelling is linked to possession, where an outside spirit takes over the physical body of another. This can be induced during voodoo rituals, during which the subject is driven into a trance, whereupon channelling begins. Occasionally, for safety, those possessed must be restrained by others participating in the ritual.

with a drug that made her body go limp, although she remained conscious. She described the stranger as a man wearing a black Iron Maiden T-shirt emblazoned with a snake coiled around a dagger. He said the reasons for killing her were that Jane was neither a good mother nor a good wife. (These were statements that Jim claimed had been part of her suicide note.) The stranger then told her that he was the angel of death and kissed her on her lips, saying that that was the kiss of death.

Just before Marcy was finally released from the spirit of Jane, Kate said that Robert was still with his father. At this, Jane's 'voice' became extremely frightened and started to cry, saying, 'My Robby. My baby Robby'. Kate later explained that Jane always called her son Robby – something her friend could not have known.

INTERROGATION BY CHANNELLING

Since the police enquiry had led nowhere, Kate's parents had started their own private investigation and prosecution. When special investigators phoned Kate to ask why she thought her sister's death was not suicide, she described what she had been told during the channelling session. There was a long pause on the line, and when Kate asked if any of it matched the evidence, they did not reply. Instead, they asked if they could provide her with a list of questions to put to 'Jane' at a future channelling session. The lawyer hired as part of the investigation sent Kate two pages of questions and commented: 'You really got those guys going with what you told them. An awful lot of what you told them has scared them.'

At the start of the second channelling session, a male spirit came through first of all. He claimed to have witnessed Jane's murder and said that she had been given a combination of two drugs, one of which was a quinine derivative. He also said that two men were present. During the session, Marcy was able to see through Jane's eyes, and she felt the young woman's panic as she stared at the lower part of the killer's face. She noted that on his neck was a tattooed version of the dagger T-shirt motif, with the weapon pointing toward his ear. Marcy said that he was a short, stocky man who looked as if he did weight training, and he had short hair and blue eyes. She also commented that Jane was wearing a black-and-white checked sweater.

As far as Kate was aware, her sister had been wearing a leather jacket when she died. She asked for postmortem pictures of Jane and found that Marcy was right – her sister had been wearing a black-and-white checked sweater under the jacket. No one, not even the family, had seen those pictures apart from officials involved in the enquiry. Kate was sure that Jim was connected with the killers through his job dealing with convicts on a prison work project.

At a third channelling session, the spirit of a woman came through, calling herself Kay, who said that a man named Donald Beckett was linked to Jane's death. She said Beckett was like Jim Neumann – 'he uses women and hurts women'. Kay said Beckett was 'a small man in a room by himself', and described what sounded like a prison. The spirit said that the man had a contact on the outside who had been hired to kill Jane. She also mentioned a date 11 months after the murder.

Kate checked these details with the lawyer handling the investigation. He said that a Donald Becker (not Beckett) had come under suspicion during their enquiries. Becker was in prison for murder at the time of Jane's death and had been participating in the project on which Jim Neumann had worked. The date mentioned by the spirit of 'Kay' was just two days after the murder had been featured in a six-minute segment on television – Kate believes that this was when a payment was made to Becker.

In the end, no direct evidence was found to prove that Jim Neumann had instigated the murder of his wife. However, there were sufficient grounds for the family to return a legal verdict of wrongful death against the man whom Kate had once regarded as a brother.

The R101, designed to serve the British empire, instead signalled the death knell of the airship. Hundreds of men were required to manoeuvre the cumbersome dirigible into position for its first – and last – flight in October 1930.

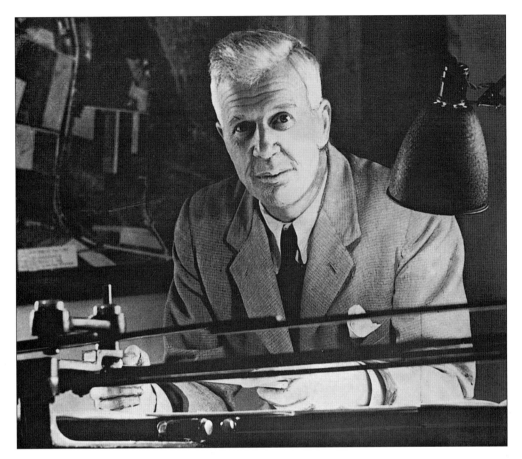

Many years before engineering genius Barnes Wallis invented the famous 'bouncing bomb', he worked for Vickers on the R101's sister ship – the R100. Wallis fitted his airship with lighter petrol engines and successfully flew it to Canada. The heavier diesel engines featured on the R101 caused its gas bags to chafe against the metal frame.

THE CRASH OF THE R101

Channelling and seances are nothing new. More than 60 years before the 'murder' of Jane Neumann, spirits had also been summoned to help explain a mysterious case of death. It was just after 2:00 a.m. on October 5, 1930, when the much-vaunted R101 airship crashed into the side of a small hill near the village of Beauvais in northern France. The aircraft exploded like a bomb, emitting searing waves of heat and light across the French countryside. It was the end of the British aircraft and its 48 passengers and crew, whose screams were heard as they perished in the inferno. All that was left was the R101's charred skeleton and its ensign, which miraculously continued to fly in the gentle breeze of the new dawn.

It was in 1924 that the British government had decided that the empire could best be served by a fleet of passenger-carrying airships. Two vessels were designed and built, far in advance of anything that had gone before. One was made by Vickers under the direction of the engineering genius Barnes Wallis, and the other by the Air Ministry. These were the largest airships the world had ever seen, kept aloft by five million tons of hydrogen. The R101 was built by the Air Ministry at Cardington, near Bedford, and was, in effect, a flying coffin.

During the design of the aircraft, Barnes Wallis had been eager to pool information with Cardington, but was rebuffed. The Air Ministry, which was under the media spotlight, took risks by increasing the gas pressure in order to lift the heavier diesel engines. This resulted in the gas bag chafing against the girders and rivets of the airship's metal frame. Test flights produced many tears in the inflated envelope. These were taped up, and more than 4,000 pads were placed over offending bits of framework.

When Vickers successfully test flew its R100 to Montreal and back in August 1930, using lighter petrol engines, Cardington was put under enormous pressure. Lord Thomson of Cardington was in charge of the project, and he became fanatical about the airship's success. He had his sights set on becoming the next Viceroy of India and was determined to organize a round trip to the subcontinent, to draw favourable attention to his candidature. He was due to attend an Imperial Conference in London, and early October was the latest departure date that would allow him to return in time. Lord Thomson was determined that the R101 would start its journey no later than October 4. Despite the fact that the airship was hardly fit for the voyage, Lord Thomson managed to wangle a

The R100 at its mooring post. While designing the craft at Vickers, Barnes Wallis asked to share information with the Air Ministry, which was producing the R101. His request was refused, with disastrous results.

Psychic researcher Harry Price organized a seance to contact Sir Arthur Conan Doyle, but instead the dead captain of the R101 appeared to come through. Several years later, Price courted controversy when he wrote a best-selling book based on his investigations of Borley rectory, supposedly 'the most haunted house in England'.

temporary Certificate of Airworthiness. An extra gas bag was added between the other two, yet she still struggled to escape her mooring mast. Half the water ballast had to be jettisoned just to get away, and as she passed over London, one of her five engines had already quit. As the R101 reached the Channel, she met with driving rain, but two hours later crossed the French coast near Dieppe.

At midnight, Cardington received the craft's final radio broadcast – an optimistic message describing an excellent meal followed by cigars and bed. It finished with, 'The crew have settled down to a watch-keeping routine'. Why were the crew unaware of the low altitude of the airship or at least showing no concern? At 1:00 a.m., she had dropped to a height of approximately 300ft (91m). One hour later came the fatal crash.

A special Court of Inquiry was set for October 28. There were just six survivors – all crewmen. They could add little evidence to determine the actual cause of the crash. In April, the court delivered its verdict, which was based on educated guesswork. It determined that, owing to the airship's low altitude, a sudden loss of gas in the forward bag – in conjunction with a sudden downdraft – had sent the R101 into the hillside. Any further answers, it seemed, could come only from those who had perished in the crash.

VOICES OF THE DEAD

Two days after the crash, while details of the tragedy were still being suppressed by the Air Ministry, a small group of people met at Harry Price's National Laboratory of Psychical Research in London. Included in the gathering was Price, medium Eileen Garrett, sceptical Australian journalist Ian Coster, and a shorthand writer to take detailed notes of the experiment that was planned. Sir Arthur Conan Doyle had died a few months earlier, and the purpose of the seance – although Eileen Garrett did not know this in advance – was to contact the celebrated author and mystic.

They settled down in the darkened room, and Mrs Garrett fell into a trance. Instead of Conan Doyle, someone else channelled himself through the medium, someone called 'Irwin'. Flight Lieutenant H. Carmichael Irwin had been the captain of the R101. He spoke through Mrs Garrett in rapid staccato bursts with barely controlled hysteria: 'The whole bulk of the dirigible was entirely and absolutely too much for her engine capacity. Engines too heavy. It was this that made me on five occasions have to scuttle back to safety. Useful lift too small. Gross lift computed badly. Inform control panel. And this idea of new elevators totally mad. Elevator jammed. Oil pipe plugged. This exorbitant scheme of carbon and hydrogen is entirely and absolutely wrong …

'Never reached cruising altitude. Same in trials. Two short trials. No one knew the ship properly. Airscrews too

Medium Eileen Garrett, allegedly in a trance, was photographed using ultraviolet flash on September 14, 1936. To channel spirits, a psychic must first enter a state of altered consciousness, which subordinates the medium's own personality. This allows the spirit to take control of the psychic's body and communicate directly with the sitters.

small. Fuel injection bad and air pump failed. Cooling system bad. Bore capacity bad. Five occasions I have had to scuttle back – three times before starting.

'Not satisfied with feed … Weather bad for long flight. Fabric all waterlogged and ship's nose down. Impossible to rise. Cannot trim … Almost scraped roofs at Achy. At enquiry to be held later it will be found that the superstructure of the envelope contained no resilience. The added middle section was entirely wrong … too heavy.'

Major Oliver Villiers had lost many friends in the disaster, particularly Flight Lieutenant Irwin, and was badly affected by it. He had driven his boss, Sir Sefton Brancker, Director of Civil Aviation at the Air Ministry, to the airship on the day of its departure and ultimately to his death. Late at night on the eve of the enquiry, Villiers suddenly had an overwhelming impression that Irwin was in the room with him. Then, in his head, he heard the airship captain cry out: 'For God's sake, let me talk to you. It's all so ghastly. I must speak to you. I must. We're all bloody murderers. For God's sake, help me speak to you.'

COMMUNING WITH SPIRITS

Villiers related the experience to a house guest who was a spiritualist. He arranged a meeting with Eileen Garrett, and from this arose several seances, the first on October 31. During this session Villiers spoke freely with Irwin, and in later seances several of his colleagues, including Sir Sefton Brancker, were channelled through Mrs Garrett. Villiers made copious notes of his conversation with the spirit of the dead airman, in which Irwin said in part: 'During the afternoon before starting, I noticed that the gas indicator was going up and down, which showed there was a leakage or escape which I could not stop or rectify any time around the valves. The goldbeater skins are porous and not strong enough. And the constant movement of the gas bags, acting like bellows, is constantly causing internal pressure of the gas, which causes a leakage of the valves.

'I told the chief engineer of this. I then knew we were almost doomed. Then later on, the meteorological charts came in, and Scottie and Johnnie [other officers] and I had a consultation. Owing to the trouble of the gas, we knew that our only chance was to leave on the scheduled time. The weather forecast was no good. But we decided we might cross the Channel and tie up at Le Bourget before the bad weather came. We three were absolutely scared stiff. And Scottie said to us, "Look here, we are in for it – but for God's sake, let's smile like damned Cheshire cats as we go on board, and leave England with a clean pair of heels"'.

Neither Harry Price nor Oliver Villiers knew about each other's seances, and quite independently of one another, they decided to put their findings to Sir John Simon, who was heading the court of enquiry, and Price also informed the Air Ministry. Not surprisingly perhaps, neither would accept the seance results as evidence.

WAS THE TRUTH REALLY OUT THERE?

In 1979, veteran mystery journalist John Fuller published a book about the R101 affair called *The Airmen Who Would Not Die*. Fuller examined the technical information from 'Irwin' in detail and cited old Cardington employees, who gave a favourable expert opinion. No one believed that Eileen Garrett was fraudulent, and yet the information that came from her mouth, allegedly from the airship captain, contained engineering concepts with which no layman – or woman – was expected to be familiar.

Fuller argued that none of those present at the seance knew anything about airship design and operation, and therefore the information could not have originated from them either consciously or unconsciously, as telepathy for instance. The disembodied Irwin also referred to the fuel as being a hydrogen–carbon mix and claimed the airship 'almost scraped the roofs of Achy'. Harry Price tried to find Achy on regular maps without success. However, when he consulted a large-scale railway map of the Beauvais area, as detailed as the charts that Irwin had in the control cabin, he found the tiny hamlet. Who would have known this other than the captain of the R101?

It was Harry Price who had the transcript minutely examined by Will Charlton and other employees at Cardington. They apparently were astonished at the technical detail, and Charlton claimed that no one but Irwin could have possessed the information. He seemed to have explained what had caused the crash.

However, critics claimed that the matter was not so clear cut. It emerged that Will Charlton was not an 'expert', but someone in charge of stores and supplies at Cardington. He was also a spiritualist. One of those challenging Charlton's views was Archie Jarman, whom Fuller credited as knowing more about the subject than any other living person.

When Price asked Charlton what 'Irwin' meant by the reference 'SL8', he had to comb the entire records of German airships to find the answer – as if this was an obscure piece of information of which only a real expert such as Irwin would be aware. The *Schutte Lanz* was one of the Zeppelins shot down over England in 1916, and, as Jarman pointed out, if Charlton was a real expert,

Through Garrett, the 'spirit' of the R101's dead captain related how the struggling airship had passed over Achy, near Beauvais. This small French village is not even marked on ordinary maps of the area, such as that below. Did the medium somehow know the obscure hamlet or was this truly a voice from beyond the grave?

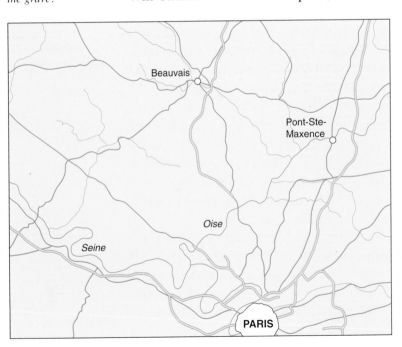

he should have known this. Also, such facts were readily available to others.

While Jarman was compiling a report on the R101 affair in the early 1960s, he consulted his own experts: Wing Commander Cave-Brown-Cave, who had been closely involved in the airship's construction, and Wing Commander Booth, who had captained the R100 on its Montreal flight. Booth said: 'I have read the description of the Price–Irwin seance with great care and am of the opinion that the messages received do not assist in any way in determining why the airship R101 crashed.'

The awesome wreck of the R101, with its steel superstructure clearly exposed – reduced to a twisted mass of metal. Only six survived the devastating crash.

SEANCE SCEPTICS

As for the Villiers seance, Booth commented: 'I am in complete disagreement with almost every paragraph ... the conversations are completely out of character; the atmosphere at Cardington is completely wrong, and the technical and handling explanation could not possibly have been messages from anyone with airship experience.' For instance, regarding 'Irwin's' comment about the gas indicator going up and down, Booth noted that no such instruments were fitted. From what was supposedly said during the seances, the officers knew they were setting off on a suicidal mission before the airship had left England. Writer Edward Horton argues that if this really was the case – and there was no indication of this before the seances – all Irwin had to do was turn the airship around and, with the wind behind them, limp back to Cardington.

Jarman believes that the statements from the Harry Price sitting attributed to Irwin could have arisen from either Mrs Garrett's own subconscious or perhaps a telepathic ability that enabled her to take in information from others present in the room, particularly the journalist Coster. There had been a lot of information published in the press about the airships during their design and construction.

With regard to the hamlet of Achy, Jarman, who knew Eileen Garrett well, claimed that she frequently drove between Calais and Paris. He claimed that Achy was signposted along the route and that the medium could have subconsciously absorbed this fact. Certainly, Harry Price did not believe that Irwin's spirit was speaking through Mrs Garrett, but nevertheless he was astonished by the amount of technical information that was recounted. Perhaps while in an altered state she had tapped into the 'collective unconscious', as postulated by the influential psychologist Carl Jung.

DISASTER FORETOLD

The debate is still open as to whether or not the dramatic utterings during these seances solved the mystery of what went so tragically wrong aboard the ill-fated R101. Yet even while the airship was being built, there had been warnings – one from beyond the grave – of the catastrophe to come. On March 13, 1928, a Captain W. R. Hinchcliffe, accompanied by the heiress Elsie Mackay, took off from Cranwell aerodrome in Lincolnshire, England, to fly the Atlantic. They completely disappeared.

Little more than two weeks later, on March 31, a Mrs Beatrice Earl received a strange message while using her Ouija board, which said: 'Hinchcliffe, tell my wife I want to speak to her.' Through Sir Arthur Conan Doyle, Mrs Earl passed on the message to the pilot's widow, Emilie. She agreed to allow the famous medium Eileen Garrett to try to contact her dead husband.

The long line of flag-draped coffins containing the victims of the R101 tragedy, as they lie in state at Westminster Abbey.

A number of sessions followed during which 'Hinchcliffe' became increasingly concerned about the R101. He commented: 'I want to say something about the new airship ... the vessel will not stand the strain.' It turned out that the navigator was his old chum Squadron Leader Johnson, whom he insisted should be told of these worries. This was duly done, but Johnson was not impressed. As the airship headed for France, the spirit delivered his last message to Mrs

Garrett: 'Storms rising, nothing but a miracle can save them.' The medium then had visions of the R101 in flames.

Just two days before the crash, Mr R. W. Boyd of London told his fiancée, Catherine Hare, that he had experienced a vision of the R101 in difficulties, before crashing into a hilltop. Boyd said that he had seen burning bodies falling from the vessel and then soldiers arriving on horseback. When details of the event were later recorded, many of these observations proved accurate.

DETECTIVE FILE:
Eileen Garrett: Medium supreme

As both the subject of study and a researcher, Eileen Garrett pioneered investigations into the paranormal.

The renowned medium Eileen Garrett was remarkably objective about her strange powers. In her book *Adventures In The Supernatural*, published in 1949, she wrote: 'I have a gift, a capacity – a delusion, if you will – which is called "psychic". I do not care what it may be called, for living with and utilizing this psychic capacity long ago inured me to a variety of epithets – ranging from expressions almost of reverence, through doubt and pity, to open vituperation. In short, I have been called many things, from a charlatan to a miracle worker. I am, at least, neither of these.'

Born in Ireland in 1893, Garrett began her career in Britain and later became an American citizen. There she founded the Parapsychology Foundation in New York, through which she promoted impartial enquiry into psychic phenomena. The foundation funded many groups and individuals in their scientific research, and it also developed a European centre in France. Garrett preferred an experimental approach, one which included exploring altered states of consciousness, such as hypnosis, and the effects of various mind-altering drugs, such as mescaline and LSD.

She was originally invited to the United States by the American Society for Psychical Research in 1931 and was studied by many researchers, including Hereward Carrington. The experimenters were satisfied that Garrett possessed a genuine ability and was not a fake. Like most mediums, she worked through a spirit guide when in trance. Her 'control' was called 'Uvani', and later she came to believe that he was an aspect of her own personality. Eileen Garrett died in 1970.

Irish-born Eileen Garrett began her career in Britain before becoming an American citizen. Among her spirit guides were 'Abdul Latif' and 'Uvani', whom she came to suspect were really facets of her own mind. Throughout her many years of work as a medium and psychic researcher, Garrett's sincerity and integrity were never questioned.

FACT FILE:
Hypnotic trance and hallucination

The exploration of altered states of consciousness – as experienced through hypnosis and hallucinations – is central in our effort to understand the nature of psychic phenomena.

Individuals receiving information psychically seem to do so while they are in a state of altered consciousness, or hypnotic trance. Victorian-era illustrations dealing with the popular subject of spiritualism often depict subjects being hypnotized in order to become receptive to clairvoyant visions. While mediums purposely put

themselves into a state of 'higher' awareness, many people who experience spontaneous flashes of enlightenment do so unconsciously. People that experience sudden psychic insights in this way are

often carrying out mundane tasks at the time, such as driving a car on a monotonous road or standing at the sink washing up the dirty dishes. Through 'automatic' chores such as these, one can seemingly enter into a light trance: as one part of the brain is kept occupied, another is allowed to open up and receive impressions from elsewhere. But what exactly is hypnosis, and how does it work?

Contrary to popular belief, people cannot be hypnotized against their will, nor do they drift into deep sleep. Subjects are both aware of their surroundings and of the place to which their mind has been directed. Dr Moyshe Kalman, a psychoanalyst who has conducted past life and alien abduction experiments, says that hypnosis enables the subject to bring together what

Stage hypnotists use showmanship to present themselves as powerful Svengali-like figures. In truth, they are merely facilitators – no one can be hypnotized against his will. Basically, subjects put themselves into a trance.

Under hypnosis, a subject is often able to do things of which they are normally physically incapable. In this demonstration, photographed in 1886, the body of the entranced subject remains rigid when elevated in mid-air, supported only by the tops of two chairs.

ordinarily are two mutually incompatible mental states – relaxation and concentration. The body is relaxed as if asleep, yet the mind is focused and uncluttered. This unique state enables one to remember and experience things that are normally out of reach.

Hallucinations are sensory perceptions that are received in the absence of external stimuli. They can be generated by removing all external stimuli – for example, by placing a subject in a sensory deprivation chamber – or through physical illness such as a severe fever, as a result of mental disorders such as schizophrenia, or by taking mind-bending drugs such as alcohol and LSD. Schizophrenics may hear the voices of their persecutors, conversations about themselves by third parties, or their own thoughts spoken aloud.

Many people have used hallucinatory drugs in the quest for personal knowledge and in order to commune with higher beings. Chief among these are shamans, or medicine men, in certain cultures. By using chemical substances as part of their rituals, they attain a state of altered consciousness in which they claim to gain new insights and foresee future events.

One leading British horror writer told the co-author of this book, Peter Hough, that all of his early work was written under the influence of cannabis, which he felt freed his mind when devising plots and characterizations. Hallucinogenic drugs are often regarded as opening up creative pathways, which is perhaps why so many artists and rock musicians experiment with such potentially harmful substances.

The widespread use of psychedelic substances is testament to people's desire to swap the mundane realities of everyday life for the initial excitement of exploring one's 'inner space'. Here, drug squad officers handle LSD tabs worth £5 million, recovered in 1995 after a raid on an illegal drug factory in north London.

Profile of a Psychic Sleuth

Are psychic abilities part of our genetic make-up and therefore a characteristic that can be passed on through the generations of one family? Can some as yet undefined DNA code explain who becomes psychic and who does not?

WHEN SHE WAS JUST A SMALL CHILD, Renie Wiley knew that she was different. Her psychic abilities first manifested themselves at school, where they soon got her into trouble. On the very first day, she told her teacher that her car had a flat tire. Thinking that this was a helpful thing to do, Renie had not considered that the woman might wonder how it was that a little girl could know this while inside the school building and with the vehicle parked out of sight. After going outside and confirming the truth, the puzzled teacher frogmarched the distraught child to the principal's office on the premise that awareness of the deflated tire could come in just one way – if she had been responsible for doing it!

Once confronted by the head teacher, Renie stood firm by her innocence, but this rather straight-laced tutor was unable to accept the word of a six-year-old in the face of physical evidence. So Renie's parents were called to observe the discipline that would be meted out. They tried to placate the principal with news that there was a history of ESP within the family and that their daughter had inherited this 'gift'. Clearly, that was not what a small-town head teacher in the early postwar years wanted to hear.

Still bemused as to why these adults were arguing over what Renie simply regarded as a helpful observation, the little girl judged that the best way forward was to prove herself again.

Renie eyed the principal coolly and said: 'I can tell you what you had for dinner, if that will help,' before regaling the startled man with the full details of his recent culinary experiences. Stunned as he was by this account, it had nothing on the revelation that followed. His pained expression moments later told Renie that she had inadvertently committed another mistake when she had added, 'Oh, and that lady you had dinner with …', before describing in detail a woman who was obviously not the headmaster's wife.

The principal promptly accepted Renie's story and dismissed the charges, telling her not to mention it to anyone again. Thus the young girl learned at a tender age the first lesson of being a psychic detective: sometimes you see things that your clients do not want you to see. She discovered that in such cases you must temper the natural desire to be open and helpful with a strong dose of tact, to avoid falsely implicating yourself or landing others in more hot water than they have bargained for.

MRI (magnetic resonance imaging) techniques help scientists to map out the functions of the brain, illuminating which sections are active during different types of physical and mental tasks, and during certain emotional experiences. Will we soon uncover the location of the psychic brain?

ATTRIBUTES OF A PSYCHIC

What makes a psychic detective? Renie Wiley's story suggests that extrasensory abilities can be genetic. Folk wisdom has long held that witches (who in less superstitious times may have been recognized as psychically aware individuals, rather than being branded satanic) are born into the seventh generation of certain families.

Witches also tend to be female, as indeed are more than three-quarters of psychic detectives. Part of the reason for this may well be that the female brain operates in a different way to the male brain. Recent scientific studies have shown that, in females, the brain tends to rely less on areas that govern manual dexterity or spatial awareness, and instead uses language and vision centres more fully. Since these functions specifically relate to the parts of the brain known to be more active during periods of psychic awareness, it is likely that women are simply more easily able than men to harness these normal abilities.

Hence, there appears to be some genuine physiological basis for the old belief in 'women's intuition'.

However, with psychics such as Renie Wiley, there may also be other factors at work. For example, she was born with a larger than normal heart located further to the right than this organ is found in most people. At birth, she had struggled to survive and did not breathe unaided for over an hour. It is impossible to say how this trauma may have affected the development of her psychic abilities, but it could have left her disposed to have 'out-of-body' or near-death experiences. As Renie grew, she had a number of these, where she found herself floating in

Psychics such as Renie Wiley often report out-of-body experiences, in which their spirit leaves their physical being to float temporarily free of earthly shackles, as in this William Blake depiction of a soul departing at death.

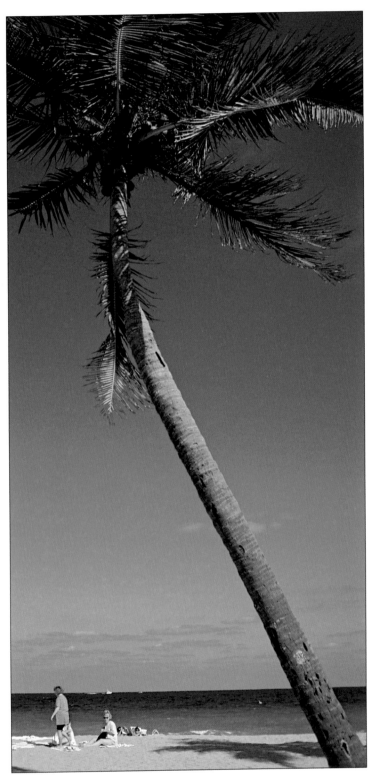

a position beyond her physical self and looking down from the edge of heaven. Regardless of whether we choose to interpret these events as psychological or physically real, they undoubtedly gave her an appreciation of the spiritual realm and an eagerness to learn more.

No doubt it was equally important that her parents did not outlaw such phenomena, in the way that most children are told from a very early age that anything supernatural is frightening or should be considered to be a mere figment of the imagination. Studies suggest that this negative teaching makes children grow out of innate abilities that most of us initially possess. Psychic detectives may develop largely because they do not have the common incentive to 'unlearn' natural skills, and thus routinely access extrasensory information.

'FEELING' THINGS

We can see how Renie Wiley's apparent powers work by looking at one of the earliest cases in which she assisted the police. This occurred in July 1981 in a suburb of Fort Lauderdale, Florida, where she lived. A six-year-old boy, Adam Walsh, had disappeared and official police searches were growing ever more frantic. Prompted by publicity for some of her psychic flashes, investigating officer Tom Rozzo asked if Renie was willing to assist. She was glad to try, but strictly on her own terms.

As Renie explains, her abilities operate through a sense of empathy.

She 'feels' the experience of the person at the centre of any incident and lets images enter her mind. She then describes these pictures (which may be symbolic and not literal), in the hope that they will yield useful information.

Because these powerful feelings often overwhelm her, Renie has two strict codes. She will not work with the family of any victim, because their own emotions are generally so strong that they 'swamp' any true insight. In addition, she always insists on steering clear of the media until a case has been solved, since the gaze of publicity and the attention of thousands of people equally complicate the delicate process.

What Renie did agree to do that summer's day was to drive with police through the streets of Fort Lauderdale, trying to 'sense' the whereabouts of the missing boy. She succeeded in a way more horrifying than she had ever expected. As they cruised the outskirts of the city, she suddenly 'tuned in' to the last moments of Adam Walsh's life and literally relived his death. His head was literally twisted off, after which his decapitated body was tossed into water.

A shocked Rozzo watched dumbfounded as the woman absorbed the pain of this sudden, violent death and then indicated where to look for the boy's body. Soon after, she was taken home to recover from this physical and emotional ordeal, Adam Walsh's body was found in a nearby canal. His death had indeed come about in just the way that the psychic had related.

Fort Lauderdale, Florida, Renie Wiley's home town, and where her 'empathic' powers were first put to the test following the disappearance of a six-year-old boy.

Psychic dreams are often laden with strange imagery the significance of which is unclear. The psychic detective's greatest challenge is learning to translate these symbols into useful information.

COMPILING CRIMINAL PROFILES

As she developed her abilities, Renie Wiley came to appreciate some of the difficulties of operating on a semi-professional level as a psychic detective. Although her visions were random and could not be made to work to order, police needed specific insights – facts that they could use to track a killer or to find a hidden weapon, for example.

The problem was that when she saw things in her mind, they often appeared as symbolic images, rather than actual visions of the event. Decoding the meaning of these symbols was the most difficult

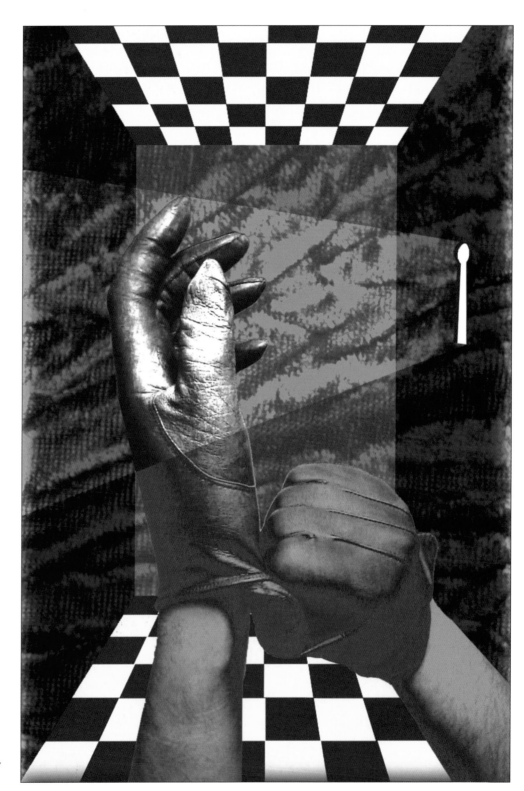

In December 1981, Renie Wiley reported that she had dreamt of a burglar in action. From the clues provided in her vision, including the observation that the man's breathing was laboured, the police were able to recognize a prime suspect.

task. On one occasion, she helped in the search for a teenager who went missing after spending New Year's Eve at a club. The images she received were imprecise and confusing, and the most that could be interpreted was that the woman was dead and her body lay 20 miles (32km) from the club. Apart from this, she sensed that a 'king' was somehow connected to the location. Such vagueness is an occupational hazard of gaining insight by psychic means.

Unfortunately, this was by no means enough to assist in the official investigation. A 20-mile (32km) radius of Florida countryside was a vast area to search, and as for the link with a 'king' – should detectives check places such as Regal Highway or a town called Monarch, or a person named Royal? It was a hopeless task. As the police told Renie, very exact locations were necessary in order to dig for a buried body. The public would not put up with huge areas of land being randomly unearthed on the whim of a psychic.

It is often easier to use supernatural skills to profile a criminal. This is because police forces operate by way of witness descriptions all the time and so are geared up to identify a person more rapidly than a location. In December 1981, Renie assisted in the hunt for a burglar by offering a picture of the man seen in her visions. To this she was able to add clues, such as that he had problems with his breathing. From this news the officers soon realized that her description was remarkably like a man that they had interviewed, but had not suspected of the crimes. When his wife confirmed that he was an asthma sufferer, they began to believe that the psychic may be onto something. Unfortunately, the delay in determining how seriously to take this 'insight' proved significant. By the time the police went after the suspect at a hotel where he was found to be staying, the man had fled. If they had gone to arrest him when the information was first provided, he may well have been captured.

RENIE'S 'BIRD DOGGING' STRATEGY

An unusual problem experienced by psychics is the difficulty they have in knowing whether images that they see relate to the past or to the future. Surprisingly, in terms of ESP, time seems not to have the same rigid meaning that we are used to in everyday life. This has often created worrying situations in which clues offered to the police in the hunt for a murderer led nowhere because – tragically – the information actually related to the killer's next victim, rather than events that had already taken place. Such failures leave psychics deeply troubled. It is human nature that they are bound to ask themselves if it was possible that they could have prevented a death by being better at their job. This feeling of frustration is something that all psychic detectives go through, despite the successes that they frequently have.

As a way of trying to minimize these problems, Renie Wiley developed a technique she calls 'bird dogging'. This means that she literally steps into the

DETECTIVE FILE:

Nancy Myer: Prolific crime-buster

Like many psychic detectives, Nancy Myer finds that her unusual work can exact a huge emotional toll.

Nancy Myer is a potential world record holder for solving the most crimes by way of psychic detection. She claims to have assisted in the resolution of well over 200 cases. Myer, a single mother now in her mid-50s, lives in Ohio and has worked all over the United States for a quarter of a century. Her 'career' began unexpectedly while she was playing with a Ouija board at home. This seems to have acted as a trigger, unleashing Myer's latent psychic abilities. Soon images began flooding in every time she tried to use the board, and in the end she had to destroy it before it destroyed her.

By the time she was 29, the strength of Myer's visions had become so intense that she had to keep away from crowded rooms, where she felt drowned by all the emotions of the many people present. Learning to control this problem was the most difficult stage in establishing herself as a psychic detective, but gradually she adopted a process by which she could home in on the most relevant images that submerged her mind. The method that worked best for her was to use a photograph of the victim as a 'prop'. By running her hands over it, she discovered that it was possible to channel the images

Nancy Myer's supernatural detection work was triggered by a 'game' – a Ouija board. This device allegedly enables the player to communicate with spirits, who move the pointer to spell out words. Psychologists believe that the movements probably stem from the collective unconscious of the participants, but in Nancy's case her innate psychic abilities were suddenly set free.

that subsequently came to her.

Since the mid-1970s, Myer has specialized in long-running murder cases and the hunt for serial killers, since the powerful emotions that these investigations generate bring her the clearest pictures. She wishes that she could escape this barrage of strong images, but considers it both a duty to society and a race against time to help police catch a killer before they strike again.

However, she admits that working on a case leaves her physically and emotionally drained. Like a human sponge, she absorbs a host of negative feelings, and is often left in a fragile mental state for days or weeks afterward.

Another difficulty Myer faces is that she often picks up so many emotional signals that she traps criminals virtually by accident. More than once, while driving with police to investigate a case, she has suddenly been

hit by a tidal wave of emotions when passing a house along the route. The police, having seen the psychic virtually collapse under the burden of this bizarre psychological assault, have subsequently investigated the premises in question and discovered it to be the home of a suspect from another crime, who would later be arrested.

Detective Leroy Landon confirmed that he had seen this eerie process in action, noting that Nancy Myer had frequently solved unconnected crimes merely by chancing to drive past a house owned by a culprit. Landon recognizes that many people would regard as utterly absurd the very notion of catching criminals in this way, but pragmatically points out that 'no one can argue with you if you are getting convictions'.

As Nancy Myer's psychic powers became more strongly established, she found that she had to avoid crowds, where she felt overwhelmed by the barrage of feelings emanating from so many people.

Psychic detection can be hazardous to one's health. Many psychics have suffered great emotional distress or even complete burn-out from the strain of being engulfed by the negative 'vibrations' of criminals and the anguish of their victims.

mind of the person that she sees in her visions. Usually this is the victim, though occasionally it is the criminal. Either way, this process roots her in time so that she observes the crime that has been committed as if it is happening there and then. On one occasion, she started bird dogging and entered the mind of a woman just as she was surprised in an office store room and then brutally

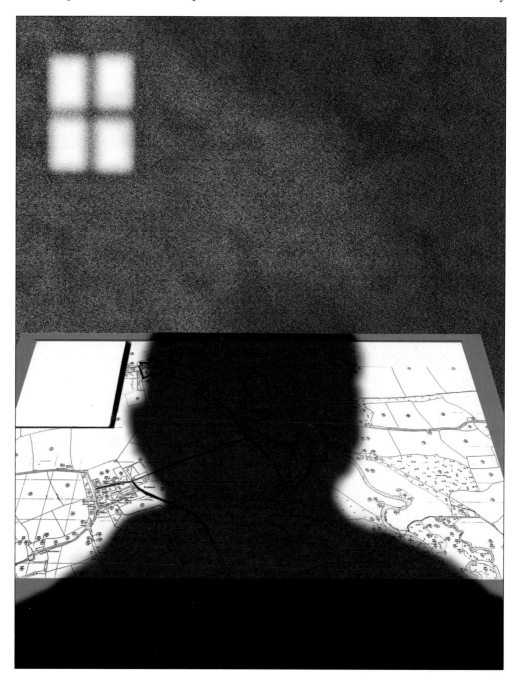

'Bird dogging' is a remarkable technique practised by psychic Renie Wiley. Using this method, she 'enters' the mind of a criminal (or a victim) and somehow observes the crime unfolding through his or her eyes.

stabbed. Renie was able to catch a glimpse of the killer, as seen by the eyes of the murdered woman just before they closed forever.

Bird dogging is an invaluable technique in bringing into focus the hunt for clues, but it is an emotionally draining experience. Because Renie is naturally a very creative person (she is an artist by trade, commercially exploiting her talent at visualization), when she enters the mind of a killer or his victim it can be extremely harrowing. More than once she has become so absorbed in those experiences that she has lost track of her current environment and ended up fearing for her own life. Since she feels all the pain as if at first hand, the situation becomes almost as dangerous as if she herself were the target of a murderer.

Clearly, no one can endure that kind of stress for very long or too often. The strain of carrying such a heavy emotional burden, and the personal responsibility of trying to interpret often baffling insights when lives may be at stake, cause many psychic detectives to retire early in their career.

THE FIRST PSYCHIC
DETECTIVE AGENCY

As Renie Wiley became more accustomed to assisting the police, and they became familiar with her capabilities, she was asked to increase the range of her support. At one stage, she was even requested to teach a course in the understanding of psychic impressions. This was to be administered to local police so that they might gain more appreciation of how to work with psychics during their investigations.

A further benefit of this course, organized by the police training officer in Broward County, Florida, was that Renie could teach officers how to use their own latent ESP to help fight crime. It was not uncommon for investigators to 'play hunches' and 'follow their nose'. Police have been doing this for years, and Sir Arthur Conan Doyle even wrote the concept into his fictional 'psychic' detective, Sherlock Holmes. However, most officers did not realize that

Psychics are increasingly being called upon to train ordinary police detectives to develop their own natural intuition, in the tradition of Sherlock Holmes. Sometimes a 'copper's hunch' may be more than just a lucky guess.

intuition could be a form of psychic ability and not merely guesswork or the result of long experience. It was hoped that by receiving this training detectives might learn how to use their own innate skills more wisely.

Renie also found advantage in working with other psychics, especially in particularly troublesome cases where serial killers were involved. Networking of psychics in this way had several benefits. First, it allowed a pooling of insights that might better trap the killer. Second, it made individual psychics feel safer, since often their greatest fear – as Renie had experienced several times by now – was that they were so 'tuned in' to the murderer that they had become vulnerable. They understandably believed that if they could 'sense' him at work, then he could sense them, too, and might decide to curtail their efforts to bring his crimes to justice by making them the next victim. Where more than one psychic was involved, it was felt that there was safety in numbers.

By 1984, Renie Wiley decided to formalize this plan. Operating from her office, which she dubbed the 'Dragon's Lair' (on the grounds that dragons were mystical, misunderstood creatures), she created the first official psychic

Renie Wiley chose to call her psychic detective agency the 'Dragon's Lair', reflecting an unsurprising empathy with these magical yet maligned beasts.

CASE FILE:
Edgar Mitchell: Space telepathy

Can mental messages be transmitted from outer space? Astronaut Edgar G. Mitchell made his own trials while on a moon mission and has continued to investigate the paranormal.

Edgar Mitchell is one of the select few to have walked on the moon. The NASA astronaut piloted the *Apollo 14* lunar module in 1971 and experienced something of a spiritual epiphany while on the moon's grey, dusty surface.

Mitchell reported that seeing the Earth as a beautiful blue orb surrounded by the infinite black void of space made him aware of how little we understood the cosmos and how we might explore our role in the wider scheme of existence.

While on his mission, Mitchell developed a strong interest in extrasensory perception and conducted experiments in which he attempted to send telepathic messages back to Earth from space. Earlier, Soviet cosmonauts had also covertly performed similar trials, reputedly with some success.

Although now retired, Mitchell has continued his interest in the paranormal. He has lectured on the subject and taken part in research examining 'the psychic potential of man and other forms of life'. He believes that the future of science could lie in a much greater awareness of the unseen powers which psychic experiences suggest that we may all possess. Mitchell hopes that by unravelling the means by which such phenomena occur, humanity can reap huge benefits.

Edgar G. Mitchell – former astronaut and present-day psychic researcher – is seen here in his space suit alongside the emblem of Apollo 14, the NASA mission which saw him become the sixth man to walk on the moon.

The lunar module piloted by Mitchell traverses the desolate surface of our airless moon, leaving clear tracks in the forlorn dust. It was here in this lonely terrain that the astronaut gained new insights into the spirituality of man.

DETECTIVE FILE:
Bulgaria's mystic 'Aunt Vanga'

Revered in her native Bulgaria, blind psychic Vangelia Gushterova predicted many major events in her lifetime and was regularly consulted by senior politicians.

Vangelia Gushterova, or Aunt Vanga, as she was known throughout Bulgaria, was born in neighbouring Macedonia in 1911 and found fame after losing her eyesight in a wind storm when she was only 12. The loss of one of her five senses seemed to have encouraged the development of a sixth – clairvoyancy.

During her long life, the blind, web-fingered peasant successfully located numerous missing people and victims of kidnappers. She also made many accurate predictions, fore-seeing the outbreak of World War II, the coming to power of the communists in 1944, the invasion of Czechoslovakia in 1968, and an earth-quake in Bulgaria in 1985. Aunt Vanga was consulted by more than a million people, including respected politicians and intellectuals. Among those who regularly sought her advice were Leonid Brezhnev, Mikhail Gorbachev, Vladimir Zhirinovsky, and the communist dictator Todor Zhivkov.

When she was pursuing information, Aunt Vanga went into an altered state of consciousness. She claimed that her powers came from an ancient city buried beneath Rupite, the village near the Greek border where she lived.

Natural boiling spring water, which many believe has special healing properties, bubbles outside her house. Coloured lights have also been seen in the sky over the area; these are attributed by some people to supernatural causes.

Vangelia Gushterova died of cancer at age 85, on August 11, 1996, in a Sofia hospital, having foretold the time of her own death. The president, prime minister, and tens of thousands of ordinary Bulgarians attended the funeral of the great psychic.

'Aunt Vanga', pictured here in 1994, was accorded saint-like status across Bulgaria for her amazing clairvoyant powers.

Britons listen intently on September 3, 1939, as it is announced that England is at war. Vangelia Gushterova predicted the outbreak of the conflict.

detective agency. Combining her unique talents with those of a retired police officer in central Florida, she formed a liaison of psychics from all over the country. Under her supervision, this most unusual group of 'private eyes' set out to offer help in cases where local police departments had requested assistance.

The novel agency has been a success but, in the interests of protecting its operatives from undue stress, has chosen to specialize in less trying cases, such as searching for stolen property. However, police still request Renie's help when in desperate straits with cases in which lives are at risk. She has made it a rule not to charge a fee in such situations, feeling that the revenue from recovering missing items is sufficient to keep the agency in business. The publicity gained from assisting in these more serious crimes invariably brings its own rewards in the form of promotion for the firm's day-to-day services.

Following Renie's lead, other psychic detective agencies have since been created around the world, giving further outlets for combining the talents of psychics with the disciplined investigative skills of the police.

The Dragon's Lair agency employs various types of psychics to assist in their casework, including psychic artists such as Coral Polge, seen here with clairaudient colleague Ron Hearne. In this picture, Polge has just sketched the image of someone seen in one of her visions.

VISUAL CREATIVITY AND STRONG EMOTIONS

A major clue about what can make an ordinary person a psychic has been uncovered during recent research, in which experimenters have sought to 'transmit' pictures to a psychic receiver by thought alone. The participants, who profess psychic abilities, completed well-established psychological question-naires (such as the Minnesota multiphasic personality inventory). Other test subjects included witnesses to strange phenomena – from out-of-body experiences to alien contact cases.

Distinct patterns have emerged. One of the most striking results is that the subjects have shown high levels of visual creativity. Indeed, many psychic detectives are artistic, and several have been found to possess near-photographic memories, enabling them to recall and accurately reproduce a complex visual image several hours after it has been briefly shown to them. Even the handwriting of psychics tends to be relatively ornate, with an unusual number of curls and fine touches.

Experiments by Florida psychiatrist Dr Berthold Schwarz showed that a psychic who is attempting to 'receive' a transmitted image will tend to do so in a creative way that is personally significant. One man, seeking to 'tune in' to a picture of a hill being transmitted from another room by a female researcher that he admired, picked up the essence of the image, but drew it in a way that was appropriate to him and also emotionally relevant. He sketched a woman's upward-facing breast. The form was similar to the transmitted image, but the symbolism chosen was deeply personal.

At Edinburgh University in Scotland, Dr Robert Morris has, since 1997, adopted a new series of tests that seek to use the knowledge gathered in research laboratories around the world. In previous experiments, a random sample of four images was 'sent' from a separate room to psychics, who attempted to describe what they saw. They then sought to match their vision to one of the four images that might have been the target. If there is no such thing as ESP, then sheer guesswork would yield an average success rate of one in four, or 25 percent.

In earlier research using test images that lacked psychological resonance, results tended to only slightly exceed the level expected through pure chance. The findings were slightly significant in a statistical sense, but not enough to persuade most scientists that paranormal effects could be seen. However, when visual images with a strong emotional component were transmitted, scores rose dramatically to a level of nearly 50 percent. This is well above chance expectation and good evidence for the reality of ESP.

Applied on a wider scale outside the laboratory, this suggests that psychic detectives will also have greater success in highly emotive cases. It also seems to explain why Renie Wiley feels that she works better when not distracted by the powerful emotions inevitably 'sent out' by the distraught family of a victim.

A major finding by researchers into the characteristics of psychics is that they have a well-above-average tendency to be visually creative. This trait often manifests as artistic talent in pursuits such as painting, sculpture, or poetry.

The Police View

W HAT DO THE AUTHORITIES themselves think about obtaining information from 'supernatural' sources? During major criminal investigations, detectives may be eager for any leads that they can get. Yet, while it may seem dramatic and positive for officers to enlist a psychic to help solve a difficult case, such open-minded tactics nevertheless have drawbacks when compared with normal police procedures.

It is easy to picture the dilemma faced by police in Lincoln, England, during the summer of 1992 when medium Bryan Gibson first got in touch. In January of that year, Norman Allen had died in his betting shop. He had been struck on the head during what was assumed to be an aborted robbery and the police had not been able to catch his killer. Six months later, Gibson called detectives to tell them that the dead man had spoken to him during two separate seances and wished to help solve his own murder.

The 'spirit' of Allen had first turned up as a 'drop-in' – literally appearing unannounced during a session that Gibson was having with a woman client, who was hoping to contact a relative. The medium knew nothing about the man's death, but the woman recognized Allen, because she had once worked part-time in his shop.

The dead man's second appearance was pre-planned. A business acquaintance of his wanted to build upon the earlier snatches of communication to see if anything helpful to the police enquiry could be provided. The entire seance was recorded, as Allen conveyed what he knew about his own sudden death. Afterward, the medium passed the transcript to Lincoln police.

The investigating officer, Graham White, received it graciously, but was understandably guarded. All he was willing to put on record was that it would be taken seriously, 'as we do all information that we receive from the public'. Although, of course, this was not your typical eyewitness statement. How

Solving serious crimes, such as cases of murder or missing persons, can be a daunting and lonely task for the police, but they are getting some unexpected help from supernatural means. Just how should the investigating officer deal with offers of help from a psychic detective?

The 1940s movie Blithe Spirit *poked gentle fun at the world of mediums and seances, but what should a real-life police force do if a murder victim seemingly returns from beyond the grave to give clues to his death?*

could the detectives persuade their superiors to launch lines of enquiry based on testimony allegedly from the murder victim himself? And what would any arrested suspect's lawyers make of the legality of such action? If a house was searched on the supposed word of a dead man, would any evidence found be subsequently deemed inadmissible in court?

POLICE PROBLEMS WITH PSYCHICS

Magician and psychic Loyd Auerbach has spoken with many police forces regarding the detection of crimes. He has found that they are usually fearful of openly admitting that a psychic has played a major role in an investigation, but privately can be much more forthcoming. They tend to emphasize their own abilities and the importance of routine police methods, at best arguing that a psychic may have pushed them in the right direction.

Auerbach also discovered that police are often faced with a barrage of contacts from psychics – or would-be psychics – during any well-publicized enquiry. While most are sincere in their attempts to help and have strong belief in the power of their own visions, the vast majority bring no fruitful information. So it is always difficult for police, with no expertise in such matters, to know in advance whether a particularly insistent medium or clairvoyant is likely to be helpful or to lead them astray.

Of course, some practising psychic detectives are registered as official informants. They are recorded on a list, allowing any officer to check their credentials as soon as they report a dream or vision. Auerbach claims that in an experiment in California a psychic who was so registered was taken much less seriously when trying to report without identifying themselves as a recognized informant.

Psychics who court publicity are anathema to investigating officers, who may in turn develop a prejudice against turning to a psychic. Detectives can also be unrealistic in their expectations – assuming that a psychic will work like a crime laboratory does, immediately supplying detailed information that can be scientifically verified. In fact, psychics can be amazingly accurate – and spectacularly wrong. On each occasion, they themselves cannot tell which it will be. Nor can they turn on their abilities like a tap; some days, things just do not 'flow'.

The most successful psychics tend to be those that respond to spontaneous visions, rather than trying to create answers to order. Yet while interpreting these images, they must make choices as to what they might mean. Nearly all psychics say that this is where most errors occur.

STRATEGY TO DETECT

Former chief constable of Devon and Cornwall, John Alderson, explained why he used psychics as part of a 'strategy to detect' during a particularly harrowing case when a young girl disappeared. No trace could be found of her, despite lengthy searches. Alderson describes: 'We decided we would give the case maximum publicity. The high profile and longevity of publicity was desirable because someone might see the missing girl even months later … This publicity

During his time as chief constable of the Devon and Cornwall police, John Alderson sanctioned the use of psychics as part of his 'strategy to detect', reasoning that no chance – however unlikely – of obtaining a lead should be refused.

CRIME FILE:
Missing on
the Moors

The fate of two suspected victims of the infamous 'Moors Murderers' remains unsolved to this day.

Major murder cases attract the attentions of psychics in droves. Many of these individuals are self-deluded or merely wish to further their careers by gaining national recognition. While in some high-profile crimes, psychics offer valuable new leads, in many others nothing comes of their pronouncements. In one of England's most heinous cases – the so-called 'Moors Murders' in Lancashire – scores of psychics offered their assistance, but in the end were of no real help.

The case was unusual in that no one had realized that a pair of serial killers

Faces of evil – Myra Hindley and Ian Brady, the heinous 'Moors Murderers'. The couple were convicted in 1966 for torturing and killing three youngsters.

The market at Ashton-under-Lyne, near Manchester. Here, Hindley and Brady allegedly lured one of their child victims away from the crowds, to meet a horrifying death.

was on the loose until they were caught shortly after claiming their last victim. The police had not connected the disappearances of several children in the Manchester area over a number of months. Now they knew who the killers were, but not where the bodies were hidden.

The murderers, Ian Brady and Myra Hindley, had met at work. Brady, aged 24, and his 19-year-old girlfriend soon embarked on a killing spree, eventually becoming so depraved and arrogant that they saw no danger in committing murder in front of a witness. They had already tortured and killed at least two children when they invited Hindley's brother-in-law, 17-year-old David Smith, to help them entice away a youth his own age.

Smith, not knowing what he was getting into, agreed to chat to Edward Evans in a pub before inviting him back to the couple's council house on Wardle Brook Avenue in Manchester. Brady had said that there they would rob him. Smith was not prepared for the carnage that ensued.

He was in the kitchen when his sister-in-law ran in and screamed at him to help Brady. He followed her into the living room and saw Brady smashing a hatchet into Evans's head. When he had killed the youth, he handed the weapon to Smith, saying: 'Feel the weight of that!' Then he added: 'It's done. It's the messiest yet. It normally only takes one blow.'

As soon as he could, the horrified youth slunk off home and told his young wife what had just happened. Maureen was Myra's sister, but she was terrified, and the couple armed themselves with a screwdriver, hiding in a public telephone until dawn. They then decided to call the police. Officers surrounded the house in Wardle Brook Avenue and tricked their way inside when one of them posed as a delivery man and knocked on the door.

Edward Evans's battered body was found upstairs. Hindley and Brady were

arrested, but the horror had only just begun. Hidden in the spine of a white missal that Hindley had been given for her First Communion was a luggage deposit ticket. This led detectives to two suitcases at one of the city's railway stations. They contained sadomasochistic equipment, including whips and restraints, plus pornographic material. Most horrifying of all, however, was an audio tape that solved the mystery of the disappearance of 10-year-old Lesley Ann Downey. The girl had gone missing without trace nearly a year before, in December 1964. Now the police had in their possession photographs showing Lesley Ann standing before the camera naked, plus an appalling audio tape made by the killers. Officers heard the child begging to be released, and Hindley ordering her to do unspeakable things.

The couple were given life sentences in 1966 for the murders of Edward Evans, Lesley Ann Downey, and John Kilbride, and they are also suspected of killing still-missing Pauline Reade and Keith Bennett. Lesley Ann Downey and John Kilbride were found buried on Saddleworth Moor, but the lonely gravesites of the other likely victims remain a mystery, having defied the efforts of police, map dowsers, and other psychics for decades.

The search continues for the bodies of Keith Bennett (12) and Pauline Reade (16), who disappeared around the same time and place as the victims of the 'Moors Murderers'. In 1986, police revisited misty Saddleworth Moor near Oldham, where Lesley Ann Downey and John Kilbride had been buried. However, no further remains were found.

in turn attracted people like mediums to offer their services … Just in case, we did not say no. But we did not treat [these sources] on the same level as we would treat hard information.'

In fact, the use of psychic detection methods here was simply part of the plan to 'try anything'. This also included hypnotically regressing witnesses (a controversial technique often frowned upon) to see if this helped them to recall any further information. Nothing useful resulted.

Nor were the psychics unduly helpful, Alderson recalls: 'We couldn't find a body – if there was a body. We literally did everything, orthodox and unorthodox. We had one from Holland [Gerard Croiset] and one from Leicester [Bob Cracknell]. But they all drew a blank.'

Nevertheless, crime writer Colin Wilson, who worked with Cracknell on this case, was impressed with his dedication in seeking the missing girl. Furthermore, since – more than 20 years later – she has still not been found, the information Cracknell provided (including the claim that she had been snatched, killed, and her body buried under water) could well have been true. We may simply never know.

And that, of course, is often the problem with the use of psychics in police detection. If they succeed, we hear about it. Much more often they will fail, and naturally this is not reported. Yet how many failures are simply failures to understand leads that might otherwise have taken police to the killer or to the body?

Alderson still believes that he was right to use psychics. 'If a police force cannot solve a mystery and some people say they can, even if they may seem a little odd, then you have a moral responsibility to let them try … But you have to have anything they tell you corroborated by real clues. It might start you on a line of enquiry. That's about the best that you can hope for'.

A line of policemen, with dogs, prod the frosty ground as they hunt for evidence in the 1970 disappearance of a woman in rural England. Even intensive searches such as this are often fruitless, and the intervention of a psychic can sometimes yield valuable new lines of enquiry.

TRAINING IN THE USE OF INTUITION

One surprising way in which the police find psychics to be useful is in the training of their own officers. Several psychic detectives, especially in the United States, run courses for police departments helping to show how to make the most of intuition and perception.

Much routine police work is actually a combination of trusting to one's own instincts and making logical deductions based on the evidence. Often police rely so much on the clues provided by the evidence that they pay too little attention to that 'little voice inside' that might tell them what to make of it all. This is the voice that many psychics seem to have honed to expert effect.

Therefore, it has become increasingly common for psychics to offer seminars to teach detectives how to recognize when they should pay attention to their own instincts. Despite this insightful training, however, when officers actually solve a case by psychic means, they are usually reluctant to draw attention to that fact in court.

Keith Charles, a now retired British police officer who is also a practising spiritualist medium, says that even he was prone to do this. He explains that, when he received a psychic impression that he thought might help in a case, it was often in the long-term interests of securing a prosecution not to reveal the source of his 'instinct'. Instead, it was often wiser to use it as a springboard to make the criminal slip up in a way that would provide more mundane clues that could be used as hard evidence.

Keith Charles (real name Keith Wright) combined his work as a police officer in southeast England with a double life as a medium. He has been a bobby on the beat and a bodyguard protecting the Queen and the Prime Minister, as well as a murder squad investigator. In his role as 'Keith Charles – clairvoyant', he is often asked about the value of messages provided to the force during any high-profile case.

In his autobiography *Psychic Cop*, Charles says: 'The police

Celebrity clairvoyant Keith Charles, surrounded by photographs of some of the famous people with whom he has collaborated. Now retired, Charles spent many years as a working police officer, and his psychic abilities were sometimes used to aid investigations.

DETECTIVE FILE:

Casebook of a 'Psychic Cop'

Keith Charles achieved unique fame as a policeman with paranormal powers and now works as a medium.

Detective Constable Keith Wright, now retired from the British police force, assumed the alter ego 'Keith Charles' when working as a psychic detective. He wrote of his experiences in the book *Psychic Cop*, co-authored with Derek Shuff. Having joined the police at the age of 17, he supplemented his normal detective work with clairvoyant powers and later became a spiritualist medium.

Charles, who earned the nickname 'Psychic Cop', has also been consulted by numerous celebrities. He believes that being a medium made him a better policeman, and that his police training gave his psychic talents a critical edge.

In his autobiography, he describes how 'spirit' has often led him to the perpetrators of crime, although these leads are often anecdotal and lacking in any real objective proof. His visions regarding the fate of Suzy Lamplugh, who went missing in London in July 1986, may yet be put to the test, since in December 2000 a man was questioned in connection with this long-unsolved crime. Regardless, like many other self-styled psychic detectives, Charles seems at times to have yielded information that is outside the realms of coincidence.

Detective Inspector Alan Wilson of the London Transport Police consulted him over the suspicious death of a man at a party that had taken place in a Ministry of Defence building in Kensington. No witnesses had come forward, even when the case was reconstructed for the popular BBC prime-time television show 'Crimewatch'. Charles agreed to help and, without knowing anything about the case, instructed Wilson to send him a photograph of the victim in a sealed envelope. Just a few days later, Charles provided 30 details that were to prove relevant to the case.

For instance, he accurately claimed that the victim had fallen down stairs near railings, and he also stated that a basement was involved – the body had been found at the bottom of a shaft. Charles described other features, including a bank, a girl with a satchel, and a taxi rank. Wilson later told researcher Robert Irving: 'What we had not released was that the victim came down with a female to get some money from a hole-in-the-wall [ATM, or automated teller machine], and then he put her in a taxi – so the satchel was probably her bag.'

Charles also gave correct names and descriptions of people who had been at the party, including those he said were responsible for the death – but there was no objective evidence that would stand up in court. Although all the information that the psychic provided that could be checked did seem to match the facts, in the end his impressions did not help police to solve the crime.

A notice displayed outside a spiritualist church advertising a public appearance by the 'psychic cop', Keith Charles.

A police underwater team plumbs the depths of a pond near Norton, Worcester, in their ongoing investigation into the disappearance of estate agent Suzy Lamplugh, who vanished in July 1986 after going to meet a client in London.

are regularly swamped with offers of assistance from self-proclaimed psychics. Well-meaning callers they may be, but few of them are genuine clairvoyants. We deal with these people politely, our attitude being that when, for example, a murder is under investigation, any offer of help is gratefully received and considered, whatever its source.' Yet all too often the information provided is next to useless. Psychic visions can be very imprecise, and that is not what a detective requires.

He cites the case of a young London boy, Lee Boxall, who disappeared on his way to a football match. The investigators were contacted by more than 50 psychics claiming to know what had happened – although they rarely agreed on what that was. One man alleged that the boy would be found 'within 50 miles [80km] of water'. Aside from the fact that this information (even if true) has absolutely no value in narrowing down the search, it is also so vague as to be meaningless in a country such as Britain. On an island with a narrow spine and many rivers and lakes, there is probably no place where this description does not apply. Psychic detectives have to be a great deal more specific than this to be successful.

A POLICEMAN'S HUNCH

Rod Englert is one detective who has honed his intuition to a level that might easily be described as psychic. But he does not consider what he is doing to be paranormal. Rather, he feels that it is an ability that all police officers could learn to use to advantage during their investigations.

Englert, who works with the sheriff's office in Portland, Oregon, says that he has developed the capacity to react when he gets a gut feeling and to understand what this sudden insight means. He cites an incident from August 1974, when a local tax adviser was attacked and strangled in his office. The motive for his murder seemed difficult to resolve, yet as soon as Englert arrived to interview the dead man's business partner, his intuition went into overdrive and he knew instinctively that this man was the killer.

There was, in fact, no logical reason to have presumed this. The man was not even a suspect and apparently had not been in the office when his colleague died. He had also proved amenable and co-operative throughout the investigation. Nevertheless, something simply lit up inside the detective's mind when he first saw him, and he knew without question that this man was the killer. All he had to do now was prove it.

Armed with this certainty, Englert began a lengthy investigation in which he paid particular attention to the story of his perceived 'suspect'. At first, there seemed nothing wrong with his account, but the detective, convinced of his guilt, began to notice small details suggesting that the man was not as innocent as he seemed.

It transpired that the partner had made a fatal error, making a phone call from the office at a time when he was not supposed to be there. With this traced call

Police officers put together the clues regarding a case much like pieces of a jigsaw puzzle. Intuition, gut feelings, and low-level ESP often play a part in defining the picture that finally emerges.

on record, the suspect's protestations of innocence gradually fell apart. He admitted that he and another colleague had lured their partner to the office on a false pretext and then killed him. Englert had known this almost from the first moment he entered the case, yet had no idea how he had come to see through an exterior that appeared far from guilty.

In the courses that Englert now teaches to other detectives, he stresses methods of using such intuitive skills to best effect. For example, he advises reading through all the files regarding a case and digesting the witness statements, paying special attention to anything that suddenly 'leaps out' as you do so. It is also useful to have free-thinking sessions in which the case is discussed with others – even people who are not part of the police operation. In this way, your mind can be freed from the normal restraints of logical thinking, allowing an awareness of that inner creative process that seems to characterize the 'hunch'.

Englert also believes that when a detective experiences a 'gut feeling' about a case, it is because pieces of the puzzle have connected at a subconscious level. Intuition is then a type of internal appreciation of this revelation, trying to alert the attention of the conscious mind. To Englert, this phenomenon is not mysterious, but simply a skill that some are better at than others, but upon which all of us can potentially improve.

What is the difference, then, between someone getting a 'gut feeling' and the full-blown vision of a professed psychic? Perhaps there is no difference. It may be that the 'psychic' person is simply more visually creative (as psychological profile tests on psychic detectives suggest them to be), and thus what to others is just a nagging sensation manifests itself in the psychic as some sort of 'mental flash'. The two processes may simply be one, expressed in different degrees. Indeed, psychic Michael Bentine, when asked how he distinguished between imagination, intuition, and psychic inspiration, explained that often he could not do so because in his opinion there was no fundamental difference. To him, they are all the same phenomenon given different names.

Psychic police officer Keith Charles (who feels that he is a clairvoyant and not just instinctive) notes that while investigating cases he often feels certain that a particular person is the culprit long before there is any reason to believe this from actual evidence. He then uses this insight to good advantage, rarely telling the suspect that he has obtained information by psychic means proving that they are guilty, but merely saying what he 'knows'. This creates the impression that he

Missing schoolgirl Genette Tate vanished while delivering newspapers on August 19, 1978. Her fate sparked an unprecedented level of 'psychic support', with reports of dreams and visions being submitted to the police by the sackload.

is a brilliant detective or has somehow discovered the truth about their lives. Unnerved, the suspect then often lets slip some vital clue that will lead to his prosecution, without psychic powers ever becoming an issue.

THE VALUE OF PUBLICITY

As a public relations officer for the Devon and Cornwall police force in England, Roger Busby had to cope with enormous press attention when psychics became involved in a major enquiry in August 1978, after 13-year-old Genette Tate disappeared from Aylesbeare, Devon. He described the position he faced: 'In the case of a missing teenager, all the classic mystery elements attracted investigators into the paranormal right away. But it was important for us to keep a story like this newsworthy and in the headlines. The psychics and paranormal sources certainly helped us to do that.'

But was this co-operation to the police's advantage? Bubsy reported: 'The assistance that we had from these people was very interesting, but it was inconclusive. A Professor Croiset, hailed as the world's leading expert in finding missing people,

The disappearance of young Genette Tate remains unsolved. Her discarded bicycle yielded few forensic clues, and increasingly frustrated investigators were happy to accept offers of assistance from psychics.

spent two days here. He was brought over by a newspaper, not by us. But we listened to what he had to say. He was able, without prompting, to describe the location where the missing girl had last been seen delivering newspapers. But at the end of the day all he could say was that he got this information, but he did not know where it came from. He could not say if it referred to the past, present, or future. And he added, "If I say go to the right or to the left, then it might be the opposite. Because I can get a mirror image". Although it led nowhere, he obviously could detect something from the environment … All told, we had countless contacts from psychics. It was all fascinating, but vague and inconclusive – with statements like, "She's in a car boot [trunk]" – but when you ask for details like the registration number, they just say: "Sorry, it doesn't work like that."

'We were open-minded and carried out many hours of interviews with psychics, and even conducted digs for a body at sites they suggested. This helped to keep the case on the front pages, but it sadly did not bring us any closer to finding the missing girl. Such a case was a peculiar – almost unique – set of circumstances. This was a holiday time. We knew someone might visit the area with vital information even weeks later. So it lent itself to psychic involvement. But normally we would not want this kind of help'. Sadly, in this instance nothing worked, and Genette Tate has never been found.

CASE FILE:
Mobius: Psychic task force

Does the novel Mobius group offer the way forward in collaboration between psychics and the police?

Stephen Schwarz has a fascinating approach to working with the police. He has created a task force of psychics to work all over the United States. From its base in Los Angeles, California, the so-called Mobius group sets its team of 25 'intuitives' to work on a case, then creates a composite picture from the information and sends this to the investigating authorities. It believes that such a joint effort provides a more accurate portrait.

Mobius is not composed of pro-active psychics who court the media. Indeed, they are all professionals in other fields (including a physicist, an aeronautical engineer, and a psychiatrist). Their abilities range from finely tuned intuition to ESP, and they simply feel that they have honed skills that most people possess to some degree.

Both the strengths and weaknesses of psychics working with police are illustrated by the Mobius case files. In one instance, the group's composite report indicated that a missing 14-year-old girl was dead and had been sexually assaulted by a man who worked near the girl's home. Information such as this seems impressive when it proves to be true (as it did here), but in reality such a tragic scenario is not that unexpected in today's world. However, the report offered additional details that would have been

harder to guess, including the fact that the girl had been suffocated, and that the killer was a teacher and had buried her in a heavily wooded area.

One of the difficulties that the police faced was in knowing which parts of the report to act upon, since they knew that, in such cases, some information always later turns out to be inaccurate. Further, in this instance even the certain knowledge that the body was in a wood would not be a great deal of help, since there was miles of local woodland to check. Neither was the identification of the killer as a teacher likely to lead to an arrest, since there are generally many teachers within close range of any murder scene. Here, the description of the man as a 'teacher' was also slightly misleading, since he was actually a student at a night class who occasionally demonstrated to other students. Only after his arrest would much of the truth of the Mobius findings become evident.

Unfortunately, police investigators need information that will unambiguously lead them to criminals, not vague clues that merely allow culprits to be recognized later. Psychic detectives often struggle to achieve this goal.

The Mobius group are an unusual team of experts, ranging from a psychiatrist to an engineer, who pool their intuitions in an effort to offer clues about perplexing cases. They claim some success, in one instance directing police to a heavily wooded area where they 'deduced' that a girl's body had been taken after her murder.

One of the most
intractable mysteries
in twentieth-century
Britain is the fate
of Lord Lucan, who
vanished in November
1974 while under
suspicion for the
murder of his nanny.
No trace of the peer
has ever been found,
despite attempts by
numerous psychics
to establish leads.

What Happened to Lord Lucan?

One of the most famous disappearances of all time is that of Britain's Lord Lucan. Since vanishing in November 1974, his fate remains a total mystery. Inevitably, this baffling case has attracted the attention of various psychics and it is interesting to examine their contrasting approaches.

Lucan was last seen at Grants Hill House, Uckfield, Sussex, the home of a gambling friend. Allegedly unknown to his host at the time, Lucan was wanted in connection with the death of his nanny, who had been found murdered at her employer's residence in London's Belgravia district. The case sparked tremendous media speculation and is still unresolved today. A popular theory is that Lucan fled abroad and changed his identity, but no significant leads were ever found to support this.

Clairvoyant Bob Cracknell was offered money by the press on several occasions during the late 1970s to try to locate Lord Lucan. He declined, since he had no personal belongings of the missing man upon which to practise his psychometry; without such items, all he could offer were 'intuitions'.

However, Cracknell reported in 1980 that he had received certain impressions about the case and was willing to put on record a number of things. First, he sensed that Lucan was alive and had fled the United Kingdom under pressure from people placed high in the establishment. Even so, he was not convinced that Lucan was a killer – only that he felt intimidated. Cracknell believed that he may have been in southern France but had then returned to Britain, possibly to Wales. One prediction the psychic was confident enough to issue was this: 'I am convinced it will not remain an unsolved mystery.' He added that 'if he is not found by the police', then Lucan will 'give himself up'.

Cracknell mentions no time limit on these events, nor does he specifically state that Lucan was in France and is now in Wales – simply that there is a 'connection' with these places. Still, many years have passed since these comments, and Lucan seems no closer to being traced.

Keith Charles's Strange Vision

However, Bob Cracknell is not the only psychic to pass comment on this intriguing case. Britain's 'psychic cop', Keith Charles, a serving police officer and medium, spoke on the matter in 1995. He claimed that, many years after the disappearance, he was relaxing following a night shift at the police station when he suddenly saw 'a country scene'. The words 'Uckfield' and 'Lucan' formed in his head, and he began to sketch what his mind's eye was showing him.

Essentially, he saw a large house on a hill with a tree and a body face down in a concrete drain or storm sewer. Standing over the body was a man in a tweed jacket, like that of a gamekeeper, carrying a smoking gun. What did all of this mean? It seemed to suggest that Lucan was dead – murdered by someone unknown in a large country house, perhaps in Uckfield, and that his body had been placed in a drain.

When checking the facts of the case, Charles learned of the connection with Grants Hill House, yet there was no evidence of foul play there. The wife of Lucan's gambling colleague, Ian Maxwell-Scott, confirmed that Lucan had arrived late at night, but said that her husband was then in London. She testified that Lucan had stayed just two hours, writing letters to his brother-in-law, and drove away at 1:30 a.m. Nobody, apparently, saw him again.

Charles went so far as to visit the area to inspect the site of Grants Hill House to see if it matched his vision. It did not. The 'big house on the hill' was missing, having been demolished and replaced by a senior citizens home. There was also no sign of a large tree, but Charles learned that there had indeed been one at that location until it was flattened, along with thousands of others, in October 1987, when a violent storm struck southeast England.

Medium Keith Charles claims to have had a vision regarding Lord Lucan, showing a large house on a hill and a man wearing a tweed jacket, carrying a gun, and standing over a body.

As for the storm sewer, it was discovered that at the time of Lucan's disappearance, drains had been laid in preparation for the building of a large housing estate nearby. Charles began to wonder whether Lucan could have been killed as he left Grants Hill House late that night. If so, he thought, could his body now be lost somewhere beneath a 25-year-old building?

To this day, no one knows if Lord Lucan is innocent or guilty, alive or dead, or in the United Kingdom or anywhere else. The information provided by Cracknell and Charles – both of whom have had previous success assisting the police in similar cases – can only be said to be confusing and contradictory. If and when the truth is ever learned about this strange disappearance, perhaps then we will know whether either psychic really did gain some mysterious insight.

THE HUNT FOR THE YORKSHIRE RIPPER

Among the few murder cases in modern Britain that is known worldwide is the investigation into the serial killer dubbed the 'Yorkshire Ripper'. Between 1975 and 1980, he killed 13 women, mostly in Yorkshire, although (especially when the police were sealing off his usual active locations) he occasionally moved a few miles across the Pennines to Manchester. His frenzied attacks were mostly on prostitutes in the red-light areas of Bradford and Leeds. However, particularly as the killing went on, he also targeted innocent women and teenage girls who were clearly just in the wrong place at the wrong time.

It is hardly a surprise that what proved to be the most expensive manhunt in criminal history attracted the attention of psychics in record numbers. This was especially apparent when police became ever more frustrated by their failure to get their man, and after the apparent taunting of this lack of success by the killer himself. (The Ripper was believed to be behind a series of letters and tapes chiding George Oldfield, the detective who put his heart and soul into ending this killing spree.) Yet what help did this flock of 'psychic sleuths' give to the struggling police force? Ironically, the vast majority were of so little use that when one was spectacularly right, she was all but ignored.

A Baffling Case

The first victim of the Ripper was Wilma McCann, brutally slaughtered in Leeds on October 29, 1975. As the list of dead grew and the manhunt led nowhere, the usual problems of a long-term investigation mounted. There was now a vast array of information, hundreds of suspects, and mountains of interview transcripts and collated facts, but no easy way to make connections between them all. Without the benefit of modern computer systems, critical leads were overlooked.

As it turned out, the man eventually convicted as the Ripper had been interviewed quite early in the case. Picked up after being seen cruising the red-light districts near the murder sites, he had somehow managed to bluff his way through the questioning. What police had not done was to connect this incident with what was later recognized as a vital clue found on the victim Jean Jordan,

Photofit images of the Ripper from witness testimony were compared with dozens of descriptions supplied by psychics.

Letters and tapes reputedly from the serial killer, calling himself 'Jack', were sent to Yorkshire police and dangerously misled their enquiries. Many psychics were also fooled by these convincing fakes, whose true sender has never been identified.

whose body was dumped at Southern Cemetery in Chorlton, Manchester, on October 1, 1977. A £5 note discovered on the body was traced to a recent payroll of a trucking company in Yorkshire (where the victim had no connections). The man interviewed was a driver at this firm. Tragically, because this link was missed, the string of murders continued for three more years. At the time, the overlooking of such a 'coincidence' was regarded as inevitable in an enquiry involving so many people and facts.

FALSE COMMUNICATIONS

Another major obstacle developed in 1978, when the police received letters that seemingly played along with the media, which had nicknamed the killer 'Jack'

(after the original Victorian Ripper). Scrawled with the motto 'I'm Jack', these letters seemed to have intimate knowledge of the brutal methods used to mutilate the bodies after the killings. Since the police were, for obvious reasons, keeping such facts secret, this implied that the letter writer had to be the real murderer.

However, the situation became even more confused on June 26, 1979, when the first of several cassette tapes arrived at a newspaper office, bearing the same handwriting on the envelope as on the letters. But the voice on the tapes, teasing the police with cries that he would kill again, was that of a 'Geordie'. This distinctive accent meant that he was from northeast England (the city of Sunderland was specified after study by linguistic experts). Police had until then assumed the killer was local to the Leeds/Bradford area. This new development seemed to point the finger 100 miles (161km) to the north, and police refocused the investigation accordingly.

As it turned out, this was a completely false lead. The Yorkshire Ripper, when finally caught, did not come from Sunderland and claimed that he had not sent the tapes or letters. Indeed, that person has never been caught. It is unclear whether this was the work of a cruel hoaxster, whose actions very possibly cost further lives, or whether it was an attempt by an accomplice of the Ripper to throw the police off the scent.

THE PSYCHIC SEARCH FOR THE MURDERER

As the police became increasingly desperate in their search for the serial killer, many psychics offered their services. As a whole, their assistance was minimal. In 1980, the magazine *The Unexplained* set up a repository for visions by psychics, and a number received related to the elusive Ripper. Typical of them was the vague suggestion that the killer would struggle when eventually cornered – hardly the psychic prediction of the century! Yet among the dozens of useless pieces of information, there were two or three insights that proved stunning.

John Pope, from the county of Hertfordshire, described seeing the Yorkshire Ripper in a vision. He was in his 30s and with a small goatee beard and black hair that stuck up as if held in place by a perm. This proved to be an eerily precise description of Peter Sutcliffe, the man eventually convicted of the killings.

The media, however, were turning their sights toward well-known mystics. Doris Stokes, at the time the world's best-known medium, was asked to examine one of the Ripper audio tapes recently sent to the tabloid newspaper the *Sunday People*. She did so and claimed to receive a message from the 'afterlife' – allegedly via the Ripper's dead mother – saying that her son, the killer, was a clean-shaven truck driver who lived in Sunderland, had a scar on his face, and was called Ronnie or Johnnie.

A 'Most Wanted' poster-style drawing based on her description was plastered across the front page of the paper, with the headline 'Face of the Ripper'. Unfortunately, it was no such

Renowned medium Doris Stokes was one of countless psychics consulted by the media in the battle to publish exclusive 'breakthroughs' as the murderer continued to elude police.

Peter Sutcliffe, a truck driver, was eventually arrested in 1981, after a five-year killing spree as the 'Yorkshire Ripper'. This artist's portrait, released during his trial, showed that psychic Doris Stokes had been correct on only one fact – Sutcliffe was indeed a truck driver.

thing. Doris Stokes, however sincere in her belief that the serial killer's mother had been in touch, proved right on just one point. The real murderer was indeed a truck driver. Everything else was a giant red herring. Stokes had perhaps been misled by hearing the Sunderland accent of the man on the tape. But she was not the only one.

Not about to be outdone, *The Sun* newspaper flew famed psychic Gerard Croiset over from the Netherlands to try his hand. On November 28, 1979, he also announced that the Ripper was from Sunderland – even pinpointing a block of flats on a map and providing a physical description of the man (this profile was, however, rather different to that provided by Doris Stokes). The media circus culminated in yet another newspaper, the *Daily Star*, bringing in a medium who claimed to be in contact with the killer's dead relatives. This time, a complete biography of the Ripper was offered up, with no fewer than seven 'identikit' artist's portraits displayed, showing everyone from the murderer's mother to his car mechanic.

When the real killer was caught, none of these images – nor the medium's description of the culprit as an unmarried plumber of about 45, with fair hair, and living in Bolton, Lancashire – proved remotely correct.

Other insights into the murderer from various psychics 'revealed' that he worked on a submarine, changed clothes in a green railway carriage, and dressed as a woman during his crimes. Again, despite the quite specific nature of this information, none was accurate.

FIASCO FOR POLICE

The police were naturally disturbed by all this media interest, especially Doris Stokes's intervention, which brought them huge embarrassment. After the massive publicity for her vision of Ripper Ronnie (allegedly a truck driver from Sunderland – Stokes even suggested that he lived in a street with a name similar to 'Berwick'), one man gave himself up to the police. He was a truck driver called Ronnie from Berwick Avenue, Sunderland, who resembled the artist's reconstruction on the front page of the *Sunday People*. The only problem was that he insisted he was completely innocent, which police subsequently confirmed. The poor man said: 'I didn't mind having my leg pulled ... [but] there are bound to be people who take this clairvoyant stuff seriously.'

This public relations catastrophe, however, did not deter other psychics from coming forward. Bob Cracknell, whose work on other cases has been described, announced on November 11, 1980, that the Ripper would strike again 'in two weeks' and that this could be the last murder, because he would soon be caught. He recorded this news in front of several witnesses, including sceptical paranormal researcher Kevin McClure. On November 17, student Jacqueline Hill was murdered. Although the psychic was off target by a week, the Ripper had not killed for a year, after he had narrowly escaped capture when his violent assault on one woman had been interrupted by her boyfriend.

Cracknell's vision that this might be the last death was reported by the *Yorkshire Post* on December 4, 1980. Ten days later, the psychic went with a *Sunday Mirror* reporter to Yorkshire to get more 'insights'. He confirmed that the end was near and that the killer lived in Bradford. On January 4, 1981, just three weeks later, Peter Sutcliffe – who was indeed from Bradford – was finally caught. Jacqueline Hill was his final victim.

Bob Cracknell's late success occurred after a catalogue of false visions and predictions that had made the police increasingly dismissive of paranormal powers – especially since the least accurate information came from those

An artist's impression of the courtroom scene at the Old Bailey on May 22, 1981, when Peter Sutcliffe was found guilty of the 13 'Yorkshire Ripper' murders and given a life sentence.

widely believed to be 'expert' psychic detectives, such as Gerard Croiset. Therefore, it is not surprising that investigating officers, weary after five years of failure and the fairly awful track record of other psychic assistants up until that time, were less than enthusiastic when clairvoyant Nella Jones entered the case. But Nella Jones, perhaps uniquely, seemed to be right on target with a series of very specific comments. Had the police known that these were bona fide impressions of the killer, Sutcliffe may have been behind bars on the day he killed Jacqueline Hill.

Jones had assisted the police in many cases and been praised for her success rate. Detective Neil Pratt, from her local area in Kent, conceded that officers are usually reluctant to call in psychic help – 'admitting they have failed goes against the grain' – but accepted that in some cases 'Nella has come up trumps'. He cited one instance in which she led him straight to the spot in a south London park where a woman had been murdered, providing a lead that was invaluable in further investigations.

In early 1980, about a year before Peter Sutcliffe was arrested, and while the police still believed that the killer was from the northeast, Nella Jones was interviewed about her psychic abilities by Yorkshire journalist Shirley Davenport. Davenport later confirmed their conversation with Jenny Randles, co-author of this book, putting Nella Jones's visions on record long before the killer was identified. According to Jones, she 'saw the killer' in a sudden mental image after watching a news report on the case in January 1980. This vision was sufficiently detailed to provide a great deal of information. The man was called Peter. He was a truck driver from Bradford. He lived in a house atop a flight of stone steps with the number 6 on the door. She even saw the side of the cab of his truck, which had the firm's name written on it. This started with the letter 'C', but she couldn't quite get the full name.

THE PRICE OF SCEPTICISM

Aware of her success in previous cases, Shirley Davenport urged Jones to tell the police what she knew, but she felt uneasy, given the recent high-profile failures by other mediums. However, particularly because she foresaw the date of the Ripper's next murder – November 17 – she eventually agreed. Jones gave a statement and hoped that the police would catch the killer before that fateful day. Unfortunately, detectives simply filed her story away with all the other 'ravings' sent in by so-called psychics, and nothing was done.

Yet Jones's description of the killer matched the already recorded clues from the investigation, in which Peter Sutcliffe, who drove for Clark's in Bradford, had been a suspect. When Sutcliffe was finally arrested a year later – as a result of chance police enquiries, with no psychic intervention – Nella Jones's visions were seen to be stunningly accurate. The killer had even lived in a house numbered '6' in Garden Lane, Bradford, which was approached by climbing steps from the main road.

If a modern-day computer had been used to cross-match the wealth of data collected from the routine investigation with the very precise details offered by Jones, then it might have issued a 'probability warning'

Psychic Nella Jones correctly 'saw' the killer as living in a house with stone steps leading up the front door. She also predicted the date of one of the murders. Unfortunately, after the spectacularly inaccurate reports of scores of other psychics, sceptical police disregarded Nella's visions.

Computer systems such as this one at the Forensic Science Services laboratory in Birmingham are now regularly used in crime investigations. Here, a technician works with one of the world's first DNA databases. Police hunting the Yorkshire Ripper did not have sophisticated equipment for cross-checking the vast amounts of data they received, both from routine enquiries and from psychics.

that Sutcliffe was worth checking out again. Unfortunately, in old-fashioned police work there is often a sea of information to deal with, making such comparisons virtually impossible.

In any case, one hit among a hundred misses is not a strike rate that will endear the authorities to the quirks of psychic detection. Even so, if lives can be saved, it really does not matter how many self-professed psychics give the police useless information, if just one points right at the killer. We simply need a way of determining which information can be regarded as worthwhile. This is not easy. For example, can we truly know why many psychics, like the police, were misled about the Yorkshire Ripper coming from Sunderland?

Peter Sutcliffe's job had in fact taken him to Sunderland, where he met other drivers. He also told one woman whom he corresponded with from his prison cell that someone had helped him with his crimes. Could this someone have sent the letters and tapes? If that person is ever identified, perhaps we will see the apparently inaccurate comments made by some of the psychic detectives in a very different light.

Native American medicine men believe in many levels of reality. They often contact their ancestors before making major decisions affecting their tribes and claim to commune with beings from other dimensions to bring change in this world.

After spending seven years developing his psychic skills with Native Americans, Michael Bromley returned to England. Bromley's mentors in the United States dubbed him a 'Celtic shaman'.

MICHAEL BROMLEY:
SHAMAN FOR THE POLICE

Psychic Michael Bromley describes himself as a 'Celtic shaman'. Usually used to denote a Native American medicine man, the word 'shaman' is an ancient term originating in Siberia. Shamanism is based on the belief that there are many levels of reality, both in the spirit dimension and on the earthly plane.

In the 1980s, Bromley spent seven years in the United States working with Native Americans, helping police search for missing persons, and detecting security loopholes at the Olympic Games held in Los Angeles. He presented researcher Peter Hough, co-author of this book, with a

The opening ceremony of the 1984 Olympic Games in Los Angeles. Michael Bromley was hired by Chief of Police Patrick Connolly to assess security risks, using his recognized extra-sensory perception. His predictions of high-risk areas, and even specific days posing danger, proved remarkably on target.

number of signed statements from law enforcement officers attesting to his various successes. In 1984, he was approached by organizers of the Los Angeles Olympic Games to assist them in pinpointing security problem areas. Bromley was introduced to Patrick Connolly, Los Angeles Chief of Police, and they discussed how he could help them. The tall, bearded Englishman was assigned a police officer who was instructed to drive him around the vast Olympic site. After spending weeks visiting different sites and studying maps of the area, Bromley compiled his report.

As he explained to Hough, 'It was no use using airy-fairy language; this was for the corporate mind. I had to be specific and include many photographs. It had to be the sort of thing a tough-nosed cop could read and understand. What I didn't know at the time was that copies were sent to the CIA, the FBI, and five other security forces'.

Bromley 'sensed' the probability of trouble at particular locations. Westwood, he wrote in his report, was an area of tremendous negativity. On the opening day of the Games, a young man drove down the main street and deliberately ran over about 20 people. At his trial, he claimed that he felt 'waves of energy' hitting him. Was this the product of a disturbed mind, or was it an objective phenomenon? Bromley had his own theory.

'I lived outside of LA. Quite independently, people were calling me from the city saying they felt waves of energy coming into the area. The Soviets didn't come to the Games. All the phone lines from that country to America were engaged a lot of the time. I realized the phone lines were carriers of energy. Now if it was possible to send psychic energy down the lines …

'I believe the Soviets were projecting negative energy into Los Angeles. I know it sounds far-fetched, but we all do it every day. It's the same as wishing someone well, sending our love, or wishing them harm. The Russians had been carrying out scientific experiments in parapsychology for decades'.

PERFECT HIT RATE IN PREDICTING DANGER

After the Games were over, Bromley sat down with Patrick Connolly to determine how accurate his dossier had been. 'I had predicted low-, medium-, and high-risk days. I was 100 percent on that. There was some terrible violence on the high-risk days, although I couldn't always predict where. But I was right about some shootings on one of the freeways. I also accurately predicted that a private security guard would attempt to rape one of the women athletes. I actually predicted the area. There was even a bomb hoax at LA Airport, although it occurred two days after the Games.' The Chief of Police later commented, 'Mr Bromley pinpointed certain problem areas with more than a high degree of reliability'. Bromley had similar successes at the 1986 San Francisco Bay Olympic Games for gay athletes and the Seoul Olympic Games in 1988, as South Korean government minister Ri Hoon Hur confirmed.

The publicity that these roles generated drew individuals to Bromley, to seek his help. One such person was the wife of an elderly man who had gone missing on November 1, 1985, in Mariposa County, California, after setting out for an afternoon walk.

The police were inclined to believe

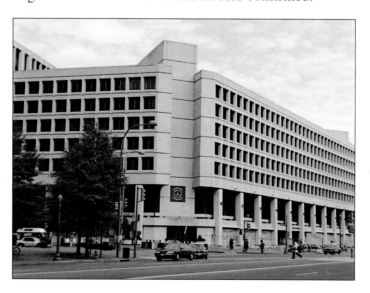

The FBI building in Washington, D.C. In the television series 'The X Files', the FBI takes a covert interest in the paranormal through its agents Fox Mulder and Dana Scully. Publicly, the bureau claims to have no involvement with psychics, yet in 1984 it requested a copy of Michael Bromley's report on security issues surrounding the Los Angeles Olympic Games.

that the man had just absconded, but his wife feared the worst. Acting Sheriff-Coroner Tom Strickland headed the investigation. He described their progress: 'An extensive search was started by the Mariposa County Sheriff's Department using search dogs, helicopters, four-wheel-drive vehicles, and horses. After nine days, the search had to be suspended due to heavy snowfall, and the difficulty of the terrain. At that time, not a trace of the gentleman had been found.'

Bromley contacted the sheriff, who invited him to assist. He explained to Peter Hough what happened: 'I meditated on the man's life-force, but could detect nothing at all. I was convinced he had been murdered. I pinpointed the area where the body lay, and said it would be discovered by two people. I was right on both counts.'

Tom Strickland verified this. 'On February 9, 1986, the remains of the gentleman were found by prospectors. The remains were out of the search area and were in the direction described by Michael Bromley. He had also given us many new leads and had been extremely accurate on the conclusion of the search for the missing man'.

INSIGHTS ON AN UNSOLVED DOUBLE MURDER

The 'Celtic shaman' also gave the police a description of the killers, but since the body had been exposed to the elements for three months, there was no conclusive evidence of murder. Therefore, the case was written off as misadventure. 'He was an old man', Bromley said resignedly. 'There was little chance of getting the murderers, I suppose'.

Later in 1986, a local publication called the *Mariposa Guide* tested Bromley's psychic abilities by asking him to throw light on an unsolved double murder. Inez and Robert Roos had been discovered shot dead 18 months previously. Bromley told Hough that he had come up with some concrete information about the case, which he had passed on to the police.

'I told them it was a Mafia killing. The man gambled heavily and owed money. The assassins came and ordered him to pay up or they were prepared to kill him. He thought they were joking. They took his wife outside and shot her, then they killed him'.

Bromley gave the authorities a great deal of new information, including details regarding a corrupt bank official who was involved. Nevertheless, the police, who had already spent hundreds of man-hours on the case, decided to drop the matter, since tangible proof was not forthcoming. However, the senior editor of the *Mariposa Guide* made these comments: 'Mr Bromley did pinpoint certain questions, offering a surprising amount of original information, giving new leads and direction to the investigations.'

By and large, most police officers are relatively neutral when it comes to accepting the help of psychics. They neither believe nor disbelieve, but are

The lighting of the Olympic torch in Seoul, Korea, in 1988. Government minister Ri Hoon Hur confirmed that Michael Bromley had worked with Games officials to pinpoint trouble hot spots using his psychic talents.

open-minded enough to explore all avenues of investigation. Unfortunately, whenever there are high-profile murder cases or missing persons enquiries, would-be psychics seem to creep out of the woodwork. Most of these 'assistants' bombard the police with useless information and exploit human misery for their own purposes of self-promotion and aggrandizement.

Occasionally, however, certain gifted individuals produce startling new insights which set the police along fresh lines of enquiry, leading to arrest and prosecution. Many authorities recognize that these genuine psychic detectives can provide a valuable extra tool in the armoury of the crime fighter.

In the Courtroom

T O RESOLVE A CRIME, THE PERPETRATOR must first be apprehended by law enforcement agencies and then prosecuted by the courts. While the use of psychics in the first stage of this process is growing year by year, what happens when judicial procedures come into play? How can a court interpret evidence based on the existence of powers that much of modern science still denies? Will this help, or hinder, the road to justice?

The judiciary takes a dim view of evidence obtained through psychic means, feeling that it can interfere with the normal running of criminal cases. In the murder case of Regina v. Young, the British jury solicited the help of a Ouija board. They used it to contact the victim, who then named his killer. The jury accordingly found the defendant guilty. When it emerged that a Ouija board had been employed to reach the decision, an appeal court judge ordered a retrial.

In March 1993, Stephen Young received a life sentence for shooting Harry and Nicola Fuller during a robbery at their cottage in Wadhurst, East Sussex. The jury had been unanimous in their verdict, but a month later Young's lawyers received an anonymous note purportedly from one of the jurors. It alleged that several other jurors had used a Ouija board to contact the spirit of Harry Fuller in their Brighton hotel the night before the verdict was returned.

On June 23, three Appeal Court judges decided that the claim could be investigated by the Treasury Solicitor and a senior police officer. Counsel for Young argued that the jurors had breached their oath to decide the case according to the evidence presented in the court. Further, they pointed out that the alleged breach had taken place in a hotel after they had been warned not to discuss the case.

Court cases featuring testimony from psychics are few, mainly because the establishment does not accept the reality of paranormal phenomena. When such evidence is given, it is invariably ridiculed, sidelined, or used to 'prove' fraud. Scottish nanny Carole Compton ran the risk of a life sentence for attempted murder

The Old Court of the Old Bailey, in London, around the time of the Jack the Ripper murders, among the first of many high-profile cases to attract the attentions of psychic detectives.

A Ouija board has the letters of the alphabet written in a crescent along one side, and the words 'Yes' and 'No'. It is used to contact spirits and other supernatural entities. The participants each place their fingertips on the planchette, and it begins to move, spelling out words and responding 'Yes' or 'No' to specific questions. Frequently the result is gibberish, but sometimes whole sentences are spelled out in this way.

because her lawyers did not allow expert witnesses to present proof of supernatural fires.

Carole was barely out of her teens when she went to Italy in 1982 to be with her Italian boyfriend. Her first job was with the wealthy Ricci family in Ortisei, Bolzano, looking after their little boy. When he was first introduced to Carole, he turned to his mother and complained, 'My hand burns!' The child never did like Carole, and neither did the Ricci's maid, Rosa. When an ancient painting of the Madonna crashed to the floor, a boiler started to gurgle, and an electricity meter went berserk with Carole standing nearby, Rosa blamed the girl, saying they were omens.

On July 11, Carole was at home with the baby and his grandfather when a fire broke out in the villa. They all escaped, but £5,000 worth of damage was done. The Morovers, friends of the Riccis, offered them shelter, but then fire broke out twice at the Morover house. The first occasion involved a rubbish bin; in the second, Mr Ricci's brother narrowly escaped after a mattress on which the grandfather had been sleeping was found smouldering. The finger of suspicion was pointed at Carole Compton, even though there was no direct evidence, and she was fired.

Within two weeks, she had a new job with a well-to-do young couple, the Cecchinis, who worked in television. Carole was sent to join their three-year-old daughter, Agnese, who was staying in the family's summer house on the island of Elba with her grandparents. Carole found that she had walked into an emotional battle zone, as the grandmother firmly believed that a mother's place was in the home and that child care should not be handed over to a nanny, especially a foreigner.

The Cecchini family's summer house, where two fires broke out – one involving the grandfather's mattress, and the other the little girl's bed.

Not long after the Scottish girl arrived, strange things began to happen. A small statue toppled from a shelf, a glass fruit bowl fell, and a terrible noise was heard when a three-tier cake stand 'dropped' to the floor, but was found standing upright and undamaged. The maid, Maria Annasuri, claimed to have seen a key turning in its lock by itself, and the old Corsican grandmother told everyone that Carole was a witch.

MATTRESS FOUND IN FLAMES

On August 1, the child's parents were in Rome, and Carole was relaxing after dinner with the grandfather, Mario Cecchini, in the sitting room, when the mattress in his bedroom was discovered ablaze. But worse was to come. Just one day later, little Agnese's mattress was found burning, with the child actually laying on it. Fortunately, she was saved in time, but by now the house was in uproar. The parents returned, Carole was blamed, and the police were called to arrest her.

If things were not already bad enough for Carole Compton, they became much more desperate one month later when the Riccis came forward with information about their fires. Carole was indicted on one charge of attempted murder and five of arson. On the face of it, it seemed an open-and-shut case.

Carole Compton, the Scottish nanny who supposedly was the catalyst for psychic powers which started fires in the homes of her Italian employers. The court chose to ignore expert witnesses and instead believed that Carole was an arsonist.

She was the only common denominator in the crimes – evidently, the Scottish nanny had maliciously set fire to the homes of her employers, endangering life in the process.

It was 16 months before Carole came to trial, and during the whole of this time she was incarcerated in prison. She always maintained her innocence, and there was speculation regarding discarded cigarettes and faulty wiring. But while such prosaic explanations might seem credible for one fire, to say that they were the source of five fires in three different houses was beyond the bounds of coincidence. The truth was that Carole Compton was in the vicinity when each fire broke out – but equally, there was no direct evidence that she had set them.

The court proceedings made international headlines, particularly in Britain. But long before it came to trial, the case had attracted the attention of parapsychologists, who saw similarities with other occurrences recorded around the world. They believed that Carole Compton was the catalyst for the outbreak of spontaneous fires. The cornerstone of this line of enquiry was Dr Hugh Pincott, founder of the Association for the Scientific Study of Anomalous Phenomena (ASSAP), and researcher Guy Lyon Playfair. A diverse range of scientists from around the globe was approached and submissions obtained from them regarding their research into poltergeist activity.

The result was a 40-page dossier, which was sent to Carole Compton's legal team to be used as evidence in court. While this dossier did maintain the link between Carole and the fires, it not only offered an explanation showing that she was not an arsonist, but was also

Numerous accidents in the Cecchini household were blamed on Carole, whom the family maid claimed was a witch. Yet could this have been the work of a poltergeist?

the only theory that fitted all the facts. The report indicated that the fires had been triggered by an unconscious burst of emotional energy that exteriorized itself in this dramatic physical way.

The scientists found Carole a likely candidate for spontaneous poltergeist activity. She was young and came from a broken home, and she had followed her boyfriend to Italy only for him to end the relationship. Carole was a stranger in a strange land, who hardly spoke the language and had to endure the hostility of people she worked with who did not like 'foreigners'. Yet her lawyers did not use the scientific dossier in her defence – despite some compelling evidence as to the strangeness of the fires which came to light during the investigation.

BAFFLING COURTROOM TESTIMONY

A fire officer from Bolzano was the first to testify in court. He had examined the sites of the three fires involving the Ricci family and had 38 years' experience in his field. He noted the peculiarity of the fires, which had burned downward with a ferocity indicative of a blaze that had been going for hours, not minutes.

Commenting on the two mattress fires, Professor Vitolo Nicolo of Pisa University told the packed courtroom: 'In all my 45 years' experience of this kind of investigation, I have never seen fires like this before. They were created by an intense source of heat, but not by a naked flame. Strangely, both mattresses had been burned only on the surface and at the same spot. The burn marks could have been caused by a hot iron, but not by a cigarette lighter, a match, or any naked flame.

Carole Compton is escorted by carabinieri (Italian military policemen) *to the courtroom, where she was placed in a cage. The nanny had been arrested on August 2, 1982, and charged with the attempted murder of little Agnese Cecchini.*

207

FACT FILE:
Profile of a poltergeist

What is the phenomenon known as a poltergeist, and what behaviour can this restless 'spirit energy' display?

The term 'poltergeist' is German and, roughly translated, means 'noisy spirit'. This is apt, since poltergeists are often alleged to exhibit violent tendencies, including (in some cases) instigating spontaneous fires.

There is no doubt among parapsychologists that the phenomenon revolves around a focus, usually a young woman, but once aroused it can become independent. Some researchers believe that a poltergeist is an unconscious exteriorization of pent-up emotions – a physical manifestation of psychic energy. Others argue that the human focus of the spirit merely acts as a facilitator to allow entities to enter our world from theirs.

Poltergeists have been attributed with numerous characteristics, although usually just two or three of these features appear in any one case:

1. Auditory effects such as knocking and rapping sounds
2. Mysterious movement of objects
3. Disappearance of objects, which usually turn up weeks or months later
4. Materialization of small objects 'from out of thin air', such as coins and rusty nails, which do not belong there
5. The appearance of writing by an unknown hand
6. Vandalization of furniture
7. Destruction of household objects such as crockery
8. Arrangement of things in neat, child-like patterns
9. The slaughter of pets
10. Footsteps, voices, and the appearance of apparitions
11. The throwing of stones at buildings
12. Violence against witnesses
13. The eruption of fires

A classic case of poltergeist activity occurred in Enfield, London, in 1977. The events revolved around the Harper family, comprising a mother and her children, separated from their father.

It began on the evening of August 30, when the beds of two of the children began to shake. The following night, the same children and their mother heard a sound like someone shuffling across the carpet in slippers. Four loud knocks followed, and they watched a heavy chest of drawers move across the room. When more knocks sounded, the family fetched a neighbour, who searched the house, along with a police officer. They found nothing.

The next night, marbles and Lego bricks were thrown around the house by an invisible hand. When touched, one of the marbles was found to be burning hot. The *Daily Mirror* became involved and, through it, Maurice Grosse and Guy Lyon Playfair of the Society for Psychical

Films such as Poltergeist III, though fictional, are based on documented case histories. While horror films provide scary entertainment, the real-life cases from which they are derived give serious food for thought.

Research (SPR), who then proceeded to investigate the allegations.

There were many witnesses to the movement of furniture and the appearance of apparitions. At one point, the disturbed spirit of a little girl suffocated by her father in a neighbouring house was suspected. (The Harpers had bought some of the family's furniture.) A medium contacted several entities who allegedly claimed reponsibility, saying that they were feeding off the negative energy leaked by 11-year-old Janet and her mother, who was very bitter toward her estranged husband.

After stopping for a few weeks, the activities resumed. The investigators recorded 400 incidents, including the appearance of a pool of water on the kitchen floor in the shape of a figure. A gas fire was ripped off the wall and an iron grill landed near one of the children. After a visit by psychic Matthew Manning, messages were left on the wall.

More of the phenomena centred on Janet, who went into convulsions and on one occasion was hurled out of bed. While in a trance, she produced a picture of a woman with blood pouring from her throat. Underneath, she wrote 'Watson'. Mrs Watson had been a previous tenant who had died of throat cancer. Did Janet know this? In December, a voice claiming to be Joe Watson started communicating. It sounded masculine but electronic, producing each word with difficulty. Later, it claimed to be various other people, including an old man buried nearby.

Some SPR members were convinced that the phenomena were a hoax perpetrated by the Harper children, who were caught on one occasion throwing something across the room. Grosse and Playfair did not agree, feeling that it would have been impossible for the children to have faked most of the incidents. The haunting eventually faded out during the summer of 1978.

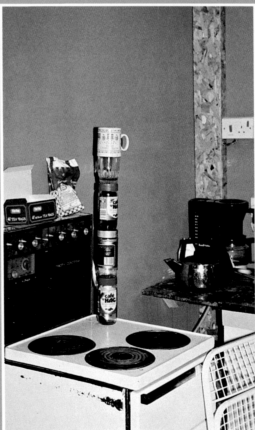

One of several pieces of furniture damaged by an invisible slasher during the 1973 Guarulhos poltergeist case in Brazil. Poltergeist manifestations can be very violent, but individuals are very rarely hurt.

Kitchen items are often found stacked during poltergeist activity, as here in Dodleston, Chester, in 1985. At the same time, messages were allegedly received on a computer from a man living in the sixteenth century.

Both fires had the same characteristics: great heat, but no flames. I have never seen anything like it before.'

Documentary film-makers for the British television company '20/20 Vision' hired forensic expert Dr Keith Borer to carry out his own tests on scaled-down versions of the original wool and horsehair mattresses. Borer was a sceptic when it came to psychic matters, but he was bemused by his findings. The Cecchini grandfather's mattress had been scorched in a long, even strip along the entire length of one side. It had been verified that no inflammable liquids had been used, but when Dr Borer tried to replicate the fire, he encountered difficulties. First of all, it took many minutes to get the mattress to light, then it burnt in an irregular upward pattern. He was also mystified by the first major fire at Ortisei.

The wooden stool where the fire apparently started was only slightly damaged, while the rest of the room was destroyed. Seemingly, the fire had 'leapt' a couple of feet from the stool and 'dropped' into a drawer.

To her credit, Carole Compton did not jump on the paranormal bandwagon and merely stuck to her guns, stating that she was not responsible for starting the fires. Nevertheless, the case's mysterious aspects were not lost on certain individuals and the media, who branded Carole a witch.

Despite having no clear evidence to connect Carole with any of the fires, nor an established motive, the jury found the Scottish nanny guilty of arson. She was given a two-and-a-half year prison sentence, but released immediately, owing to the time she had already spent in custody awaiting trial.

CASE FILE:
Possessed by an evil spirit

What was the horrifying presence that nearly led to murder one night in the grounds of a quiet house?

Abney Hall, located in Cheadle, Cheshire, England, then in use as council offices, had once been a grand home, and it was also said to be where crime writer Agatha Christie fled during her still mysterious 11-day disappearance in 1926. In 1988, it was being used as an evening practice ground by a group of martial arts students.

One night, a powerful force seemed to take control of the group. One student was seen to walk zombie-like toward a lake, as if to drown herself, before being grabbed at the last moment. Another nearly strangled a fellow student before being pulled away and awoken from his 'trance' state. A strange imp-like figure was also witnessed standing near a waterfall before disappearing into the undergrowth, bringing the frightening experiences to an end.

During this bizarre episode, building work was being carried out on the nearby estate. Previous studies have shown that construction is often connected with poltergeist outbreaks.

The waterfall in the grounds of Abney Hall, in Cheadle, Cheshire, where a suspected poltergeist attack wreaked havoc on a group of martial arts students in 1988.

Inexplicable spontaneous fires have occurred during poltergeist outbreaks, as evidenced here by a burned blanket in a case from Suzano, Brazil, in 1970.

CRIME FILE:
The New York fires

Was a teenage girl really guilty of arson – or did these mysterious blazes have a supernatural cause?

Among the many incidents of spontaneous fires, there are curious parallels between the Carole Compton case and a series of blazes in a New York suburb toward the end of the nineteenth century. Both involved a large number of fires in two households and centred on a young woman who was accused of arson.

In 1895, the *New York Herald* reported on 'the many fires' that had plagued the house of Adam Colwell during January 4 and 5. The final outbreak burnt the building to the ground. There were many witnesses, including police officers and fire fighters, who concluded at the time that the fires were of an unknown origin. Colwell's 16-year-old stepdaughter, Rhoda, was initially considered as a suspect, but the possibility of her involvement was dismissed by the Fire Marshall, who commented: 'It might be thought that Rhoda started two of the fires, but she cannot be considered guilty of the others, as she was being questioned when some of them began.'

He described also how furniture had reportedly been thrown around in the house by an unseen hand. Colwell stated that he, his wife, and Rhoda had all been together when they heard a loud crash. A large stove had fallen over. Later, pictures fell from the walls, and then a bed was found on fire. A police officer who helped extinguish the blaze then saw some wallpaper begin to burn. Another officer, Detective Sergeant Dunn, witnessed another fire and saw a heavy lamp fall from its hook. Finally, the house burned down completely and the family was taken to the police station. Dunn said: 'There were things that happened before my eyes that I did not believe were possible.'

Captain Rhoads of the Greenpoint Precinct told the press: 'The people we arrested had nothing to do with the strange fires. The more I look into it, the deeper the mystery. So far I can attribute it to no other cause than a supernatural agency. Why, the fires broke out under the very noses of the men I sent to investigate.'

Despite these public statements, the next day the police claimed that Rhoda was responsible for all the events through trickery. This conclusion was based on the allegations of a Mr Hope, who had come forward to state that, in November and December, four blazes had broken out in his house while Rhoda was working there as a maid. Rhoads now believed that the young woman had utilized her feminine charms in order to distract his officers while she set the fires and knocked things over. Placed under extreme pressure to 'confess', Rhoda dutifully obliged. Yet there was never any concrete evidence to prove her guilt.

In a bizarre echo of the 1895 New York fires, the poltergeist energy allegedly released nearly 100 years later at Dodleston, Chester, showed the same violent tendencies when it upended a heavy cooker.

THE TRIAL OF HELEN DUNCAN

In another bizarre case, Helen Duncan was the last person to be tried under England's Witchcraft Act of 1735 – in April 1944. Duncan, a very successful clairvoyant, was on trial for fraud after a member of the public had complained about her. According to some, the reasons for her conviction were far from straightforward. The prosecution's star witness had close links with Scotland Yard and social connections with the upper echelons of the Portsmouth police.

A portrait of the famous medium Helen Duncan, dated May 1931. Was she a fraud, a genuine psychic, or in fact a mixture of the two?

Supporters of Helen Duncan claimed it was a 'put-up job' to take the medium out of circulation because she had used her psychic powers to predict the sinking of two British ships by the Germans. During wartime, this was seen as a treasonable act.

The ships were HMS *Hood* and HMS *Barham*. The *Hood* was sunk following an engagement with the *Bismarck* on May 24, 1941. Before even the Admiralty knew that she had gone down, Duncan told a roomful of witnesses while in a trance that 'a battleship has been sunk'. Brigadier R. C. Firebrace was at the seance and confirmed the details. Sceptics pointed out that a war was on, and therefore it was to be expected that battleships would be lost. It would have been more significant, they said, had Duncan named the ship.

Helen Duncan was a physical, or materialization, medium. This meant that she could allegedly produce a substance called 'ectoplasm' from her body, which then took the physical form of the spirit with which she was in contact.

HMS Hood *at full speed in the Moray Firth in 1933, eight years before she was sunk by the* Bismarck. *Brigadier R. C. Firebrace heard an entranced Duncan announce the tragedy in front of a room full of witnesses.*

According to witnesses, during another seance the figure of a sailor materialized, who was identified by a woman in the audience as her son, who was aboard the *Barham*. He supposedly told the audience it had been sunk. HMS *Barham* went down in the Mediterranean on November 25, 1941. There is some confusion, however, over the date of the seance during which Duncan made her 'prophetic' statement – one version of events places it in 1943, and the other at the time of the sinking, which makes rather more sense.

After giving a series of seances in January 1944, Duncan was arrested and charged with pretending to raise the dead and obtaining money under false pretences. She had previously been convicted of fraud in 1933, but at the new trial more than 40 witnesses gave evidence in her defence. Many of these witnesses were intelligent people of good standing. Duncan denied all of the charges against her, but was found guilty and served nine months in prison.

There are many photographs that supposedly show ectoplasm emanating

The British battleship Barham. *Did a sailor from the sunken ship materialize at one of Helen Duncan's seances to announce that the vessel had gone down?*

FACT FILE:
What is ectoplasm?

Physical, or materialization, mediums are known to produce a substance by which 'spirits' can take shape.

Ectoplasm, in spiritualist terminology, is a whitish substance alleged to exude from the body of a medium while in a trance state. Supposedly, the material appears alive and sensitive to touch and light, upon contact with which it will shoot back into the psychic, causing physical pain. It is conceived as some sort of supernatural modelling clay used by spirits to manifest in our world. Variously described as having the texture of muslin, liquid, or paste, it is cold, slightly luminous, and has a characteristic smell.

In the nineteenth and early twentieth century, mediums commonly produced ectoplasm, but it is rarely seen today. The substance is usually extruded from natural orifices such as the ears, eyes, nostrils, navel, nipples, and genitals. However, the medium known as 'Eva C.' was apparently witnessed with ectoplasm coming from her thumb. This early twentieth-century medium, whose real name was Marthe Beraud, was famous for producing materialized spirit figures However, when she was examined in 1920 by the Society for Psychical Research, they found that the 'ectoplasm' comprised regurgitated paper and fabric.

The only documented scientific analysis of ectoplasm produced by a psychic took place at the Massachusetts Institute of Technology. It was reported as being composed of sodium, potassium, water, chlorine, albumen, epithelial cells, and fresh red blood corpuscles.

from the entranced body of Helen Duncan; in some cases, the material has assumed recognizable features such as a face. Many of these pictures were taken at seances by Harry Price, a psychic investigator who was convinced that Duncan was a fraud. In several of the photographs, the 'ectoplasm' appears to be white muslin or cheesecloth, while the 'faces' look as if they were manufactured from papier-mâché. If these 'materializations' seem obvious fakes to us, why was this not clear to the people present at the time? Were they deluding themselves? Did they see what they wanted to see?

Perhaps Helen Duncan had a genuine talent for physical mediumship and did, on occasions, really produce ectoplasm that manifested as the image of someone who had died. However, she was clearly in the business of earning a living, and people expect results when they have bought a ticket. Psychics have often supplemented real talents with trickery, in order to satisfy an audience – the late medium Doris Stokes admitted to cheating when she was under pressure to perform. Nevertheless, many witnesses attested to the authenticity of Helen Duncan's powers. After her trial, the Witchcraft Act was replaced by the Fraudulent Medium's Act.

Helen Duncan supposedly producing ectoplasm for psychic researcher, Harry Price, in May 1931. Was this really the fabled substance or merely cheesecloth that the medium had regurgitated from her stomach?

The business of cheating

Accusations of fraud have long dogged the paranormal field. How just are the claims of sceptics?

Harry Price earned a reputation for uncovering the fraudulent exploits of professional mediums, yet ironically, several years later, it was his turn to be accused of manufacturing phenomena in 'haunted' Borley Rectory on the Essex border.

Some sceptics are on a mission to 'prove', by hook or by crook, that all supposed psychic phenomena are nothing more than misperception or fraud. It became very acrimonious when Uri Geller and American stage

magician James Randi began throwing libel lawsuits at one another. They eventually agreed to call a truce.

One of the most successful films of the 1980s was *The Amityville Horror*, based on the novel by Jay Anson. The movie told the supposedly true story of what happened to the Lutz family after they moved into 112 Ocean Avenue, Amityville, Long Island. The previous tenants of the house had been slaughtered there by Ronald Defoe, a family member.

George and Kathy Lutz claimed that they had come under demonic attack. Swarms of flies appeared, doors were torn off their hinges, slime dripped over everything, and malevolent entities tried to kill them. In the end, they were driven from the house. The book became a bestseller, and the Lutz family appeared on chat shows talking about their experiences. However, when investigators became involved, they found that there was little substance to the story. Dr Stephan Kaplan of the Parapsychology Institute of America commented: 'After several months of extensive research and interviews with those who were involved … we found no evidence to support any claim of a "haunted house". What we did find was a couple who had purchased a house that they economically could not afford. It is our professional opinion that the story of its haunting is mostly fiction.'

Others had the same opinion, and investigators Rick Moran and Peter Jordan discovered that police officers and priests who supposedly had been involved in the haunting had not even set foot in the house and denied what was said about them in the book.

Helen Duncan materializes a figure while her hands are held by sitters. The figure, supposedly formed from ecto-plasm, looks as if it is composed of papier-mâché and muslin.

Investigator Harry Price demonstrating the electrical device he built to detect any movement of hand or foot by a medium during a seance.

DEATH BY SPONTANEOUS COMBUSTION?

The authors of this book were able to witness first-hand how courts deal with the tricky issue of the supernatural when they were invited by the police in Cheshire, England, to attend an inquest and give evidence to the jury. This opportunity arose because of our acknowledged record of investigating strange phenomena and seeking rational explanations behind them wherever possible. The incident that had baffled both the police and the fire service was a tragedy that befell a young student, Jacqueline Fitzsimon, at the Halton College of Further Education in Widnes, on the banks of the River Mersey.

It was midmorning on January 28, 1985, and Jacqueline, who was on a youth training program, had just finished a cookery class. She set off down the stairs,

Spontaneous human combustion is a highly contentious phenomenon in which a human being allegedly bursts into flame of supernatural origin, as depicted in this 1885 illustration.

laughing and joking with some friends. Then – in the blink of an eye – she became engulfed in a mass of flames. The fire was beaten out by her shocked friends and college employees who had wrestled her to the ground, but the burns were so severe that Jacqueline died a few days later in hospital.

No one knew what had caused this blaze to erupt so suddenly and to burn so fiercely. There were stories aired about certain students playing 'flame throwers' with hairspray cans (although this was never proven), as well as an eyewitness account of a 'light' that fell like a blazing speck from midair onto the unfortunate teenager's back. The spectre of the supernatural also reared its head when, in an off-guard moment, an investigating fire officer – clearly shocked by the horrific incident – said that they would investigate every angle, including the possibility of spontaneous human combustion.

Those that endorse the existence of spontaneous human combustion describe it as a rare phenomenon during which a person allegedly bursts into flames and is consumed within minutes – sometimes to little more than a pile of ash. The source of the fire is unknown, but is believed to be internally generated. Theories on its genesis range from fluke combinations of natural events – such as human body fat cooking the bones in the same way that wax burns around a candle wick – to more esoteric notions about an imbalance of psychic forces.

Although the subject is still intensely controversial, several hundred cases have been recorded over 400 years, some based on eyewitness testimony and

During Victorian times, when court reporter Charles Dickens came upon several cases of reputed spontaneous combustion, the popular view was that an excess of alcohol caused drunkards to become flammable. This was a frequent topic of social commentary in cartoon images, where the threat was used as a warning against the evils of the demon drink.

others on fire service records. In Victorian times, the novelist Charles Dickens, who had been a court reporter, encountered several such incidents. Indeed, he was so intrigued that he killed off one of his villains – Krook, in *Bleak House* – by this mysterious means.

When called upon to attend the inquest, we conducted our own investigation of both this case and the general phenomenon of spontaneous human combustion, by interviewing eyewitnesses at the college, forensic scientists, fire officers who had witnessed the aftermath of events of this alleged nature, and numerous others with clues to offer. We concluded in our report that many fires reported as spontaneous human combustion are in reality of mundane origin, but that in perhaps a handful of cases worldwide each year, there is sufficient evidence that an unusual scientific phenomenon may be involved. In these incidents, the most likely cause

seems to be an increased level of electrical energy within the body, literally providing a spark to trigger the combustion of gases created by natural biological processes (production of these gases being heightened by modern Western diets and alcohol consumption).

However, we were not convinced that Jacqueline Fitzsimon had died through spontaneous human combustion. Instead, we felt that this ignition was due to an as-yet unidentified external source, with the updraft from the stairwell a contributing factor. Yet there were conflicting pieces of evidence. For example, the tests conducted on the girl's clothing by forensic officers failed to demonstrate that they could catch fire so dramatically. An independent scientific report

Spontaneous human combustion, though a rare occurrence, still apparently happens, and inquest juries are occasionally forced to consider the prospect of the supernatural at work.

221

commissioned by the Cheshire Fire Brigade via a leading Manchester laboratory also failed to support the viability of our theory, which was basically that the clothing had smouldered and was then fanned into ferocious life by the air currents on the stairs.

At the inquest, we were prepared to inform the jury on the myths and realities of spontaneous human combustion, as we saw them. Instead, the coroner opened the proceedings by staring pointedly at us and advising the jury to discount all talk they might have heard about the supernatural. This somewhat aggrieved us, since we were not intent on trying to prove a paranormal connection in this case. On the contrary, we were likely to help dispel the idea.

As the case unfolded, our frustration grew. Key witnesses that we had interviewed were not present at the inquest; nor was there a representative from the fire department. Moreover, the science lab report – which reached conclusions that at least in part contradicted the ultimate verdict (that the girl's clothing had been smouldering) – was not shown to the jury. In a fire death enquiry, such omissions seemed odd.

Perhaps we will never know the full truth, but spontaneous human combustion was at least a possible explanation for this tragedy. However, the court appeared to dismiss such an idea as unworthy of any sort of rational debate, rejecting much of the evidence in the process. We spoke to several other coroners, who admitted that they, too, would be reluctant to allow such contentious discussion in their courtrooms. They explained that this did not reflect any conspiracy against the paranormal, but a very valid concern that to raise such issues would increase the suffering of the bereaved by attracting unwelcome publicity. Nor would it resolve matters, since the existence of supernatural phenomena cannot be determined at an inquest.

This may be so, yet if a mysterious death

How do modern courts deal with apparently 'miraculous' events such as spontaneous combustion? Judgements that accept the paranormal as reality could set precedents and lead to challenges to rulings on appeal. Few judges relish taking such a risk.

CASE FILE:
What happened to Mary Reeser?

When a woman died in a household fire, the evidence baffled investigators. While her body had been reduced to ash, the rest of her home was left miraculously unscathed.

One of the most extensively investigated cases of spontaneous human combustion involved the death of 67-year-old Mary Reeser. In the early morning of July 1, 1951, her body – reduced to little more than a pile of ash and a few shrunken skull fragments – was found in her apartment in St Petersberg, Florida. There were traces of a fire in the room, but it was limited to a small area and did little damage, not even affecting flammable materials found inches from the utterly consumed body of the woman.

Police suspected foul play, but their investigations drew a total blank. Because of the bizarre nature of the case, the FBI were called in, thus making this one of the first-ever real-life 'X Files'. The agents conducted a major forensic investigation and a detailed follow-up of the evidence, interviewing neighbours and other witnesses. They also failed to find an explanation, but ruled out any criminal act.

The dead woman's son, a doctor, told the authors of this book in 1993 that he believed his mother's death was a tragic accident. He proposed that she had consumed sleeping pills and had fallen asleep with a cigarette in her hand. This had apparently dropped onto the chair, which then caught alight.

The original FBI reports, however, record that the room's electric clock had stopped in the middle of the night – presumably when the socket burnt out. Yet it worked perfectly when plugged in elsewhere. The timing of the fire (as noted by the clock) and the hour at which the body was known to be found are difficult to reconcile with the precise manner of Mary Reeser's death. Experiments by forensic scientists to discover how human bone can be turned to ash – something not even achieved in a modern crematorium – indicated that at least 12 hours would be required to leave the total devastation seen in Mary Reeser's room. In fact, the evidence shows that, in this case, just two hours elapsed before the consummation to ash – nothing like long enough for these horrifying consequences.

Police sift through the shocking evidence found in Mary Reeser's apartment following her mysterious death. The fire was so intense that it reduced Reeser to little more than a pile of ash, yet strangely it did not spread beyond her body. Despite forensic study by the police and the FBI, the case has never been fully explained.

occurs, surely it is important to examine all options – no matter how bizarre – on the premise that doing so might prevent something similar happening again. It is strange that despite the fact that judgements on the reality of spontaneous human combustion are largely the result of observations made by fire officers, forensic scientists, and other experts, the subject is still perceived as taboo. Imagine then the prospect of any court taking seriously evidence generated by psychic visions, premonitions, or someone's dreams!

ARSON IN COLORADO

Elisabeth Allison knows all too well how difficult it can be to use a premonition to help secure a criminal conviction. In the spring of 1940, she and her husband, Ed, were running a farm machinery store in a small western Colorado town. The area's towering mountains and wide valleys made for lush farmland, and business was good, as ranchers from miles around relied upon the Allisons for their parts and equipment.

Yet, earlier that year, things had turned a little sour. A local odd-job man had decided to set up a rival operation across the street, but was soon in financial difficulty. The Allisons had been respected locally for many years, and customers stayed with them, rather than defect to the new dealership. Even when their competitor slashed his prices, he still did not win trade.

One April day, after preparing dinner, Elisabeth decided to walk the few hundred yards to meet Ed as he left the store, but along the route she passed the owner of the competing business on the street. As she did so, she was struck by a wave of nausea and a strange sensation. She literally 'knew' what was about

to happen. The man was going to seek to ruin them in order to save his own skin. It was a powerful psychic vision that Elizabeth could not explain, but was certain would come true.

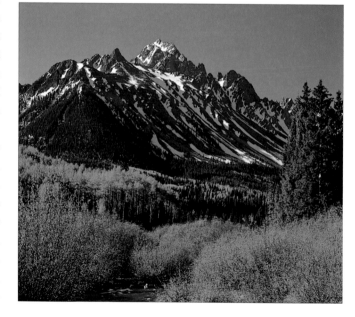

As soon as her husband appeared, Elisabeth asked him if he had insurance to cover the cost of the large intake of equipment that had just arrived. He replied that he had not taken out a policy as yet; he

The rural idyll of a small Colorado farming town was shattered when envy led a frustrated man to commit arson against his local business rival.

did not consider it a priority, since crime in the area was rare. She insisted that he do so right away, saying that she knew the warehouse was going to be destroyed by their business rival, in an attempt to wipe them out.

Ed was less than convinced, saying it was just her imagination. The man concerned had no reputation for lawlessness and it seemed absurd that he would do such a thing. Desperate to persuade her husband, Elisabeth shared her fears with her friend, Martha Campbell, who agreed to speak to Ed on the matter. The tactic worked, and, somewhat reluctantly, Mr Allison agreed that as a precaution that he would enquire about taking out insurance to cover their stock and premises.

Despite an eerie premonition of the arson attack that was to destroy a family warehouse, a reluctance to believe in the power of the paranormal was to cost one couple very dearly.

Sadly, this was all too late. Less than a week later, before he had had the chance to sign any insurance forms, the Allisons were awoken at 3:00 a.m. with cries of 'Fire!' Rushing outside, they were confronted with the horrifying spectacle of their warehouse and all its precious stock burning to the ground. Despite every effort, there was massive damage before the fire engine could arrive to bring the blaze under control.

The next day, the fire officer visited the Allisons and was full of suspicious questions. He had realized immediately that there was something not right about the fire. He was convinced that it was deliberate. But the fact that Ed had no valid insurance – not to mention the healthy state of the business – ruled out any motive for setting the fire for his own purposes.

The town doctor asked Elisabeth Allison if the rumours were true – had the fire been arson? She replied that yes, it was looking that way. The doctor nodded and said that he had just treated the odd-job man, who appeared to be in deep shock and plainly terrified. His demeanour convinced the doctor that he had set the fire and was now bitterly regretting his actions.

The Allisons told the sheriff of the doctor's suspicions and that Elisabeth had somehow 'known' that their rival was going to burn down their property. The police confirmed that there was now no doubt. The fire was without question arson – petrol had been strewn all over the warehouse floor. Yet they could not find anything to positively connect the matter with the person they now considered to be the prime suspect – the man across the street. The Colorado police could not act on the basis of a premonition, however, no matter how well

A lonely farmhouse, a violent, bloody crime, and a mystery that perplexed the Alberta police – until the arrival of a psychic detective.

it backed up their own suspicions, and the case never went to trial. They needed proof, and they had none. It looked as if a criminal had escaped, despite his guilt being recognized by all.

The disaster cost the Allisons dearly, but they eventually recovered. The odd-job man, however, never got over the trauma of that night. Locals shunned him as news of the story spread. A few weeks later, his business folded. He locked himself indoors, refusing even to cross the street as he avoided going near the burned-out building. He sank deeper into depression and died just two years later, a very troubled man. Perhaps justice was served after all by the culprit's own conscience.

THE MANVILLE FARM MURDERS

On July 9, 1928, Mannville Farm near Edmonton, Alberta, was the scene of one of the most bloody mass murders in Canada's history. And psychic detection was to play a remarkable role.

It all started when shots were heard by neighbouring property holders at around 6:30 p.m., with further gunfire 90 minutes later. Since the shots appeared to be from a rifle, and this was an area where hunting was very popular, not too much attention was paid to these events at the time. Yet they were to prove very significant.

At just after 8 o'clock that evening, Vernon Booher called a local doctor to say that he had just arrived home – to find the farm was a slaughterhouse. At that hour the place should have been full, with his parents, his brother, Fred, and two farmhands inside. Instead, there was an eerie silence as he entered – suggesting that something was very wrong. Then he saw the blood on the floor in the kitchen.

Walking inside, he found the body of his mother, Rose, who had been shot through the head. His brother was in an adjacent room, shot through the mouth and with blood flowing everywhere. Finally, outside he came across the body of one of the farmhands, Gabriel Cronby, on the floor of his bunk room, again shot through the head. But there was no sign of the other farmhand, Herma Rosyk – or Henry Booher, Vernon's father.

Booher had rushed from this terrible discovery to his neighbour's farm to phone for help, hoping that one of the victims might still be alive – although this seemed very unlikely.

Henry Booher arrived back about an hour later, saying that he had been unexpectedly delayed. He was stunned by the horror that confronted him, with police and medics now poring over the farmhouse and quizzing his son as to the whereabouts of the family.

It was not long afterward that police found the missing farmhand; he was in a barn some distance from the house, also shot in the head.

PIECING TOGETHER THE CRIME

It took little time to establish that all four victims had been murdered by the same weapon – a rifle. The time of death, however, proved to be more of a puzzle when the forensic teams got to work. The two family members in the farmhouse and the farmhand in the outlying barn had all been killed about the same time (roughly 6:00 p.m.), but the other farmhand, found in the nearby bunk house, had definitely been killed up to two hours later.

This placed the times of death coincident with the two separate bursts of rifle fire, but also meant that the final murder – that of Gabriel Cronby – must have happened very close to the time when Vernon Booher arrived home. The police concluded that he may have missed seeing the killer by mere minutes and was probably very fortunate to be alive.

But why would the killer murder two people in the house, another some distance away, and then return to the house over an hour later (risking being disturbed by anyone who heard the original shots) in order to murder the second farm hand in his bunk room?

It made no sense at all. Detective Mike Gier from Edmonton did have a prime suspect – Charles Stevenson – the man on the neighbouring property from whose house Booher had called for a doctor. He was the registered owner of a

The Mannville Farm murders could not be resolved without the discovery of the weapon used to kill the victims. It had been hidden somewhere on the farm. But where?

rifle of the same calibre as the one used in the murders, but claimed that it had been stolen shortly before the killings.

This story did not entirely convince the police, yet despite six months of intensive investigation, nothing whatsoever could be found to link Stevenson with the murders. Nor did he appear to have any kind of motive.

Gier was at a total impasse when fate dealt him a curious hand. A most unusual scientist was passing through the area on route to Alaska, where he intended to study the paranormal experiences of the local Eskimo tribes. This man, Dr Max Langsner, had something of a reputation as a psychic, and Gier decided that he had nothing to lose by seeing what he could tell him about this perplexing case.

The rifle used to commit the crime was dug up from the spot where the killer had hidden it, following the precise directions of psychic Dr Max Langsner.

A NEW LINE OF ENQUIRY

Dr Langsner very quickly sent the case in a completely different direction with a strange combination of ESP and deduction of which Sherlock Holmes would have been proud. In fact, this fascinating man had a sound academic background, having earned a PhD from Calcutta University and studied psychology under the famous Sigmund Freud in Vienna. Whether through finely tuned insights or by psychic intuition (he claimed both), Langsner said within moments of arriving that Stevenson was not the killer – Vernon Booher was. His entire story of arriving home and finding the bodies was a deception.

Gier found this allegation difficult to take seriously, because Booher had been co-operative and apparently shell-shocked throughout the investigation. If he was lying, then his acting was impeccable. But the psychic knew how to combat this disbelief. He said that he could 'see' exactly where Booher had hidden the gun, which the police had failed to find after months of effort. It was, he said, buried under grass at the rear of the house. Amazingly, the rifle was indeed exactly where Langsner said it would be – hidden underneath a shallow mound of earth, barely detectable.

However, this alone did not persuade the police that Langsner had the right man, let alone allow them to convict him, particularly as the rifle was the one owned by Stevenson – the man they believed to be the killer. This was the same gun that he claimed had mysteriously disappeared from his farm.

Nevertheless, so certain was the psychic in his identification of the real killer that he suggested a way to trap the murderer. He persuaded Gier to take Vernon Booher into custody, on the pretext that this was a form of witness protection, saying that the police suspected that Stevenson might come after him.

What Booher did not know was that his cellmate during this period of 'protective custody' was none other than Dr Max Langsner. In such proximity to his suspect, he hoped to conduct a personal psychic reading and establish exactly what had happened and why.

PSYCHIC RESOLUTION

After spending some hours sharing a cell with the man he was certain was the murderer, Langsner told Gier that he knew what had happened. Booher had first shot his mother, then killed his brother, who was also in the house, and then trailed Rosyk to the barn because he had seen him leaving the farmhouse with the gun. He had then brooded over the one remaining possible witness – Cronby – who was still in his bunk room and had not responded to the original gunshots. Therefore, there was no reason to believe that he had seen the killings. Nevertheless, as a precaution, Booher returned to the farmhouse, shot Cronby, then feigned his own discovery of the bodies.

Langsner's proposed scenario was fascinating, but, as far as Gier was concerned, it was nothing more than a complex theory and there was really nothing he could do with the psychic's news. By now, he, too, believed that Booher was the murderer, but he also knew that in a trial there would be no way to prove it. Forensic tests had revealed nothing on the buried gun. The only lead tied the rifle to a different suspect – Stevenson. And Booher was such a clever actor that his story of grief was likely to convince a jury. There seemed no way to get a conviction.

Yet, just as the police were convinced that the killer would escape justice, the redoubtable Langsner intervened once more. He claimed that there was a witness who could crack this case open. She had appeared to him in a vision, he said, and he described her to police artists. In a community as small as Mannville, there were few women of the right age to check out, and in only a matter of days detectives had found a woman that fit Langsner's description.

This woman, Erma Higgins, did indeed have the vital clue – a piece of information that she could not have known was significant. On the day Stevenson claimed that his rifle went missing, Erma saw Vernon Booher sneak out of church. Since virtually the entire town was at the service, it seemed as though he was taking the opportunity to get up to something. What she did not know was that he was about to steal the rifle that would later be used to murder four people.

Faced with this evidence, Booher confessed. The details were precisely as Langsner had 'seen' them. A motive was also revealed. Vernon's mother had not agreed with his choice of girlfriend and had thrown her off the property. He planned to take his revenge, and the other killings had followed in an attempt to eliminate witnesses, as events spiralled out of control. Vernon Booher was found guilty and was hanged on April 26, 1929. The role of Dr Langsner was not credited in court, but without it this case would almost certainly never have been solved.

CRIME FILE:
The murder of William Edden

The bond between man and wife proved strong indeed when a woman 'heard' a final cry from her husband as he lay dying miles away.

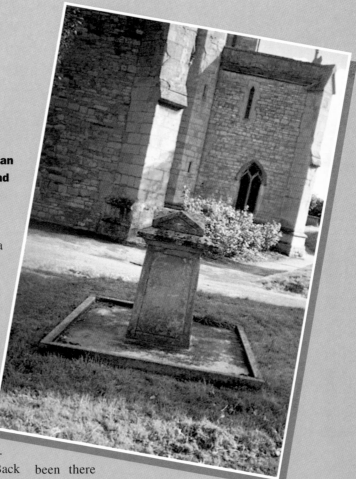

Researcher Alan Cleaver uncovered a fascinating case in nineteenth-century England in which a murder suspect was identified through a bizarre psychic vision. Two men were eventually convicted and hanged, all on the strength of one woman's extraordinary 'message' from her dying husband.

In 1828, William 'Noble' Edden lived in Thame on the Oxfordshire–Buckinghamshire border. On his way home from the market, near the village of Haddenham, he was fatally attacked. Back home in Thame, his wife experienced a sudden vision of the crime at the very time of her husband's death and was so convinced of its truth that she immediately told friends and neighbours what had occurred.

When the authorities began an investigation of the murder, they were astonished by Mrs Edden's detailed knowledge of events. They were further shocked when she named a man called Benjamin Tyler as the killer. Tyler naturally denied being involved, and without hard evidence no action could be taken.

Twelve months later, labourer Solomon Sewell confessed that he had been there when Tyler had murdered William Edden. Tyler's defence was that Sewell was a simpleton. Even the youth's mother agreed, and the labourer's testimony was dismissed as unreliable.

A year later, Mrs Edden was still insisting that her husband had appeared to her at the moment of his death and pointed out Tyler as the killer. A trial was convened, and this time both Benjamin Tyler and Solomon Sewell were charged with the crime. Largely on the evidence of Mrs Edden's vision, they were found guilty and were subsequently hanged. Tyler protested his innocence even on the scaffold.

The grave of William 'Noble' Edden in Thame churchyard. Did the spirit of the murdered man 'travel' from his dying body to tell his wife the name of his killer?

The Danger of Being Right

ALL PSYCHICS GROW UP HARDENED to ridicule and expect to have to prove themselves against inevitable prejudice. This is not easy, since they cannot fully explain their own abilities. Such gifted individuals are generally regarded as cranks or frauds by those who do not believe in the existence of paranormal powers. Within the police force, where facts and logic are the order of the day, such a reaction is quite common.

Therefore, the career of a psychic detective is inevitably fraught with difficulty. As psychic Dr John Dale explains, 'As a psychic working on crimes, you have to be prepared to accept that you might be wrong. Overconfidence can be a real enemy. From my experience, it is easy to see images or visions that might be revealing but are a great deal harder to interpret with your logical mind … Understanding psychic impressions is a very subjective process'. He points out that psychic experiences occur almost in a different reality – the part of the brain that governs imagination and creativity – and are then processed by the rational sections of the brain. During that decoding (either by the psychic or by police officers), things often go wrong. One can easily make the wrong assumptions about the meaning of a symbol or locate an image somewhere that it is not intended to be.

Dale advises: 'Psychics who put themselves forward to work on these cases must be prepared to be wrong as often as they are right. This can be harrowing, especially if lives are at stake. They can feel the burden placed upon them very

Do actors have enhanced psychic abilities? Certainly many claim to have had strange experiences – especially when entertaining troops in battle zones. Here, General George Patton greets Bob Hope as he arrives to perform for soldiers in 1943.

heavily indeed. All that they can give is of their best. Unfortunately, sometimes their best is just not good enough. But it is rarely for the want of trying. Most of these people are sincere and really do want to help.'

The emotional toll that can be wrought upon a psychic is well described by actor Bill Waddington, who played the popular character Percy Sugden in 'Coronation Street' – the world's oldest continuously produced television soap opera series, broadcast in England since December 1960. Throughout his life, the actor had many psychic flashes in which he simply 'saw' things happening, even when miles away. His revelations invariably stunned those whom he contacted to explain what he knew. Usually these were relatively minor events, such as sensing that one of his horses at a stud farm had been taken ill during the night. Sometimes, however, his experiences were highly emotional and could be very draining.

'During the war', he told us, 'I was with a field entertainment troupe. One day we visited the tank corps after a devastating battle early in the war during which many people had been killed. I could feel the emotions as if they were a living thing'. Waddington explains how he acted like a 'psychic sponge' – absorbing the negative emotions of the demoralized troops, who by now feared that Hitler was marching to victory. In response to their dejection, he emitted what today we might call 'positive vibes', allowing the tension to lift from the battle-weary soldiers. He describes it as a very real exchange of energy, after which he entered a state of deep emotional suffering, as if having contracted a psychological infection.

A number of clairvoyants have told of the mental and physical trauma that using psychic powers can bring. Medium Doris Collins told us of her need to rest during tour engagements, saying that the contacts she has with other realities completely sap her energy and emotions. Indeed, clairvoyants have long warned that disturbing mediums while they are using their powers can be life-threatening.

Imagine, then, the added pressure brought to bear upon any psychic who, day in and day out, is seeking to 'commune' with evil people who have carried out violent crimes. It is akin to being weighed down in a psychic quicksand awash with pure hate, an experience that is almost bound to leave indelible stains.

This may be why many psychic detectives have relatively short careers, with several forced to 'retire' under the overwhelming strain. Sadly, their work is not helped by authorities who distrust psychics or, even if convinced they are genuine, expect them to work miracles when in truth they are merely gifted individuals with ordinary human failings. Psychic detectives need understanding and compassion from the people with whom they work.

PSYCHICS AS HUMAN TARGETS

But psychic stress is not the only problem. Fred Hansen, a Los Angeles psychic, created a team of psychics and psychologists to work with the police on major cases. Calling this operation Unit 9 – since on any one case, nine psychics shared the burden and pooled their impressions – he soon became aware of another, unexpected, difficulty.

The more accurately the team identified culprits, the greater a threat they posed to those they were trying to help unmask. Many of the criminals were dangerous and killed without remorse; if some also believed in ESP and the work of Unit 9, they might well choose the psychics as their next target. In the early days, one team member was actually attacked and stabbed in what seemed to be a revenge mission by a criminal that they had helped bring to justice.

After this incident, Hansen sensibly decided to operate almost entirely undercover. Thereafter, Unit 9 shunned publicity and refused to reveal the psychics' identities or the cases with which they were involved. Such protection, however, did not spare independent psychic detective Ann Fisher from a harrowing ordeal when she assisted on a particularly grim case in 1976–77, as a series of violent murders took place in and around Albany, the New York State capital. The killer mutilated his victims with such rage that he appeared intent on destroying anything within his reach.

After the third murder, the day before Christmas in 1976, when a young woman's body was found with massive stab wounds inside a car, frustrated police decided to call in Fisher, a noted local psychic and a qualified psychologist. This combination made her an excellent choice as a consultant, since the courts need never suspect that she used anything other than her professional skills to lead police in the right direction.

When taken to the scene of the first two violent killings four weeks earlier – at a religious art store – Fisher immediately picked up awful waves of emotion that swamped her. She knew that the killer was a pathological criminal on a murder spree and would strike again unless he was caught.

For the first time in her life, Ann Fisher nearly lied her way out of helping the authorities. She left the building reeling and said later, 'I was half tempted to tell police that I could not pick up anything. I just wanted to get away from the evil presence that I felt'.

AN INCREDIBLE FIND
However, after recovering her composure, the psychic's conscience soon got the better of her. She knew that this man had to be caught. After giving a detailed description of the killer, she marched off down the street with the stunned detectives following like pet poodles. Several blocks away, she entered a back alley and pointed to a garbage can; astonished officers pulled from it a blood-stained vest. It was, she claimed, the killer's vest, dumped there a month earlier. Tests later established that it was undoubtedly from the murder scene, yet it had been discarded far enough away from the crime that it almost certainly would never have been found by routine methods.

Unsatisfied, Fisher continued, leading detectives to an old building where she said that the injured killer had rested (indeed, blood stains of the same type as those on the vest were subsequently found inside the building). She then directed the police just across the street to a store where she claimed the killer had worked. Enquiries soon revealed that a man fitting the description that Fisher had just given had indeed been employed there at the time of the first murders. A check into the man's background revealed him to be a violent convicted killer who had been released from a 10-year jail sentence just before the art store murders. Utterly amazed, the police knew that they had their man. Yet they faced a dilemma.

The information that Ann Fisher had provided went well beyond what any police psychologist could have deduced. The police knew that the discovery of the vest could not be used as evidence in court, since no amount of reasoning would have led any consultant to suggest that detectives should search in that specific site so far from the crime scene. This left them in a helpless situation. They were certain that this man, Smith, was the killer, but had no way to convict him. All they could do was watch him closely, under the constant fear that he would strike again.

As for Ann Fisher, her fears were very different. She felt that a 'psychic connection' had opened up between herself and Smith, placing her in very real danger every single day that the man roamed the streets. She pleaded with detectives to keep her involvement in the case secret; they complied, knowing how dangerous Smith was.

Ann Fisher reacted strongly when the police took her to a religious art store – the site of a brutal murder. She immediately received a psychic impression of the killer, and overcame her fear to lead detectives to a garbage can in a nearby alley, where the vital clue of a blood-stained vest was uncovered.

A year later, in nearby Schenectady, a fourth young woman was murdered and another was raped. The rape victim was shown Smith's mug shot and recognized him. He was arrested for the attack, yet there was still a strong chance that he would escape punishment for the other crimes that he had carried out. Thankfully, the Albany police hit upon an idea for an ingenious line-up. Sniffer dogs were used to smell the blood on the vest and then home in on a group of men – one of whom was Smith – who were out of sight behind a fence. The dogs went straight for his scent. This was sufficient evidence to charge him with murder.

Smith eventually confessed, but claimed that he was 'possessed' by the spirit of his dead brother, who made him do the killings. This insanity plea was rejected by the courts, and he was sent to jail for life in 1979.

In the meantime, the woman whose gifts had helped to catch him was forced to endure another two years of agony as the legal process ground on, afraid that any day the trial might collapse and she would again be put in danger from the man she had identified as the killer. It was only when Smith was safely behind bars that Ann Fisher's extraordinary role in this case revealed by the journalist Lawrence Cortesi.

NIGHTMARE VISION PUTS FAMILY AT RISK

Dixie Yeterian, from a small California town, is one of America's most astonishing psychic detectives. Yet, as a mother, she also must face the implications of putting her family at risk every time she has visions of a dangerous killer. All of her worst nightmares came home to roost the night that she had a terrifying dream of a teenage girl inside an old wooden shack.

It was a very realistic vision, unlike the many that she often had in which future events were merely symbolized and Dixie had to work out their meaning. This time, it was almost as if she were hovering in midair, invisible to those present, like an all-seeing spy camera.

The young girl in view was cowering in a corner as screams raged outside the shack. She was covering her ears in terror. Then, in the darkness, a man marched in carrying a flashlight, pointing it at his own face. In her dream, Dixie watched him take the teenager outside, to a scene of total horror. Several people (men and women) were sitting around a campfire, and a girl – about 14 years old – was on the ground badly bruised and bloodied. As Dixie watched, she saw the group gang-rape and mutilate her, one by one, in some kind of bizarre ritual. The terrified girl from the shack was forced to watch it all unfold and was then herself raped. Finally, Dixie saw the girl flee the campsite, while two of the men and one girl set off in pursuit. At this point, the psychic emerged, sweat-ridden, from her hideous sleep into wakefulness.

Dixie had no idea what to do. She felt that her dream vision was real, but she had no way of knowing where it was happening, or even if it had happened yet.

Since the age of four, she had had flashes of insight. But she quickly learned the price of knowing things that you should not know when she told her parents where to find a missing doll lost by a sobbing neighbourhood child. When Dixie led them to the girl's doll – she had simply 'known' where to find it – they punished her for stealing, since this seemed the only logical explanation for her knowing where to look.

Despite these occasional psychic experiences, Dixies had sought a normal life. She married her childhood sweetheart, Vahan, an aero engineer, and they later moved to the Los Angeles area. They had three children – a girl and two boys, aged five, seven, and nine at the time of the dream – and the main Yeterian family concerns were schools, cooking breakfast, and paying bills.

Horrible dreams like this one were not part of the agenda, yet this nightmare had been so vivid that, the next morning, Dixie could still recall both visual and

Bloodhounds are often used by police tracker squads to follow scent trails that may lead to missing persons or murder victims. Psychics operate in a similar way – employing a mysterious sixth sense, rather than an acute sense of smell.

auditory clues from it. She knew the name of the girl in the shack and had heard her identify two of the men (one was her boyfriend, whom she had reluctantly followed there). Dixie could also remember the very unusual knife used to murder the sacrificial victim. But was all this just a product of her imagination or was it really happening?

NAGGING VISION OF A BRUTAL MURDER

That afternoon, after sorting out her domestic duties, Dixie felt exhausted and lay down to rest. It was not long before the visions returned, picking up from where they had left off. She saw the fleeing girl – Karen – as if following her in a helicopter. She watched her fall, twist her ankle, and stumble to a road, desperately seeking to flag down a passing motorist. Most drove by, but finally one stopped. Out got three of the people – her boyfriend included – from the scene of the ritual. Karen struggled to get free, but her boyfriend murdered her in a rage. He then placed her body in the car and drove to a deep gully near the coast, into which he tossed his victim.

Two friends who called to see Dixie that evening saw her shell-shocked and asked her what was wrong. They listened to her story and reassured her that it was simply a nightmare that would fade with the passage of time. And, as the days went by, Dixie convinced herself that they had been right, as the memories receded into the background.

Then, a week later, her two friends paid another visit, this time thrusting a newspaper in front of Dixie. It showed an artist's sketch of a young girl whose body had just been found. The headline blared: 'Do you know this girl?' And Dixie certainly did. It was Karen. Her friends pleaded with her to go to the police. Clearly, they said, her dream was not just a dream. She knew things. She had to tell them. But Dixie resisted – apart from the shock and fear at what she was getting into, she had also realized that the police would surely deem her crazy. In the end, her friends called the police for her, making the decision that they knew she would want to make. It was a fateful moment.

Once at the police station, Dixie was quite naturally terrified. She had never faced a situation like this before, but nevertheless concluded that all she could do was tell the detectives everything that she had seen – which was a very great deal indeed. She could give first names of most of those involved, as well as describing their clothing and appearance. Not only that, she had seen the car they were driving (an old blue station wagon) and could indicate where evidence had been left behind – at two different sites, since Karen's murder did not take place at the same location as where the first girl had been killed.

Psychic Dixie Yeterian claims the ability to 'astrally project' her spirit from her body to a distant location, and thus witness events there. On this occasion, a violent crime unfolded in her mind's eye.

The police gazed at her with increasing astonishment as her tale unfolded. They recorded the proceedings as if Dixie was herself a suspect. Eventually, she realized that this was exactly what she was.

The detective in charge of the case told her that he was fed up with her nonsensical story about what she called 'astral projection', by which she was allegedly

A detail remembered from her vision – a discarded shoe left by the murder victim – convinced the police of Dixie's guilt. This clue had never been made public, and investigators believed only one person alive would know about it – the killer.

able to project her spirit to a distant location and see events there. He wanted to know how she really knew what she was claiming.

Dixie had expected none of this. She thought that all she was going to do was to offer help and be thanked for doing her duty as a good citizen. But then she remembered an important clue – that, as she tried to run from her attackers, Karen had taken off the shoe from her injured ankle and tossed it into the roadside. At this, the detective barked: 'How do you know that?'

The police had already found the shoe, but had deliberately withheld this news from the media as a piece of information that might help to identify the killer. Now Dixie was revealing intimate knowledge of that vital evidence, and to the authorities that meant only one thing. They had discovered the killer – her!

As Dixie became increasingly agitated, the psychic was told that the police could not accept stories about her spirit flying around the murder scene. Either there had been a security leak and a police officer had given her confidential details of the case or else Dixie was involved in these brutal events directly. In that case, she faced arrest and a long time in prison. Suddenly, using her psychic powers to help the police with their enquiries did not seem like such a good idea.

DANGEROUS TIMES

It took several days to persuade the investigators that Dixie was not actually involved in the murders and could possibly help to solve them. It was only after she had demonstrated her total co-operation and led them to the scene of the first ritual killing (where major forensic evidence was retrieved) that their suspicions were finally allayed.

But with this came a new problem. Someone at the police station told the local press about the matter. They did not reveal any names or identities – except Dixie's. Perhaps they reasoned, as police forces sometimes do, that the publicity generated by using a psychic might help to raise the profile of a flagging case. Or maybe it was just an idle slip.

Whatever the truth, the consequences on Dixie's family were devastating. Vahan went to work outside the city to escape the ridicule, while the children

The very notion of psychic powers can frighten many people. In the Middle Ages, anyone possessing inexplicable abilities was considered to be a witch, in league with the devil. Many, as Dixie Yeterian discovered, still hold a dim view of those with reputed super-natural skills.

were made cruel fun of in the school playground. Neighbours cracked jokes about witches and goblins. Life in the Yeterian household had been virtually ripped apart – all thanks to one bad dream.

However, much worse was to follow, when Dixie began to notice a car following her. It often turned up nearby, but she tried to dismiss this as a coincidence, reasoning that there must be many similar vehicles in California. What was disconcerting, however, was that this was a blue station wagon.

It was Vahan who finally made her see the truth. He told her that the news reports must have reached the man who had murdered Karen, and he had to know that she could identify him. Every day that he remained free, Dixie was now a target. More importantly, so were her family.

Then came the moment when she had no choice but to call in the police. The station wagon was parked on her street again – as if watching the house. By the time the police arrived, it had gone. But in her mailbox was an anonymous note saying, 'You have a cute little girl' and 'If you want to keep her, back off'.

The police did not hesitate. They gave the family round-the-clock protection and advised them to keep the children at home. They also released a new story to the press, saying that they had checked out Dixie's 'psychic hotline' and the information provided by her had led nowhere and was of no further value in the enquiry. This ruse, they hoped, would remove the threat.

It did. The station wagon disappeared, and the Yeterians' life returned to normal. The police withdrew their surveillance operation and it seemed as if the trauma was at last over. Sadly, it was not.

The case remained unsolved, and, several weeks later, the police conducted a radio interview/call-in in an attempt to reawaken public interest in the case. In an unguarded moment, a deputy took a phone call from a woman who proceeded to attack the psychic, who had allegedly been of no help. 'Yes, she was', he replied, inadvertently revealing that the story about Dixie's failure was not quite accurate. By spontaneously defending Dixie's reputation, the detective was in reality putting her life back on the line.

Kidnap Attempt by Killer

Just days later, a man tried to abduct Dixie Yeterian's daughter, Shannon, as she rode to school on her bicycle. Cruising alongside her in a pick-up truck, one man drove as the other leaned out to grab the girl. Fortunately, two young men on the pavement leapt to her defence and the pick-up drove away without Shannon. There seemed to be no question as to the identity of the would-be abductor, who had yelled out Shannon's name. Surely this latest incident was connected with the murders.

Two weeks later, a car tried to snatch Shannon from outside a grocery store. Luckily, her mother was close enough to drag her away from danger. After this,

*The California
Highway Patrol,
whose vigilance
helped to save the
life of a terrified
psychic detective and
her family. Once they
had accepted Dixie
Yeterian's innocence,
they rushed to protect
her when her identity
was inadvertently
revealed to the
press – and hence
the murderer.*

police provided 24-hour protection. Still, Dixie took no chances and sent the children away to live with their grandparents out of state.

Meanwhile, police kept a close watch on the house, but nothing seemed to be happening. However, detectives had at last closed in on the gang by finding a ranch that matched the description offered by Dixie. The site had been abandoned, but there they discovered the body of the teenager that Dixie had seen murdered.

An horrific satanic cult brought terror to the small communities of California in a spree of rape and murder. But one psychic detective knew who they were and put her life at risk to bring them to justice.

This find led the police to identify one man – not Karen's killer, but the man who had been with him during the apparently satanic ritual that had taken place. The detective in charge of the case, who had worked with Dixie for some months now and had become a family friend, telephoned her with the welcome news that an arrest was near.

As she took the call, Dixie let the family dog into the back yard. Suddenly the phone cut dead, and she heard breaking glass and a murmuring noise coming from the back yard. The dog was yelping furiously. The strange murmur rose to a chant, with several people clearly intoning at once. Dixie knew what this horrifying commotion meant. The gang had chanted just like this in her dream when they butchered the young girl.

In absolute terror, she instinctively hid under a table, as there seemed no other escape. Outside, her barking dog let out one final terrible sound and was then silent. Orange flames began to lick around the house as the chanting increased in volume and footsteps headed toward her hiding place. Into the room marched half a dozen people, carrying torches and holding a cross. Impaled on top of this was the poor body of Dixie's pet dog. One of the men's faces was visible, looming in the flickering light. It was Karen's boyfriend. As Dixie cowered, she believed that this was it. Death could only be seconds away.

In the gloom, the gang spotted the panicked psychic under the table and pulled her out, dragging her toward the door. Dixie tried to scream. Suddenly, there was pandemonium as several police cars screeched to a halt outside her gate and voices barked into the night. The detective had suspected that something was wrong when the phone lines were cut and had dispatched nearby officers to check out the situation.

As the gang fled into the night, one officer threw himself at the man still holding Dixie and freed her by pushing her to the ground. Unfortunately, the man – Karen's killer – escaped in the confusion.

STRING OF KILLINGS BROUGHT TO AN END

However, he was not to remain free for long. With their identities known, the group was soon apprehended, and a major investigation ensued. From this, it was eventually established that the gang had ritually slaughtered over 30 young girls in California. They were convicted of six murders – the cases for which there was the strongest physical evidence. Sadly, that did not include either Karen's death or the foiled attack on Dixie Yeterian. The police felt that it was safer to avoid initiating a court case involving a psychic and also believed that the Yeterians had suffered enough.

At last, this extraordinary family could again breathe easily – until, of course, Dixie had her next dream of a violent crime, which they accepted might happen one day. Such is the life of a psychic detective.

Bibliography

Ball, Pamela: *Jack The Ripper: A Psychic Investigation*; Arcturus, London 1998

Begg, Paul & Harris, Melvyn: 'Yorkshire Ripper' in *The Unexplained* No. 67; Orbis, London (n.d.)

Bell, D.: *Derbyshire Ghosts and Legends*; Countryside Books, Derby 1993

Bird, Christopher: *Divining*; Macdonald, London 1980

Bonkalo, Ervin: 'Murderer Reappears After Two Hundred Years' in *FATE* Vol. 41 No. 4; Llewellyn, Minnesota April 1988

Cavendish, Richard (ed.): The *Unexplained*; Routledge & Kegan Paul, London 1974

Charles, Keith & Shuff, D.: *Psychic Cop*; Blake, London 1995

Cheetham, Erica: *The Prophecies of Nostradamus*; Corgi, London 1973

Clark, Jerome: *Unexplained*; Visible Ink, Michigan 1993

Cortesi, Lawrence: 'Psychic Tracks a Killer' in *FATE*; Llewellyn, Minnesota July 1987

Cracknell, Bob: *Clues to the Unknown*; Hamlyn, London 1981

Dennis, Andrew: 'Spirit of the Law Part 2' in *Fortean Times* No. 104; London November 1997

Dennis, Andrew: 'The Lying, the Witch and the War Probe' in *Fortean Times* No. 116; London November 1998

Eysenck, Hans J. & Sargent, Carl: *Explaining the Unexplained*; Weidenfeld & Nicolson, London 1982

Geller, Uri & Playfair, Guy Lyon: *The Geller Effect*, Grafton, London 1988

Godman, Colin: 'Psychic Serendipity' in *The Unexplained* No. 101; Orbis, London (n.d.)

Graves, Tom: 'Pitfalls and the Pendulum' *The Unexplained* No. 106; Orbis, London (n.d.)

Hill, Douglas & Williams, Pat: *The Supernatural*; New American Library, New York 1965

Hilton, Kathryn: 'Psychic Finder of Lost Things' in *FATE* Vol. 41 No. 1; Llewellyn, Minnesota January 1988

Horton, Edward: 'Death of a Dream' in *The Unexplained* Nos 24, 25, 27; Orbis, London (n.d.)

Hough, Peter: *Witchcraft: A Strange Conflict*; Lutterworth, Cambridge 1991

Hough, Peter & Randles, Jenny: *Encyclopedia of the Unexplained*; O'Mara, London 1995

Jaegers, Beverly C.: 'Dowser Wins the Gold' in *FATE* Vol. 39 No. 10; Llewellyn, Minnesota October 1986

King, Stephen: *Danse Macabre*; Futura, London 1982

Kirkwood, Alex: 'Testimony From Beyond' in *FATE* Vol. 51 No. 5; Llewellyn, Minnesota May 1998

Lafferty, Peter & Rowe, Julian (eds): *The Hutchinson Dictionary of Science*; Helicon Publishing, London 1993

Leabo, Audrey: 'A Treasure Found' in *FATE* Vol. 39 No. 6; Llewellyn, Minnesota June 1986

Nielson, Greg & Polansky, Joseph: *Pendulum Power*; Aquarian Press, Wellingborough 1977

Pratt, Neil: *Psychic News*; Essex, 14 November 1992

Randles, Jenny: *Sixth Sense*; Hale, London 1987

Randles, Jenny & Hough, Peter: *Death by Supernatural Causes?*; Grafton, London 1988

Randles, Jenny & Hough, Peter: *The Afterlife*; Piatkus, London 1993

Randles, Jenny & Hough, Peter: *Strange but True?*; Piatkus, London 1994

Robinson, D. & Boot, A.: *Dream Detective*; Psychic Press, Essex 1996

Sandwell, Frank: 'Cranium' in *Strange Magazine* No 12; Rockville, Maryland 1993

Smith, K.: *Supernatural*; Pan, Sydney 1991

Stemman, Roy: 'Clues from Clairvoyance' in *The Unexplained* No. 4; Orbis, London (n.d.)

Vaughan, Alan: *Dreams and Destiny*; Llewellyn, Minnesota 1997

Yeterian, Dixie: *Casebook of a Psychic Detective*; Stein & Day, New York 1982

York, Helen C.: 'Future in the Window' in *FATE*; Llewellyn, Minnesota January 1988

Unattributed:

'Mindbender' in *The X Factor* No. 4; Marshall Cavendish, London (n.d.)

'Testimony Beyond the Grave' in *Fortean Times* No. 77; London April 1994

'The Mystery of Dowsing' in *The X Factor* No. 5; Marshall Cavendish, London (n.d.)

Index

Picture Credits
The Associated Press: 16 (b), 122, 123 (b), 130 (t), 168 (t), 207. **Amber Books Ltd**: 24, 25, 123 (t), 135, 178. **Fortean Picture Library**: 8, 17, 22, 59, 67, 68, 69, 76, 85, 89, 92, 93, 98, 101, 115, 126 (t), 130 (b), 139, 145, 169, 180 (t), 209 (both), 210, 211 (b), 212, 243.
Dave Hendley: 39, 50, 176 (b). **Images Colour Library**: 47, 52-53, 66, 136, 140, 152 (both), 156, 157, 158, 162, 204 (t), 219, 221, 224. **Mary Evans Picture Library**: 9, 14, 15, 18, 19, 20, 26 (both), 28, 29, 32, 33, 34, 36 (b), 37, 42, 49, 54, 55, 80, 81, 83, 91, 95, 96, 128, 137, 142, 146, 149, 151, 202-203, 213, 217, 218 (both), 246. **Moviestore Collection**: 27, 174, 208.
PA Photos: 10, 60-61, 64, 105, 125, 129, 153, 176 (t), 196, 204 (b), 205, 238, 240-241, 245.
Public Records Office Image Library: 35, 40, 180 (b). **Topham Picturepoint**: 23, 36 (t), 41, 44, 45, 46, 56, 56-57, 71, 73, 74, 84, 99, 100, 104, 108, 114, 118, 119, 150, 165, 175, 177, 179, 183, 186, 189, 192, 194, 198, 199, 201, 214, 215. **TRH Pictures**: 16 (t), 77, 78, 133, 143, 144, 167 (both), 168 (b), 229, 234.

With kind permission of the authors: 21, 90, 191, 197 (b), 211 (t), 220, 223, 231.

Illustrations:
Front cover: Mark Batley; **Back cover**: Georgia Denby (t); Darren Hopes (b).
Georgia Denby: 12-13, 75, 87, 102-103, 105, 111, 154-155, 164, 172-173, 222.
Peter Harper: 116, 126, 148.
Darren Hopes: 6-7, 106, 120-121, 124, 134, 184, 188, 225, 226, 232-233, 237, 242.
Kevin Jones Associates: 30, 58, 62, 107, 110, 113, 127, 132, 159, 160, 163 (both), 166, 170, 182, 185, 190, 195, 197(t), 206, 228, 241 (b).

C . S . LEWIS

THE LION, THE WITCH AND THE WARDROBE

ILLUSTRATIONS BY
PAULINE BAYNES

An imprint of HarperCollins*Publishers*

The Chronicles of Narnia

in suggested reading order

THE MAGICIAN'S NEPHEW
THE LION, THE WITCH AND THE WARDROBE
THE HORSE AND HIS BOY
PRINCE CASPIAN
THE VOYAGE OF THE *DAWN TREADER*
THE SILVER CHAIR
THE LAST BATTLE

This edition produced for Premier Direct Group Plc in 2005

First published in Great Britain by Geoffrey Bles in 1950

1 3 5 7 9 10 8 6 4 2

Collins is an imprint of HarperCollins*Publishers* Ltd,
77-85 Fulham Palace Road, Hammersmith, London, W6 8JB

Text copyright © C. S. Lewis Pte Ltd 1950
Illustrations copyright © HarperCollins*Publishers* Ltd 1950

ISBN 0 00 774804 3

"Narnia" is a UK registered trademark of C. S. Lewis Pte Ltd and
"The Chronicles of Narnia" is a trademark of C. S. Lewis Pte Ltd.

A CIP record for this book is available at the British Library.

The HarperCollins website is:
www.**fire**and**water**.com

Printed and bound in China by Imago

TO LUCY BARFIELD

My dear Lucy,

   I wrote this story for you, but when I began it I had not realized that girls grow quicker than books. As a result you are already too old for fairy tales, and by the time it is printed and bound you will be older still. But some day you will be old enough to start reading fairy tales again. You can then take it down from some upper shelf, dust it, and tell me what you think of it. I shall probably be too deaf to hear, and too old to understand, a word you say, but I shall still be

                              your affectionate Godfather,

                                        C. S. LEWIS

LIST OF PLATES

CONTENTS

'She immediately stepped into the wardrobe and got in among the coats'

CHAPTER ONE

LUCY LOOKS INTO A WARDROBE

Once there were four children whose names were Peter, Susan, Edmund and Lucy. This story is about something that happened to them when they were sent away from London during the war because of the air-raids. They were sent to the house of an old Professor who lived in the heart of the country, ten miles from the nearest railway station and two miles from the nearest post office. He had no wife and he lived in a very large house with a housekeeper called Mrs Macready and three servants. (Their names were Ivy, Margaret and Betty, but they do not come into the story much.) He himself was a very old man with shaggy white hair which grew over most of his face as well as on his head, and they liked him almost at once; but on the first evening when he came out to meet them at the front door he was so odd-looking that Lucy (who was the youngest) was a little afraid of him, and Edmund (who was the next youngest) wanted to laugh and had to keep on pretending he was blowing his nose to hide it.

As soon as they had said good night to the Professor and gone upstairs on the first night, the boys came into the girls' room and they all talked it over.

"We've fallen on our feet and no mistake," said Peter. "This is going to be perfectly splendid. That old chap will let us do anything we like."

"I think he's an old dear," said Susan.

"Oh, come off it!" said Edmund, who was tired and pretending not to be tired, which always made him bad-tempered. "Don't go on talking like that."

"Like what?" said Susan; "and anyway, it's time you were in bed."

"Trying to talk like Mother," said Edmund. "And who are you to say when I'm to go to bed? Go to bed yourself."

"Hadn't we all better go to bed?" said Lucy. "There's sure to be a row if we're heard talking here."

"No there won't," said Peter. "I tell you this is the sort of house where no one's going to mind what we do. Anyway, they won't hear us. It's about ten minutes' walk from here down to that dining-room, and any amount of stairs and passages in between."

"What's that noise?" said Lucy suddenly. It was a far larger house than she had ever been in before and the thought of all those long passages and rows of doors leading into empty rooms was beginning to make her feel a little creepy.

"It's only a bird, silly," said Edmund.

"It's an owl," said Peter. "This is going to be a wonderful place for birds. I shall go to bed now. I say, let's go and explore tomorrow. You might find anything in a place like this. Did you see those mountains as we came along? And the woods? There might be eagles. There might be stags. There'll be hawks."

"Badgers!" said Lucy.

"Foxes!" said Edmund.

"Rabbits!" said Susan.

But when next morning came there was a steady rain falling,

so thick that when you looked out of the window you could see neither the mountains nor the woods nor even the stream in the garden.

"Of course it *would* be raining!" said Edmund. They had just finished their breakfast with the Professor and were upstairs in the room he had set apart for them – a long, low room with two windows looking out in one direction and two in another.

"Do stop grumbling, Ed," said Susan. "Ten to one it'll clear up in an hour or so. And in the meantime we're pretty well off. There's a wireless and lots of books."

"Not for me," said Peter; "I'm going to explore in the house."

Everyone agreed to this and that was how the adventures began. It was the sort of house that you never seem to come to the end of, and it was full of unexpected places. The first few doors they tried led only into spare bedrooms, as everyone had expected that they would; but soon they came to a very long room full of pictures and there they found a suit of armour; and after that was a room all hung with green, with a harp in one corner; and then came three steps down and five steps up, and then a kind of little upstairs hall and a door that led out on to a balcony, and then a whole series of rooms that led into each other and were lined with books – most of them very old books and some bigger than a Bible in a church. And shortly after that they looked into a room that was quite empty except for one big wardrobe; the sort that has a looking-glass in the door. There was nothing else in the room at all except a dead blue-bottle on the window-sill.

"Nothing there!" said Peter, and they all trooped out again –

all except Lucy. She
stayed behind because
she thought it would be
worth while trying the
door of the wardrobe,
even though she felt
almost sure that it
would be locked. To
her surprise it opened
quite easily, and two
moth-balls dropped out.

Looking into the inside, she saw several coats hanging up –
mostly long fur coats. There was nothing Lucy liked so much
as the smell and feel of fur. She immediately stepped into the
wardrobe and got in among the coats and rubbed her face
against them, leaving the door open, of course, because she
knew that it is very foolish to shut oneself into any wardrobe.
Soon she went further in and found that there was a second row
of coats hanging up behind the first one. It was almost quite dark
in there and she kept her arms stretched out in front of her so as
not to bump her face into the back of the wardrobe. She took
a step further in – then two or three steps – always expecting
to feel woodwork against the tips of her fingers. But she could
not feel it.

"This must be a simply enormous wardrobe!" thought Lucy,
going still further in and pushing the soft folds of the coats
aside to make room for her. Then she noticed that there was
something crunching under her feet. "I wonder is that more
moth-balls?" she thought, stooping down to feel it with her

hand. But instead of feeling the hard, smooth wood of the floor of the wardrobe, she felt something soft and powdery and extremely cold. "This is very queer," she said, and went on a step or two further.

Next moment she found that what was rubbing against her face and hands was no longer soft fur but something hard and rough and even prickly. "Why, it is just like branches of trees!" exclaimed Lucy. And then she saw that there was a light ahead of her; not a few inches away where the back of the wardrobe ought to have been, but a long way off. Something cold and soft was falling on her. A moment later she found that she was standing in the middle of a wood at night-time with snow under her feet and snowflakes falling through the air.

Lucy felt a little frightened, but she felt very inquisitive and excited as well. She looked back over her shoulder and there, between the dark tree-trunks, she could still see the open doorway of the wardrobe and even catch a glimpse of the empty room from which she had set out. (She had, of course,
left the door open, for she knew that it is a very silly thing to shut oneself into a wardrobe.) It seemed to be still daylight there. "I can always get back if anything goes wrong," thought Lucy. She began to walk forward, *crunch-crunch* over the snow and through the wood towards the other light. In about ten minutes she reached it and found it was a

lamp-post. As she stood looking at it, wondering why there was a lamp-post in the middle of a wood and wondering what to do next, she heard a pitter patter of feet coming towards her. And soon after that a very strange person stepped out from among the trees into the light of the lamp-post.

He was only a little taller than Lucy herself and he carried over his head an umbrella, white with snow. From the waist upwards he was like a man, but his legs were shaped like a goat's (the hair on them was glossy black) and instead of feet he had goat's hoofs. He also had a tail, but Lucy did not notice this at first because it was neatly caught up over the arm that held the umbrella so as to keep it from trailing in the snow. He had a red woollen muffler round his neck and his skin was rather reddish too. He had a strange, but pleasant little face, with a short pointed beard and curly hair, and out of the hair there stuck two horns, one on each side of his forehead. One of his hands, as I have said, held the umbrella: in the other arm he carried several brown-paper parcels. What with the parcels and the snow it looked just as if he had been doing his Christmas shopping. He was a Faun. And when he saw Lucy he gave such a start of surprise that he dropped all his parcels.

"Goodness gracious me!" exclaimed the Faun.

CHAPTER TWO

WHAT LUCY FOUND THERE

"Good evening," said Lucy. But the Faun was so busy picking up its parcels that at first it did not reply. When it had finished it made her a little bow.

"Good evening, good evening," said the Faun. "Excuse me – I don't want to be inquisitive – but should I be right in thinking that you are a Daughter of Eve?"

"My name's Lucy," said she, not quite understanding him.

"But you are – forgive me – you are what they call a girl?" said the Faun.

"Of course I'm a girl," said Lucy.

"You are in fact Human?"

"Of course I'm human," said Lucy, still a little puzzled.

"To be sure, to be sure," said the Faun. "How stupid of me! But I've never seen a Son of Adam or a Daughter of Eve before. I am delighted. That is to say –" and then it stopped as if it had been going to say something it had not intended but had remembered in time. "Delighted, delighted," it went on. "Allow me to introduce myself. My name is Tumnus."

"I am very pleased to meet you, Mr Tumnus," said Lucy.

"And may I ask, O Lucy Daughter of Eve," said Mr Tumnus, "how you have come into Narnia?"

"Narnia? What's that?" said Lucy.

"This is the land of Narnia," said the Faun, "where we are

now; all that lies between the lamp-post and the great castle of Cair Paravel on the eastern sea. And you – you have come from the wild woods of the west?"

"I – I got in through the wardrobe in the spare room," said Lucy.

"Ah!" said Mr Tumnus in a rather melancholy voice, "if only I had worked harder at geography when I was a little Faun, I should no doubt know all about those strange countries. It is too late now."

"But they aren't countries at all," said Lucy, almost laughing. "It's only just back there – at least – I'm not sure. It is summer there."

"Meanwhile," said Mr Tumnus, "it is winter in Narnia, and has been for ever so long, and we shall both catch cold if we stand here talking in the snow. Daughter of Eve from the far land of Spare Oom where eternal summer reigns around the bright city of War Drobe, how would it be if you came and had tea with me?"

"Thank you very much, Mr Tumnus," said Lucy. "But I was wondering whether I ought to be getting back."

"It's only just round the corner," said the Faun, "and there'll be a roaring fire – and toast – and sardines – and cake."

"Well, it's very kind of you," said Lucy. "But I shan't be able to stay long."

"If you will take my arm, Daughter of Eve," said Mr Tumnus, "I shall be able to hold the umbrella over both of us. That's the way. Now – off we go."

And so Lucy found herself walking through the wood arm in arm with this strange creature as if they had known one another all their lives.

They had not gone far before they came to a place where the ground became rough and there were rocks all about and little hills up and little hills down. At the bottom of one small valley Mr Tumnus turned suddenly aside as if he were going to walk straight into an unusually large rock, but at the last moment Lucy found he was leading her into the entrance of a cave. As soon as they were inside she found herself blinking in the light of a wood fire. Then Mr Tumnus stooped and took a flaming piece of wood out of the fire with a neat little pair of tongs, and lit a lamp. "Now we shan't be long," he said, and immediately put a kettle on.

Lucy thought she had never been in a nicer place. It was a little, dry, clean cave of reddish stone with a carpet on the floor and two little chairs ("one for me and one for a friend," said Mr Tumnus) and a table and a dresser and a mantelpiece over the fire and above that a picture of an old Faun with a grey beard. In one corner there was a door which Lucy thought must lead to Mr Tumnus's bedroom, and on one wall was a shelf full of books. Lucy looked at these while he was setting out the tea things. They had titles like *The Life and Letters of Silenus* or *Nymphs and Their Ways* or *Men, Monks and Gamekeepers; a Study in Popular Legend* or *Is Man a Myth?*

"Now, Daughter of Eve!" said the Faun.

And really it was a wonderful tea. There was a nice brown egg, lightly boiled, for each of them, and then sardines on toast, and then buttered toast, and then toast with honey, and

then a sugar-topped cake. And when Lucy was tired of eating the Faun began to talk. He had wonderful tales to tell of life in the forest. He told about the midnight dances and how the

Nymphs who lived in the wells and the Dryads who lived in the trees came out to dance with the Fauns; about long hunting parties after the milk-white stag who could give you wishes if you caught him; about feasting and treasure-seeking with the wild Red Dwarfs in deep mines and caverns far beneath the forest floor; and then about summer when the woods were green and old Silenus on his fat donkey would come to visit them, and sometimes Bacchus himself, and then the streams would

run with wine instead of water and the whole forest would give itself up to jollification for weeks on end. "Not that it isn't always winter now," he added gloomily. Then to cheer himself up he took out from its case on the dresser a strange little flute that looked as if it were made of straw and began to play. And the tune he played made Lucy want to cry and

"'It isn't something I have done. I'm doing it now, this very moment'"

laugh and dance and go to sleep all at the same time. It must have been hours later when she shook herself and said:

"Oh, Mr Tumnus – I'm so sorry to stop you, and I do love that tune – but really, I must go home. I only meant to stay for a few minutes."

"It's no good *now*, you know," said the Faun, laying down its flute and shaking its head at her very sorrowfully.

"No good?" said Lucy, jumping up and feeling rather frightened. "What do you mean? I've got to go home at once. The others will be wondering what has happened to me." But a moment later she asked, "Mr Tumnus! Whatever is the matter?" for the Faun's brown eyes had filled with tears and then the tears began trickling down its cheeks, and soon they were running off the end of its nose; and at last it covered its face with its hands and began to howl.

"Mr Tumnus! Mr Tumnus!" said Lucy in great distress. Don't! Don't! What is the matter? Aren't you well? Dear Mr Tumnus, do tell me what is wrong." But the Faun continued sobbing as if its heart would break. And even when Lucy went over and put her arms round him and lent him her handkerchief, he did not stop. He merely took the handkerchief and kept on using it, wringing it out with both hands whenever it got too wet to be any more use, so that presently Lucy was standing in a damp patch.

"Mr Tumnus!" bawled Lucy in his ear, shaking him. "Do stop. Stop it at once! You ought to be ashamed of yourself, a great big Faun like you. What on earth are you crying about?"

"Oh – oh – oh!" sobbed Mr Tumnus, "I'm crying because I'm such a bad Faun."

"I don't think you're a bad Faun at all," said Lucy. "I think you are a very good Faun. You are the nicest Faun I've ever met."

"Oh – oh – you wouldn't say that if you knew," replied Mr Tumnus between his sobs. "No, I'm a bad Faun. I don't suppose there ever was a worse Faun since the beginning of the world."

"But what have you done?" asked Lucy.

"My old father, now," said Mr Tumnus; "that's his picture over the mantelpiece. He would never have done a thing like this."

"A thing like what?" said Lucy.

"Like what I've done," said the Faun. "Taken service under the White Witch. That's what I am. I'm in the pay of the White Witch."

"The White Witch? Who is she?"

"Why, it is she that has got all Narnia under her thumb. It's she that makes it always winter. Always winter and never Christmas; think of that!"

"How awful!" said Lucy. "But what does she pay *you* for?"

"That's the worst of it," said Mr Tumnus with a deep groan.

"I'm a kidnapper for her, that's what I am. Look at me, Daughter of Eve. Would you believe that I'm the sort of Faun to meet a poor innocent child in the wood, one that had never done me any harm, and pretend to be friendly with it, and invite it home to my cave, all for the sake of lulling it asleep and then handing it over to the White Witch?"

"No," said Lucy. "I'm sure you wouldn't do anything of the sort."

"But I have," said the Faun.

"Well," said Lucy rather slowly (for she wanted to be truthful and yet not be too hard on him), "well, that was pretty bad. But you're so sorry for it that I'm sure you will never do it again."

"Daughter of Eve, don't you understand?" said the Faun. "It isn't something I *have* done. I'm doing it now, this very moment."

"What do you mean?" cried Lucy, turning very white.

"You are the child," said Tumnus. "I had orders from the White Witch that if ever I saw a Son of Adam or a Daughter of Eve in the wood, I was to catch them and hand them over to her. And you are the first I ever met. And I've pretended to be your friend and asked you to tea, and all the time I've been meaning to wait till you were asleep and then go and tell *Her*."

"Oh, but you won't, Mr Tumnus," said Lucy. "You won't, will you? Indeed, indeed you really mustn't."

"And if I don't," said he, beginning to cry again, "she's sure to find out. And she'll have my tail cut off, and my horns sawn off, and my beard plucked out, and she'll wave her wand over my beautiful cloven hoofs and turn them into horrid solid hoofs like a wretched horse's. And if she is extra and specially angry she'll turn me into stone and I shall be only a statue of a Faun in her horrible house until the four thrones at Cair Paravel are filled – and goodness knows when that will happen, or whether it will ever happen at all."

"I'm very sorry, Mr Tumnus," said Lucy. "But please let me go home."

"Of course I will," said the Faun. "Of course I've got to. I see that now. I hadn't known what Humans were like before I met you. Of course I can't give you up to the Witch; not now that I know you. But we must be off at once. I'll see you back to the lamp-post. I suppose you can find your own way from there back to Spare Oom and War Drobe?"

"I'm sure I can," said Lucy.

"We must go as quietly as we can," said Mr Tumnus. "The

whole wood is full of *her* spies. Even some of the trees are on her side."

They both got up and left the tea things on the table, and Mr Tumnus once more put up his umbrella and gave Lucy his arm, and they went out into the snow. The journey back was not at all like the journey to the Faun's cave; they stole along as quickly as they could, without speaking a word, and Mr Tumnus kept to the darkest places. Lucy was relieved when they reached the lamp-post again.

"Do you know your way from here, Daughter of Eve?" said Tumnus.

Lucy looked very hard between the trees and could just see in the distance a patch of light that looked like daylight. "Yes," she said, "I can see the wardrobe door."

"Then be off home as quick as you can," said the Faun, "and – c-can you ever forgive me for what I meant to do?"

"Why, of course I can," said Lucy, shaking him heartily by the hand. "And I do hope you won't get into dreadful trouble on my account."

"Farewell, Daughter of Eve," said he. "Perhaps I may keep the handkerchief?"

"Rather!" said Lucy, and then ran towards the far off patch of daylight as quickly as her legs would carry her. And presently instead of rough branches brushing past her she felt coats, and instead of crunching snow under her feet she felt wooden boards, and all at once she found herself jumping out of the wardrobe into the same empty room from which the whole adventure had started. She shut the wardrobe door tightly behind her and looked around, panting for breath. It was still raining and she could hear the voices of the others in the passage.

"I'm here," she shouted. "I'm here. I've come back, I'm all right."

CHAPTER THREE

EDMUND AND THE WARDROBE

Lucy ran out of the empty room into the passage and found the other three.

"It's all right," she repeated, "I've come back."

"What on earth are you talking about, Lucy?" asked Susan.

"Why?" said Lucy in amazement, "haven't you all been wondering where I was?"

"So you've been hiding, have you?" said Peter. "Poor old Lu, hiding and nobody noticed! You'll have to hide longer than that if you want people to start looking for you."

"But I've been away for hours and hours," said Lucy.

The others all stared at one another.

"Batty!" said Edmund, tapping his head. "Quite batty."

"What do you mean, Lu?" asked Peter.

"What I said," answered Lucy. "It was just after breakfast when I went into the wardrobe, and I've been away for hours and hours, and had tea, and all sorts of things have happened."

"Don't be silly, Lucy," said Susan. "We've only just come out of that room a moment ago, and you were there then."

"She's not being silly at all," said Peter, "she's just making up a story for fun, aren't you, Lu? And why shouldn't she?"

"No, Peter, I'm not," she said. "It's – it's a magic wardrobe. There's a wood inside it, and it's snowing, and there's a Faun and a Witch and it's called Narnia; come and see."

The others did not know what to think, but Lucy was so excited that they all went back with her into the room. She rushed ahead of them, flung open the door of the wardrobe and cried, "Now! go in and see for yourselves."

"Why, you goose," said Susan, putting her head inside and pulling the fur coats apart, "it's just an ordinary wardrobe; look! there's the back of it."

Then everyone looked in and pulled the coats apart; and they all saw – Lucy herself saw – a perfectly ordinary wardrobe. There was no wood and no snow, only the back of the wardrobe, with hooks on it. Peter went in and rapped his knuckles on it to make sure that it was solid.

"A jolly good hoax, Lu," he said as he came out again; "you have really taken us in, I must admit. We half believed you."

"But it wasn't a hoax at all," said Lucy, "really and truly. It was all different a moment ago. Honestly it was. I promise."

"Come, Lu," said Peter, "that's going a bit far. You've had your joke. Hadn't you better drop it now?"

Lucy grew very red in the face and tried to say something, though she hardly knew what she was trying to say, and burst into tears.

For the next few days she was very miserable. She could have made it up with the others quite easily at any moment if she could have brought herself to say that the whole thing was only a story made up for fun. But Lucy was a very truthful girl and she knew that she was really in the right; and she could not bring herself to say this. The others who thought she was telling a lie, and a silly lie too, made her very unhappy. The two elder ones did this without meaning to do it, but Edmund could be spiteful, and on this occasion he was spiteful. He sneered and jeered at Lucy and kept on asking her if she'd found any other new countries in other cupboards all over the house. What made it worse was that these days ought to have been delightful. The weather was fine and they were out of doors from morning to night, bathing, fishing, climbing trees, and lying in the heather. But Lucy could not properly enjoy any of it. And so things went on until the next wet day.

That day, when it came to the afternoon and there was still no sign of a break in the weather, they decided to play hide-and-seek. Susan was "It" and as soon as the others scattered to hide, Lucy went to the room where the wardrobe was. She did not mean to hide in the wardrobe, because she knew that would only set the others talking again about the whole wretched business. But she did want to have one more look inside it; for by this time she was beginning to wonder herself whether Narnia and the Faun had not been a dream. The house was so large and complicated and full of hiding-places that she thought she would have time to have one look into the wardrobe and then hide somewhere else. But as soon as she reached it she heard steps in the passage outside, and then there was nothing for it but to jump into the wardrobe and hold the door closed behind her. She did not shut it properly because she knew that it is very silly to shut oneself into a wardrobe, even if it is not a magic one.

Now the steps she had heard were those of Edmund; and he came into the room just in time to see Lucy vanishing into the wardrobe. He at once decided to get into it himself – not because he thought it a particularly good place to hide but because he wanted to go on teasing her about her imaginary country. He opened the door. There were the coats hanging up as usual, and a smell of mothballs, and darkness and silence, and no sign of Lucy. "She thinks I'm Susan come to catch her," said Edmund to himself, "and so she's keeping very quiet in at the back." He jumped in and shut the door, forgetting what a very foolish thing this is to do. Then he began feeling about for Lucy in the dark. He had expected to find her in a few seconds and was very surprised when he did not. He decided to open the door again and let in some light. But he could not find the door either. He didn't like this at all and began groping wildly in every direction; he even shouted out, "Lucy! Lu! Where are you? I know you're here."

There was no answer and Edmund noticed that his own voice had a curious sound – not the sound you expect in a cupboard, but a kind of open-air sound. He also noticed that he was unexpectedly cold; and then he saw a light.

"Thank goodness," said Edmund, "the door must have swung open of its own accord." He forgot all about Lucy and went towards the light, which he thought was the open door of the wardrobe. But instead of finding himself stepping out into the spare room he found himself stepping out from the shadow of some thick dark fir trees into an open place in the middle of a wood.

There was crisp, dry snow under his feet and more snow lying on the branches of the trees. Overhead there was pale blue sky, the sort of sky one sees on a fine winter day in the morning. Straight ahead of him he saw between the tree-trunks the sun, just rising, very red and clear. Everything was perfectly still, as if he were the only living creature in that country. There was not even a robin or a squirrel among the trees, and the wood stretched as far as he could see in every direction. He shivered.

He now remembered that he had been looking for Lucy; and also how unpleasant he had been to her about her "imaginary country" which now turned out not to have been imaginary at all. He thought that she must be somewhere quite close and so he shouted, "Lucy! Lucy! I'm here too – Edmund."

There was no answer.

"She's angry about all the things I've been saying lately," thought Edmund. And though he did not like to admit that he had been wrong, he also did not much like being alone in this strange, cold, quiet place; so he shouted again.

"I say, Lu! I'm sorry I didn't believe you. I see now you were right all along. Do come out. Make it Pax."

Still there was no answer.

"Just like a girl," said Edmund to himself, "sulking some-where, and won't accept an apology." He looked round him again and decided he did not much like this place, and had almost made up his mind to go home, when he heard, very far off in the wood, a sound of bells. He listened and the sound came nearer and nearer and at last there swept into sight a sledge drawn by two reindeer.

The reindeer were about the size of Shetland ponies and their hair was so white that even the snow hardly looked white compared with them; their branching horns were gilded and shone like something on fire when the sunrise caught them. Their harness was of scarlet leather and covered with bells. On the sledge, driving the reindeer, sat a fat dwarf who would have been about three feet high if he had been standing. He was dressed in polar bear's fur and on his head he wore a red hood with a long gold tassel hanging down from its point; his huge beard covered his knees and served him instead of a rug. But behind him, on a much higher seat in the middle of the sledge sat a very different person – a great lady, taller than any woman that Edmund had ever seen. She also was covered in white fur up to her throat and held a long straight golden wand in her right hand and wore a golden crown on her head. Her face was white – not merely pale, but white like snow or paper or icing-sugar, except for her very red mouth. It was a beautiful face in other respects, but proud and cold and stern.

The sledge was a fine sight as it came sweeping towards Edmund with the bells jingling and the dwarf cracking his whip and the snow flying up on each side of it.

"Stop!" said the Lady, and the dwarf pulled the reindeer up so sharp that they almost sat down. Then they recovered themselves and stood champing their bits and blowing. In the frosty air the breath coming out of their nostrils looked like smoke.

'at last there swept into sight a sledge drawn by two reindeer'

"And what, pray, are you?" said the Lady, looking hard at Edmund.

"I'm – I'm – my name's Edmund," said Edmund rather awkwardly. He did not like the way she looked at him.

The Lady frowned. "Is that how you address a Queen?" she asked, looking sterner than ever.

"I beg your pardon, your Majesty, I didn't know," said Edmund.

"Not know the Queen of Narnia?" cried she. "Ha! You shall know us better hereafter. But I repeat – what are you?"

"Please, your Majesty," said Edmund, "I don't know what you mean. I'm at school – at least I was – it's the holidays now."

CHAPTER FOUR

TURKISH DELIGHT

"But what *are* you?" said the Queen again. "Are you a great overgrown dwarf that has cut off its beard?"

"No, your Majesty," said Edmund, "I never had a beard, I'm a boy."

"A boy!" said she. "Do you mean you are a Son of Adam?"

Edmund stood still, saying nothing. He was too confused by this time to understand what the question meant.

"I see you are an idiot, whatever else you may be," said the Queen. "Answer me, once and for all, or I shall lose my patience. Are you human?"

"Yes, your Majesty," said Edmund.

"And how, pray, did you come to enter my dominions?"

"Please, your Majesty, I came in through a wardrobe."

"A wardrobe? What do you mean?"

"I – I opened a door and just found myself here, your Majesty," said Edmund.

"Ha!" said the Queen, speaking more to herself than to him. "A door. A door from the world of men! I have heard of such things. This may wreck all. But he is only one, and he is easily dealt with." As she spoke these words she rose from her seat and looked Edmund full in the face, her eyes flaming; at the same moment she raised her wand. Edmund felt sure that she was going to do something dreadful but he seemed unable to move. Then, just as he gave himself up for lost, she appeared to change her mind.

"My poor child," she said in quite a different voice, "how cold you look! Come and sit with me here on the sledge and I will put my mantle round you and we will talk."

Edmund did not like this arrangement at all but he dared not disobey; he stepped on to the sledge and sat at her feet, and she put a fold of her fur mantle round him and tucked it well in.

"Perhaps something hot to drink?" said the Queen. "Should you like that?"

"Yes please, your Majesty," said Edmund, whose teeth were chattering.

The Queen took from somewhere among her wrappings a very small bottle which looked as if it were made of copper. Then, holding out her arm, she let one drop fall from it on the snow beside the sledge. Edmund saw the drop for a second in mid-air, shining like a diamond. But the moment it touched the snow there was a hissing sound and there stood a jewelled cup full of something that steamed. The dwarf immediately took this and handed it to Edmund with a bow and a smile; not a very nice smile. Edmund felt much better as he began to sip the hot drink. It was something he had never tasted before, very sweet and foamy and creamy, and it warmed him right down to his toes.

'there appeared a round box, tied with green silk ribbon'

"It is dull, Son of Adam, to drink without eating," said the Queen presently. "What would you like best to eat?"

"Turkish Delight, please, your Majesty," said Edmund.

The Queen let another drop fall from her bottle on to the snow, and instantly there appeared a round box, tied with green silk ribbon, which, when opened, turned out to contain several pounds of the best Turkish Delight. Each piece was sweet and light to the very centre and Edmund had never tasted anything more delicious. He was quite warm now, and very comfortable.

While he was eating the Queen kept asking him questions. At first Edmund tried to remember that it is rude to speak with one's mouth full, but soon he forgot about this and thought only of trying to shovel down as much Turkish Delight as he could, and the more he ate the more he wanted to eat, and he never asked himself why the Queen should be so inquisitive. She got him to tell her that he had one brother and two sisters, and that one of his sisters had already been in Narnia and had met a Faun there, and that no one except himself and his brother and his sisters knew anything about Narnia. She seemed especially interested in the fact that there were four of them, and kept on coming back to it. "You are sure there are just four of you?" she asked. "Two Sons of Adam and two Daughters of Eve, neither more nor less?" and Edmund, with his mouth full of Turkish Delight, kept on saying, "Yes, I told you that before," and forgetting to call her "Your Majesty", but she didn't seem to mind now.

At last the Turkish Delight was all finished and Edmund was looking very hard at the empty box and wishing that she would ask him whether he would like some more. Probably the Queen knew quite well what he was thinking; for she knew, though Edmund did not, that this was enchanted Turkish Delight and that anyone who had once tasted it would want more and more of it, and would even, if they were allowed, go on eating it till they killed themselves. But she did not offer him any more. Instead, she said to him,

"Son of Adam, I should so much like to see your brother and your two sisters. Will you bring them to see me?"

"I'll try," said Edmund, still looking at the empty box.

"Because, if you did come again – bringing them with you of course – I'd be able to give you some more Turkish Delight. I can't do it now, the magic will only work once. In my own house it would be another matter."

"Why can't we go to your house now?" said Edmund. When he had first got on to the sledge he had been afraid that she might drive away with him to some unknown place from which he would not be able to get back; but he had forgotten about that fear now.

"It is a lovely place, my house," said the Queen. "I am sure you would like it. There are whole rooms full of Turkish Delight, and what's more, I have no children of my own. I want a nice boy whom I could bring up as a Prince and who would be King of Narnia when I am gone. While he was Prince he would wear a gold crown and eat Turkish Delight all day long; and you are much the cleverest and handsomest young man I've ever met. I think I would like to make you the Prince – some day, when you bring the others to visit me."

"Why not now?" said Edmund. His face had become very

red and his mouth and fingers were sticky. He did not look either clever or handsome, whatever the Queen might say.

"Oh, but if I took you there now," said she, "I shouldn't see your brother and your sisters. I very much want to know your charming relations. You are to be the Prince and – later on – the King; that is understood. But you must have courtiers and nobles. I will make your brother a Duke and your sisters Duchesses."

"There's nothing special about *them*," said Edmund, "and, anyway, I could always bring them some other time."

"Ah, but once you were in my house," said the Queen, "you might forget all about them. You would be enjoying yourself so much that you wouldn't want the bother of going to fetch them. No. You must go back to your own country now and come to me another day, *with them*, you understand. It is no good coming without them."

"But I don't even know the way back to my own country," pleaded Edmund. "That's easy," answered the Queen. "Do you see that lamp?" She pointed with her wand and Edmund turned and saw the same lamp-post under which Lucy had met the Faun. "Straight on, beyond that, is the way to the World of Men. And now look the other way" – here she pointed in the opposite direction – "and tell me if you can see two little hills rising above the trees."

"I think I can," said Edmund.

"Well, my house is between those two hills. So next time you come you have only to find the lamp-post and look for those two hills and walk through the wood till you reach my house. But remember – you must bring the others with you. I might have to be very angry with you if you came alone."

"I'll do my best," said Edmund.

"And, by the way," said the Queen, "you needn't tell them about me. It would be fun to keep it a secret between us two, wouldn't it? Make it a surprise for them. Just bring them along to the two hills – a clever boy like you will easily think of some excuse for doing that – and when you come to my house you could just say 'Let's see who lives here' or something like that. I am sure that would be best. If your sister has met one of the Fauns, she may have heard strange stories about me – nasty stories that might make her afraid to come to me. Fauns will say anything, you know, and now –"

"Please, please," said Edmund suddenly, "please couldn't I have just one piece of Turkish Delight to eat on the way home?"

"No, no," said the Queen with a laugh, "you must wait till next time." While she spoke, she signalled to the dwarf to drive on, but as the sledge swept away out of sight, the Queen waved to Edmund, calling out, "Next time! Next time! Don't forget. Come soon."

Edmund was still staring after the sledge when he heard someone calling his own name, and looking round he saw Lucy coming towards him from another part of the wood.

"Oh, Edmund!" she cried. "So you've got in too! Isn't it wonderful, and now –"

"All right," said Edmund, "I see you were right and it is a magic wardrobe after all. I'll say I'm sorry if you like. But where on earth have you been all this time? I've been looking for you everywhere."

"If I'd known you had got in I'd have waited for you," said Lucy, who was too happy and excited to notice how snappishly Edmund spoke or how flushed and strange his face was. "I've been having lunch with dear Mr Tumnus, the Faun, and he's very well and the White Witch has done nothing to him for letting me go, so he thinks she can't have found out and perhaps everything is going to be all right after all."

"The White Witch?" said Edmund; "who's she?"

"She is a perfectly terrible person," said Lucy. "She calls herself the Queen of Narnia though she has no right to be queen at all, and all the Fauns and Dryads and Naiads and Dwarfs and Animals – at least all the good ones – simply hate her. And she can turn people into stone and do all kinds of horrible things. And she has made a magic so that it is always winter in Narnia – always winter, but it never gets to Christmas. And she drives about on a sledge, drawn by reindeer, with her wand in her hand and a crown on her head."

Edmund was already feeling uncomfortable from having eaten too many sweets, and when he heard that the Lady he had made friends with was a dangerous witch he felt even more uncomfortable. But he still wanted to taste that Turkish Delight again more than he wanted anything else.

"Who told you all that stuff about the White Witch?" he asked.

"Mr Tumnus, the Faun," said Lucy.

"You can't always believe what Fauns say," said Edmund, trying to sound as if he knew far more about them than Lucy.

"Who said so?" asked Lucy.

"Everyone knows it," said Edmund; "ask anybody you like.

But it's pretty poor sport standing here in the snow. Let's go home."

"Yes, let's," said Lucy. "Oh, Edmund, I *am* glad you've got in too. The others will have to believe in Narnia now that both of us have been there. What fun it will be!"

But Edmund secretly thought that it would not be as good fun for him as for her. He would have to admit that Lucy had been right, before all the others, and he felt sure the others would all be on the side of the Fauns and the animals; but he was already more than half on the side of the Witch. He did not know what he would say, or how he would keep his secret once they were all talking about Narnia.

By this time they had walked a good way. Then suddenly they felt coats around them instead of branches and next moment they were both standing outside the wardrobe in the empty room.

"I say," said Lucy, "you do look awful, Edmund. Don't you feel well?"

"I'm all right," said Edmund, but this was not true. He was feeling very sick.

"Come on then," said Lucy, "let's find the others. What a lot we shall have to tell them! And what wonderful adventures we shall have now that we're all in it together."

Because the game of hide-and-seek was still going on, it took Edmund and Lucy some time to find the others. But when at last they were all together (which happened in the long room, where the suit of armour was) Lucy burst out:

"Peter! Susan! It's all true. Edmund has seen it too. There *is* a country you can get to through the wardrobe. Edmund and I both got in. We met one another in there, in the wood. Go on, Edmund; tell them all about it."

"What's all this about, Ed?" said Peter.

And now we come to one of the nastiest things in this story. Up to that moment Edmund had been feeling sick, and sulky, and annoyed with Lucy for being right, but he hadn't made up his mind what to do. When Peter suddenly asked him the question he decided all at once to do the meanest and most spiteful thing he could think of. He decided to let Lucy down.

"Tell us, Ed," said Susan.

And Edmund gave a very superior look as if he were far older than Lucy (there was really only a year's difference) and then a little snigger and said, "Oh, yes, Lucy and I have been playing – pretending that all her story about a country in the wardrobe is true. Just for fun, of course. There's nothing there really."

Poor Lucy gave Edmund one look and rushed out of the room.

Edmund, who was becoming a nastier person every minute, thought that he had scored a great success, and went on at once to say, "There she goes again. What's the matter with her? That's the worst of young kids, they always –"

"Look here," said Peter, turning on him savagely, "shut up! You've been perfectly beastly to Lu ever since she started this nonsense about the wardrobe, and now you go playing games with her about it and setting her off again. I believe you did it simply out of spite."

"But it's all nonsense," said Edmund, very taken aback.

"Of course it's all nonsense," said Peter, "that's just the point. Lu was perfectly all right when we left home, but since we've been down here she seems to be either going queer in the head or else turning into a most frightful liar. But whichever it is, what good do you think you'll do by jeering and nagging at her one day and encouraging her the next?"

"I thought – I thought," said Edmund; but he couldn't think of anything to say.

"You didn't think anything at all," said Peter; "it's just spite. You've always liked being beastly to anyone smaller than yourself; we've seen that at school before now."

"Do stop it," said Susan; "it won't make things any better having a row between you two. Let's go and find Lucy."

It was not surprising that when they found Lucy, a good deal later, everyone could see that she had been crying. Nothing they could say to her made any difference. She stuck to her story and said:

"I don't care what you think, and I don't care what you say. You can tell the Professor or you can write to Mother or you can do anything you like. I know I've met a Faun in there and – I wish I'd stayed there and you are all beasts, beasts."

It was an unpleasant evening. Lucy was miserable and Edmund was beginning to feel that his plan wasn't working as well as he had expected. The two older ones were really beginning to think that Lucy was out of her mind. They stood in the passage talking about it in whispers long after she had gone to bed.

The result was the next morning they decided that they really would go and tell the whole thing to the Professor. "He'll write to Father if he thinks there is really something wrong with Lu," said Peter; "it's getting beyond us." So they went and knocked at the study door, and the Professor said "Come in," and got up and found chairs for them and said he was quite at their disposal. Then he sat listening to them with the tips of his fingers pressed together and never interrupting, till they had finished the whole story. After that he said nothing for quite a long time. Then he cleared his throat and said the last thing either of them expected:

"How do you know," he asked, "that your sister's story is not true?"

"Oh, but –" began Susan, and then stopped. Anyone could see from the old man's face that he was perfectly serious. Then Susan pulled herself together and said, "But Edmund said they had only been pretending."

"That is a point," said the Professor, "which certainly deserves consideration; very careful consideration. For instance – if you will excuse me for asking the question – does your experience lead you to regard your brother or your sister as the more reliable? I mean, which is the more truthful?"

"That's just the funny thing about it, sir," said Peter. "Up till now, I'd have said Lucy every time."

"And what do you think, my dear?" said the Professor, turning to Susan.

"Well," said Susan, "in general, I'd say the same as Peter, but this couldn't be true – all this about the wood and the Faun."

"That is more than I know," said the Professor, "and a charge of lying against someone whom you have always found truthful is a very serious thing; a very serious thing indeed."

"We were afraid it mightn't even be lying," said Susan; "we thought there might be something wrong with Lucy."

"Madness, you mean?" said the Professor quite coolly. "Oh, you can make your minds easy about that. One has only to look at her and talk to her to see that she is not mad."

"But then," said Susan, and stopped. She had never dreamed that a grown-up would talk like the Professor and didn't know what to think.

"Logic!" said the Professor half to himself. "Why don't they teach logic at these schools? There are only three possibilities. Either your sister is telling lies, or she is mad, or she is telling the truth. You know she doesn't tell lies and it is obvious that she is not mad. For the moment then and unless any further evidence turns up, we must assume that she is telling the truth."

Susan looked at him very hard and was quite sure from the expression on his face that he was not making fun of them.

"But how could it be true, sir?" said Peter.

"Why do you say that?" asked the Professor.

"Well, for one thing," said Peter, "if it was real why doesn't everyone find this country every time they go to the wardrobe? I mean, there was nothing there when we looked; even Lucy didn't pretend there was."

"What has that to do with it?" said the Professor.

"Well, sir, if things are real, they're there all the time."

"Are they?" said the Professor; and Peter did not know quite what to say.

"But there was no time," said Susan. "Lucy had had no time to have gone anywhere, even if there was such a place. She came running after us the very moment we were out of the room. It was less than a minute, and she pretended to have been away for hours."

"That is the very thing that makes her story so likely to be true," said the Professor. "If there really is a door in this house that leads to some other world (and I should warn you that this is a very strange house, and even I know very little about it) – if, I say, she had got into another world, I should not be at all surprised to find that the other world had a separate time of its own; so that however long you stayed there it would never take up any of *our* time. On the other hand, I don't think many girls of her age would invent that idea for themselves. If she had been pretending, she would have hidden for a reasonable time before coming out and telling her story."

"But do you really mean, sir," said Peter, "that there could be other worlds – all over the place, just round the corner – like that?"

"Nothing is more probable," said the Professor, taking off his spectacles and beginning to polish them, while he muttered to himself, "I wonder what they *do* teach them at these schools."

"But what are we to do?" said Susan. She felt that the conversation was beginning to get off the point.

"My dear young lady," said the Professor, suddenly looking up with a very sharp expression at both of them, "there is one plan which no one has yet suggested and which is well worth trying."

"What's that?" said Susan.

"We might all try minding our own business," said he. And that was the end of that conversation.

After this things were a good deal better for Lucy. Peter saw to it that Edmund stopped jeering at her, and neither she nor anyone else felt inclined to talk about the wardrobe at all. It had become a rather alarming subject. And so for a time it looked as if all the adventures were coming to an end; but that was not to be.

This house of the Professor's – which even he knew so little about – was so old and famous that people from all over England used to come and ask permission to see over it. It was the sort of house that is mentioned in guide books and even in histories; and well it might be, for all manner of stories were told about it, some of them even stranger than the one I am telling you now. And when parties of sightseers arrived and asked to see

'A few mornings later Peter and Edmund were looking at the suit of armour'

the house, the Professor always gave them permission, and Mrs Macready, the housekeeper, showed them round, telling them

about the pictures and the armour, and the rare books in the library. Mrs Macready was not fond of children, and did not like to be interrupted when she was telling visitors all the things she knew. She had said to Susan and Peter almost on the first morning (along with a good many other instructions), "And please remember you're to keep out of the way whenever I'm taking a party over the house."

"Just as if any of us would *want* to waste half the morning trailing round with a crowd of strange grown-ups!" said Edmund, and the other three thought the same. That was how the adventures began for the second time.

A few mornings later Peter and Edmund were looking at the suit of armour and wondering if they could take it to bits when the two girls rushed into the room and said, "Look out! Here comes the Macready and a whole gang with her."

"Sharp's the word," said Peter, and all four made off through the door at the far end of the room. But when they had got out into the Green Room and beyond it, into the Library, they suddenly heard voices ahead of them, and realized that Mrs Macready must be bringing her party of sightseers up the back stairs – instead of up the front stairs as they had expected. And after that – whether it was that they lost their heads, or that Mrs Macready was trying to catch them, or that some magic in the house had come to life and was chasing them into Narnia – they seemed to find themselves being followed everywhere, until at last Susan said, "Oh bother those trippers! Here – let's get into the Wardrobe Room till they've passed. No one will follow us in there." But the moment they were inside they heard the voices in the passage – and then someone fumbling at the door – and then they saw the handle turning.

"Quick!" said Peter, "there's nowhere else," and flung open the wardrobe. All four of them bundled inside it and sat there, panting, in the dark. Peter held the door closed but did not shut it; for, of course, he remembered, as every sensible person does, that you should never never shut yourself up in a wardrobe.

CHAPTER SIX

INTO THE FOREST

"I wish the Macready would hurry up and take all these people away," said Susan presently, "I'm getting horribly cramped."

"And what a filthy smell of camphor!" said Edmund.

"I expect the pockets of these coats are full of it," said Susan, "to keep away the moths."

"There's something sticking into my back," said Peter.

"And isn't it cold?" said Susan.

"Now that you mention it, it is cold," said Peter, "and hang it all, it's wet too. What's the matter with this place? I'm sitting on something wet. It's getting wetter every minute." He struggled to his feet.

"Let's get out," said Edmund, "they've gone."

"O-o-oh!" said Susan suddenly, and everyone asked her what was the matter.

"I'm sitting against a tree," said Susan, "and look! It's getting light – over there."

"By jove, you're right," said Peter, "and look there – and there. It's trees all round. And this wet stuff is snow. Why, I do believe we've got into Lucy's wood after all."

And now there was no mistaking it and all four children stood blinking in the daylight of a winter day. Behind them were coats hanging on pegs, in front of them were snow-covered trees.

Peter turned at once to Lucy.

"I apologize for not believing you," he said, "I'm sorry. Will you shake hands?"

"Of course," said Lucy, and did.

"And now," said Susan, "what do we do next?"

"Do?" said Peter, "why, go and explore the wood, of course."

"Ugh!" said Susan, stamping her feet, "it's pretty cold. What about putting on some of these coats?"

"They're not ours," said Peter doubtfully.

"I am sure nobody would mind," said Susan; "it isn't as if we wanted to take them out of the house; we shan't take them even out of the wardrobe."

"I never thought of that, Su," said Peter. "Of course, now you put it that way, I see. No one could say you had bagged a coat as long as you leave it in the wardrobe where you found it. And I suppose this whole country is in the wardrobe."

They immediately carried out Susan's very sensible plan. The coats were rather too big for them so that they came down to their heels and looked more like royal robes than coats when they had put them on. But they all felt a good deal warmer and each thought the others looked better in their new get-up and more suitable to the landscape.

"We can pretend we are Arctic explorers," said Lucy.

"This is going to be exciting enough without pretending," said Peter, as he began leading the way forward into the forest. There were heavy darkish clouds overhead and it looked as if there might be more snow before night.

"I say," began Edmund presently, "oughtn't we to be bearing a bit more to the left, that is, if we are aiming for the lamp-post?" He had forgotten for the moment that he must pretend never to have been in the wood before. The moment the words were out of his mouth he realized that he had given himself away. Everyone stopped; everyone stared at him. Peter whistled.

"So you really were here," he said, "that time Lu said she'd met you in here – and you made out she was telling lies."

There was a dead silence. "Well, of all the poisonous little beasts –" said Peter, and shrugged his shoulders and said no more. There seemed, indeed, no more to say, and presently the four resumed their journey; but Edmund was saying to himself, "I'll pay you all out for this, you pack of stuck-up, self-satisfied prigs."

"Where *are* we going anyway?" said Susan, chiefly for the sake of changing the subject.

"I think Lu ought to be the leader," said Peter; "goodness knows she deserves it. Where will you take us, Lu?"

"What about going to see Mr Tumnus?" said Lucy. "He's the nice Faun I told you about."

Everyone agreed to this and off they went walking briskly and stamping their feet. Lucy proved a good leader. At first she wondered whether she would be able to find the way, but she recognized an odd-looking tree in one place and a stump in another and brought them on to where the ground became uneven and into the little valley and at last to the very door of Mr Tumnus's cave. But there a terrible surprise awaited them.

The door had been wrenched off its hinges and broken to bits. Inside, the cave was dark and cold and had the damp feel and smell of a place that had not been lived in for several days. Snow had drifted in from the doorway and was heaped on the floor, mixed with something black, which turned out to be the charred sticks and ashes from the fire. Someone had apparently flung it about the room and then stamped it out. The crockery lay smashed on the floor and the picture of the Faun's father had been slashed into shreds with a knife.

"This is a pretty good wash-out," said Edmund; "not much good coming here."

"What is this?" said Peter, stooping down. He had just noticed a piece of paper which had been nailed through the carpet to the floor.

"Is there anything written on it?" asked Susan.

"Yes, I think there is," answered Peter, "but I can't read it in this light. Let's get out into the open air."

They all went out in the daylight and crowded round Peter as he read out the following words:

The former occupant of these premises, the Faun Tumnus, is under arrest and awaiting his trial on a charge of High Treason against her Imperial Majesty Jadis, Queen of Narnia, Chatelaine of Cair Paravel, Empress of the Lone Islands, etc., also of comforting her said Majesty's enemies, harbouring spies and fraternizing with Humans.

signed MAUGRIM, Captain of the Secret Police,

LONG LIVE THE QUEEN!

The children stared at each other.

"I don't know that I'm going to like this place after all," said Susan.

"Who is this Queen, Lu?" said Peter. "Do you know anything about her?"

"She isn't a real queen at all," answered Lucy; "she's a horrible witch, the White Witch. Everyone – all the wood people – hate her. She has made an enchantment over the whole country so that it is always winter here and never Christmas."

"I – I wonder if there's any point in going on," said Susan. "I mean, it doesn't seem particularly safe here and it looks as if it won't be much fun either. And it's getting colder every minute, and we've brought nothing to eat. What about just going home?"

"Oh, but we can't, we can't," said Lucy suddenly; "don't you see? We can't just go home, not after this. It is all on my account that the poor Faun has got into this trouble. He hid me from the Witch and showed me the way back. That's what

"'I say," began Edmund presently, "oughtn't we to be bearing a bit more to the left"'

it means by comforting the Queen's enemies and fraternizing with Humans. We simply must try to rescue him."

"A lot *we* could do!" said Edmund, "when we haven't even got anything to eat!"

"Shut up – you!" said Peter, who was still very angry with Edmund. "What do you think, Susan?"

"I've a horrid feeling that Lu is right," said Susan. "I don't want to go a step further and I wish we'd never come. But I think we must try to do something for Mr Whatever-his-name is – I mean the Faun."

"That's what I feel too," said Peter. "I'm worried about having no food with us. I'd vote for going back and getting something from the larder, only there doesn't seem to be any certainty of getting into this country again when once you've got out of it. I think we'll have to go on."

"So do I," said both the girls.

"If only we knew where the poor chap was imprisoned!" said Peter.

They were all still wondering what to do next, when Lucy said, "Look! There's a robin, with such a red breast. It's the first bird I've seen here. I say! – I wonder can birds talk in Narnia? It almost looks as if it wanted to say something to us." Then she turned to the Robin and said, "Please, can you tell us where Tumnus the Faun has been taken to?" As she said this she took a step towards the bird. It at once flew away but only as far as to the next tree. There it perched and looked at them very hard as if it understood all they had been saying. Almost without noticing that they had done so, the four children went a step or two nearer to it. At this the Robin flew away again to the next tree and once more looked at them very hard. (You couldn't have found a robin with a redder chest or a brighter eye.)

"Do you know," said Lucy, "I really believe he means us to follow him."

"I've an idea he does," said Susan. "What do you think, Peter?"

"Well, we might as well try it," answered Peter.

The Robin appeared to understand the matter thoroughly. It kept going from tree to tree, always a few yards ahead of them, but always so near that they could easily follow it. In this way it led them on, slightly downhill. Wherever the Robin alighted a little shower of snow would fall off the branch. Presently the clouds parted overhead and the winter sun came out and the snow all around them grew dazzlingly bright. They had been travelling in this way for about half an hour, with the two girls in front, when Edmund said to Peter, "if you're not still too high and mighty to talk to me, I've something to say which you'd better listen to."

"What is it?" asked Peter.

"Hush! Not so loud," said Edmund; "there's no good frightening the girls. But have you realized what we're doing?"

"What?" said Peter, lowering his voice to a whisper.

"We're following a guide we know nothing about. How do we know which side that bird is on? Why shouldn't it be leading us into a trap?"

"That's a nasty idea. Still – a robin, you know. They're good birds in all the stories I've ever read. I'm sure a robin wouldn't be on the wrong side."

"If it comes to that, which *is* the right side? How do we know that the Fauns are in the right and the Queen (yes, I know we've been *told* she's a witch) is in the wrong? We don't really know anything about either."

"The Faun saved Lucy."

"He *said* he did. But how do we know? And there's another thing too. Has anyone the least idea of the way home from here?"

"Great Scott!" said Peter, "I hadn't thought of that."

"And no chance of dinner either," said Edmund.

CHAPTER SEVEN

A DAY WITH THE BEAVERS

While the two boys were whispering behind, both the girls suddenly cried "Oh!" and stopped.

"The robin!" cried Lucy, "the robin. It's flown away." And so it had – right out of sight.

"And now what are we to do?" said Edmund, giving Peter a look which was as much as to say "What did I tell you?"

"Sh! Look!" said Susan.

"What?" said Peter.

"There's something moving among the trees over there to the left."

They all stared as hard as they could, and no one felt very comfortable.

"There it goes again," said Susan presently.

"I saw it that time too," said Peter. "It's still there. It's just gone behind that big tree."

"What is it?" asked Lucy, trying very hard not to sound nervous.

"Whatever it is," said Peter, "it's dodging us. It's something that doesn't want to be seen."

"Let's go home," said Susan. And then, though nobody said it out loud, everyone suddenly realized the same fact that Edmund had whispered to Peter at the end of the last chapter. They were lost.

"What's it like?" said Lucy.

"It's – it's a kind of animal," said Susan; and then, "Look! Look! Quick! There it is."

They all saw it this time, a whiskered furry face which had looked out at them from behind a tree. But this time it didn't immediately draw back. Instead, the animal put its paw against its mouth just as humans put their finger on their lips when they are signalling to you to be quiet. Then it disappeared again. The children all stood holding their breath.

A moment later the stranger came out from behind the tree, glanced all round as if it were afraid someone was watching, said "Hush", made signs to them to join it in the thicker bit of wood where it was standing, and then once more disappeared.

"I know what it is," said Peter; "it's a beaver. I saw the tail."

"It wants us to go to it," said Susan, "and it is warning us not to make a noise."

"I know," said Peter. "The question is, are we to go to it or not? What do you think, Lu?"

"I think it's a nice beaver," said Lucy.

"Yes, but how do we *know?*" said Edmund.

"Shan't we have to risk it?" said Susan. "I mean, it's no good just standing here and I feel I want some dinner."

At this moment the Beaver again popped its head out from behind the tree and beckoned earnestly to them.

"Come on," said Peter, "let's give it a try. All keep close together. We ought to be a match for one beaver if it turns out to be an enemy."

So the children all got close together and walked up to the tree and in behind it, and there, sure enough, they found the Beaver; but it still drew back, saying to them in a hoarse throaty whisper, "Further in, come further in. Right in here. We're not safe in the open!" Only when it had led them into a dark spot where four trees grew so close together that their boughs met and the brown earth and pine needles could be seen underfoot because no snow had been able to fall there, did it begin to talk to them.

"Are you the Sons of Adam and the Daughters of Eve?" it said.

"We're some of them," said Peter.

"S-s-s-sh!" said the Beaver, "not so loud please. We're not safe even here."

"Why, who are you afraid of?" said Peter. "There's no one here but ourselves."

"There are the trees," said the Beaver. "They're always listening. Most of them are on our side, but there *are* trees that would betray us to *her*; you know who I mean," and it nodded its head several times.

"If it comes to talking about sides," said Edmund, "how do

we know you're a friend?"

"Not meaning to be rude, Mr Beaver," added Peter, "but you see, we're strangers."

"Quite right, quite right," said the Beaver. "Here is my token." With these words it held up to them a little white object. They all looked at it in surprise, till suddenly Lucy said, "Oh, of course. It's my handkerchief – the one I gave to poor Mr Tumnus."

"That's right," said the Beaver. "Poor fellow, he got wind of the arrest before it actually happened and handed this over to me. He said that if anything happened to him I must meet you here and take you on to –" Here the Beaver's voice sank into silence and it gave one or two very mysterious nods. Then signalling to the children to stand as close around it as they possibly could, so that their faces were actually tickled by its whiskers, it added in a low whisper –

"They say Aslan is on the move – perhaps has already landed."

And now a very curious thing happened. None of the children knew who Aslan was any more than you do; but the moment the Beaver had spoken these words everyone felt quite different. Perhaps it has sometimes happened to you in a dream that someone says something which you don't understand but in the dream it feels as if it had some enormous meaning – either a terrifying one which turns the whole dream into a nightmare or else a lovely meaning too lovely to put into words, which makes the dream so beautiful that you remember it all your life and are always wishing you could get into that dream again. It was like that now. At the name of Aslan each one of the children felt something jump in its inside. Edmund felt a sensation of mysterious horror. Peter felt suddenly brave and adventurous. Susan felt as if some delicious smell or some delightful strain of music had just floated by her. And Lucy got the feeling you have when you wake up in the morning and realize that it is the beginning of the holidays or the beginning of summer.

"And what about Mr Tumnus," said Lucy; "where is he?"

"S-s-s-sh," said the Beaver, "not here. I must bring you where we can have a real talk and also dinner."

No one except Edmund felt any difficulty about trusting the Beaver now, and everyone, including Edmund, was very glad to hear the word "dinner". They therefore all hurried along behind their new friend who led them at a surprisingly quick pace, and always in the thickest parts of the forest, for over an hour. Everyone was feeling very tired and very hungry when suddenly the trees began to get thinner in front of them and the ground to fall steeply downhill. A minute later they came out under the open sky (the sun was still shining) and found themselves looking down on a fine sight.

They were standing on the edge of a steep, narrow valley at the bottom of which ran – at least it would have been running if it hadn't been frozen – a fairly large river. Just below them a dam had been built across this river, and when they saw it everyone suddenly remembered that of course beavers are always making dams and felt quite sure that Mr Beaver had made this one. They also noticed that he now had a sort of modest expression on his face – the sort of look people have when you are visiting a garden they've made or reading a story they've written. So it was only common politeness when Susan said, "What a lovely dam!" And Mr Beaver didn't say "Hush" this time but "Merely a trifle! Merely a trifle! And it isn't really finished!"

Above the dam there was what ought to have been a deep pool but was now, of course, a level floor of dark green ice. And below the dam, much lower down, was more ice, but instead of being smooth this was all frozen into the foamy and wavy shapes in which the water had been rushing along at the very moment when the frost came. And where the water had been trickling over and spurting through the dam there was now a glittering wall of icicles, as if the side of the dam had been covered all over with flowers and wreaths and festoons of the purest sugar. And out in the middle, and partly on top of the dam was a funny little house shaped rather like an enormous beehive and from a hole in the roof smoke was going up, so that when you saw it (especially if you were hungry) you at once thought of cooking and became hungrier than you were before.

That was what the others chiefly noticed, but Edmund noticed something else. A little lower down the river there was another small river which came down another small valley to join it. And looking up that valley, Edmund could see two small hills, and he was almost sure they were the two hills which the White Witch had pointed out to him when he parted from her at the lamp-post that other day. And then between them, he thought, must be her palace, only a mile off or less. And he thought about Turkish Delight and about being a King ("And I wonder how Peter will like that?" he asked himself) and horrible ideas came into his head.

"Here we are," said Mr Beaver, "and it looks as if Mrs Beaver is expecting us. I'll lead the way. But be careful and don't slip."

The top of the dam was wide enough to walk on, though not (for humans) a very nice place to walk because it was covered with ice, and though the frozen pool was level with it on one side, there was a nasty drop to the lower river on the other.

Along this route Mr Beaver led them in single file right out to the middle where they could look a long way up the river and a long way down it. And when they had reached the middle they were at the door of the house.

"Here we are, Mrs Beaver," said Mr Beaver, "I've found them. Here are the Sons and Daughters of Adam and Eve" – and they all went in. The first thing Lucy noticed as she went in was a burring sound, and the first thing she saw was a kind-looking old

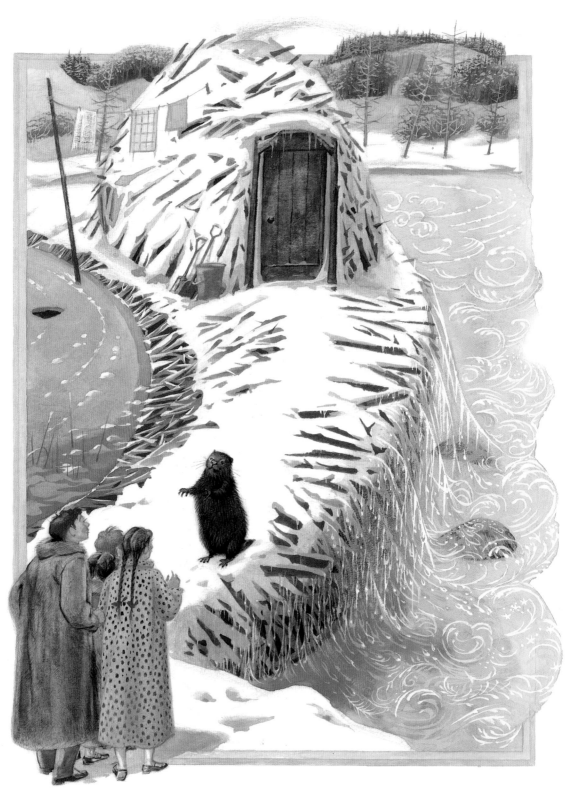

'"Here we are," said Mr Beaver, "and it looks as if Mrs Beaver is expecting us"'

she-beaver sitting in the corner with a thread in her mouth working busily at her sewing machine, and it was from it that the sound came. She stopped her work and got up as soon as the children came in.

"So you've come at last!" she said, holding out both her wrinkled old paws. "At last! To think that ever I should live to see this day! The potatoes are on boiling and the kettle's singing and I daresay, Mr Beaver, you'll get us some fish."

"That I will," said Mr Beaver, and he went out of the house (Peter went with him), and across the ice of the deep pool to where he had a little hole in the ice which he kept open every day with his hatchet. They took a pail with them. Mr Beaver sat down quietly at the edge of the hole (he didn't seem to mind it being so chilly), looked hard into it, then suddenly shot in his paw, and before you could say Jack Robinson had whisked out a beautiful trout. Then he did it all over again until they had a fine catch of fish.

Meanwhile the girls were helping Mrs Beaver to fill the kettle and lay the table and cut the bread and put the plates in the oven to heat and draw a huge jug of beer for Mr Beaver from a barrel which stood in one corner of the house, and to put on the frying-pan and get the dripping hot. Lucy thought the Beavers had a very snug little home though it was not at all like Mr Tumnus's cave. There were no books or pictures, and instead of beds there were bunks, like on board ship, built into the wall. And there were hams and strings of onions hanging from the roof, and against the walls were gum boots and oilskins and hatchets and pairs of shears and spades and trowels and things for carrying mortar in and fishing-rods and fishing-nets and sacks. And the cloth on the table, though very clean, was very rough.

Just as the frying-pan was nicely hissing Peter and Mr Beaver came in with the fish which Mr Beaver had already opened with his knife and cleaned out in the open air. You can think how good the new-caught fish smelled while they were frying and how the hungry children longed for them to be done and how very much hungrier still they had become before Mr Beaver said, "Now we're nearly ready." Susan drained the potatoes and then put them all back in the empty pot to dry on the side of the range while Lucy was helping Mrs Beaver to dish up the trout, so that in a very few minutes everyone was drawing up their stools (it was all three-legged stools in the Beavers' house except for Mrs Beaver's own special rocking-chair beside the fire) and preparing to enjoy themselves. There was a jug of creamy milk for the children (Mr Beaver stuck to beer) and a great big lump of deep yellow butter in the middle of the table from which everyone took as much as he wanted to go with his potatoes, and all the children thought – and I agree with them – that there's nothing to beat good freshwater fish if you eat it when it has been alive half an hour ago and has come out of the pan half a minute ago. And when they had finished the fish Mrs Beaver brought unexpectedly out of the oven a great and gloriously sticky marmalade roll, steaming hot, and at the same time moved the kettle on to the fire, so that when they had finished the marmalade roll the tea was made and ready to be poured out. And when each person had got his (or her) cup of tea, each person shoved back his (or her) stool so as to be able to lean against the wall and gave a long sigh of contentment.

"And now," said Mr Beaver, pushing away his empty beer mug and pulling his cup of tea towards him, "if you'll just wait till I've got my pipe lit up and going nicely – why, now we can get to business. It's snowing again," he added, cocking his eye at the window. "That's all the better, because it means we shan't have any visitors; and if anyone should have been trying to follow you, why he won't find any tracks."

CHAPTER EIGHT

WHAT HAPPENED AFTER DINNER

"And now," said Lucy, "do please tell us what's happened to Mr Tumnus."

"Ah, that's bad," said Mr Beaver, shaking his head. "That's a very, very bad business. There's no doubt he was taken off by the police. I got that from a bird who saw it done."

"But where's he been taken to?" asked Lucy.

"Well, they were heading northwards when they were last seen and we all know what that means."

"No, *we* don't," said Susan. Mr Beaver shook his head in a very gloomy fashion.

"I'm afraid it means they were taking him to her House," he said.

"But what'll they do to him, Mr Beaver?" gasped Lucy.

"Well," said Mr Beaver, "you can't exactly say for sure. But there's not many taken in there that ever comes out again. Statues. All full of statues they say it is – in the courtyard and up the stairs and in the hall. People she's turned" – (he paused and shuddered) "turned into stone."

"But, Mr Beaver," said Lucy, "can't we – I mean we *must* do something to save him. It's too dreadful and it's all on my account."

"I don't doubt you'd save him if you could, dearie," said Mrs Beaver, "but you've no chance of getting into that House against her will and ever coming out alive."

"Couldn't we have some stratagem?" said Peter. "I mean couldn't we dress up as something, or pretend to be – oh, pedlars or anything – or watch till she was gone out – or – oh, hang it all, there must be *some* way. This Faun saved my sister at his own risk, Mr Beaver. We can't just leave him to be – to be – to have that done to him."

"It's no good, Son of Adam," said Mr Beaver, "no good *your* trying, of all people. But now that Aslan is on the move –"

"Oh, yes! Tell us about Aslan!" said several voices at once; for once again that strange feeling – like the first signs of spring, like good news, had come over them.

"Who is Aslan?" asked Susan.

"Aslan?" said Mr Beaver. "Why, don't you know? He's the King. He's the Lord of the whole wood, but not often here, you understand. Never in my time or my father's time. But the word has reached us that he has come back. He is in Narnia at this moment. He'll settle the White Queen all right. It is he, not you, that will save Mr Tumnus."

"She won't turn him into stone too?" said Edmund.

"Lord love you, Son of Adam, what a simple thing to say!" answered Mr Beaver with a great laugh. "Turn *him* into stone? If she can stand on her two feet and look him in the face it'll be the most she can do and more than I expect of her. No, no. He'll put all to rights as it says in an old rhyme in these parts:

> Wrong will be right, when Aslan comes in sight,
> At the sound of his roar, sorrows will be no more,
> When he bares his teeth, winter meets its death,
> And when he shakes his mane, we shall have spring again.

You'll understand when you see him."

"But shall we see him?" asked Susan.

"Why, Daughter of Eve, that's what I brought you here for. I'm to lead you where you shall meet him," said Mr Beaver.

"Is – is he a man?" asked Lucy.

"Aslan a man!" said Mr Beaver sternly. "Certainly not. I tell you he is the King of the wood and the son of the great Emperor-beyond-the-Sea. Don't you know who is the King of Beasts? Aslan is a lion – *the* Lion, the great Lion."

"Ooh!" said Susan, "I'd thought he was a man. Is he – quite safe? I shall feel rather nervous about meeting a lion."

"That you will, dearie, and no mistake," said Mrs Beaver; "if there's anyone who can appear before Aslan without their knees knocking, they're either braver than most or else just silly."

"Then he isn't safe?" said Lucy.

"Safe?" said Mr Beaver; "don't you hear what Mrs Beaver tells you? Who said anything about safe? 'Course he isn't safe. But he's good. He's the King, I tell you."

"I'm longing to see him," said Peter, "even if I do feel frightened when it comes to the point."

"That's right, Son of Adam," said Mr Beaver, bringing his paw down on the table with a crash that made all the cups and saucers rattle. "And so you shall. Word has been sent that you *are* to meet him, tomorrow if you can, at the Stone Table."

"Where's that?" said Lucy.

"I'll show you," said Mr Beaver. "It's down the river, a good step from here. I'll take you to it!"

"But meanwhile what about poor Mr Tumnus?" said Lucy.

"The quickest way you can help him is by going to meet

Aslan," said Mr Beaver, "once he's with us, then we can begin doing things. Not that we don't need you too. For that's another of the old rhymes:

When Adam's flesh and Adam's bone
Sits at Cair Paravel in throne,
The evil time will be over and done.

So things must be drawing near their end now he's come and you've come. We've heard of Aslan coming into these parts before – long ago, nobody can say when. But there's never been any of your race here before."

"That's what I don't understand, Mr Beaver," said Peter, "I mean isn't the Witch herself human?"

"She'd like us to believe it," said Mr Beaver, "and it's on that that she bases her claim to be Queen. But she's no Daughter of Eve. She comes of your father Adam's" – (here Mr Beaver bowed) "your father Adam's first wife, her they called Lilith. And she was one of the Jinn. That's what she comes from on one side. And on the other she comes of the giants. No, no, there isn't a drop of real human blood in the Witch."

"That's why she's bad all through, Mr Beaver," said Mrs Beaver.

"True enough, Mrs Beaver," replied he, "there may be two views about humans (meaning no offence to the present company). But there's no two views about things that look like humans and aren't."

"I've known good Dwarfs," said Mrs Beaver.

"So've I, now you come to speak of it," said her husband, "but precious few, and they were the ones least like men. But in general, take my advice, when you meet anything that's going to be human and isn't yet, or used to be human once and isn't now, or ought to be human and isn't, you keep your eyes on it and feel for your hatchet. And that's why the Witch is always on the lookout for any humans in Narnia. She's been watching for you this many a year, and if she knew there were four of you she'd be more dangerous still."

"What's that to do with it?" asked Peter.

"Because of another prophecy," said Mr Beaver. "Down at Cair Paravel – that's the castle on the sea coast down at the mouth of this river which ought to be the capital of the whole country if all was as it should be – down at Cair Paravel there are four thrones and it's a saying in Narnia time out of mind that when two Sons of Adam and two Daughters of Eve sit in those four thrones, then it will be the end not only of the White Witch's reign but of her life, and that is why we had to be so cautious as we came along, for if she knew about you four, your lives wouldn't be worth a shake of my whiskers!"

All the children had been attending so hard to what Mr Beaver was telling them that they had noticed nothing else for a long time. Then during the moment of silence that followed his last remark, Lucy suddenly said:

"I say – where's Edmund?"

There was a dreadful pause, and then everyone began asking "Who saw him last? How long has he been missing? Is he outside?" and then all rushed to the door and looked out. The snow was falling thickly and steadily, the green ice of the pool had vanished under a thick white blanket, and from where the little house stood in the centre of the dam you could hardly see

"'Word has been sent that you are to meet him, tomorrow if you can, at the Stone Table'"

either bank. Out they went, plunging well over their ankles into the soft new snow, and went round the house in every direction. "Edmund! Edmund!" they called till they were hoarse. But the silently falling snow seemed to muffle their voices and there was not even an echo in answer.

"How perfectly dreadful!" said Susan as they at last came back in despair. "Oh, how I wish we'd never come."

"What on earth are we to do, Mr Beaver?" said Peter.

"Do?" said Mr Beaver, who was already putting on his snow-boots, "do? We must be off at once. We haven't a moment to spare!"

"We'd better divide into four search parties," said Peter, "and all go in different directions. Whoever finds him must come back here at once and –"

"Search parties, Son of Adam?" said Mr Beaver; "what for?"

"Why, to look for Edmund, of course!"

"There's no point in looking for him," said Mr Beaver.

"What do you mean?" said Susan. "He can't be far away yet. And we've got to find him. What do you mean when you say there's no use looking for him?"

"The reason there's no use looking," said Mr Beaver, "is that we know already where he's gone!" Everyone stared in amazement. "Don't you understand?" said Mr Beaver. "He's gone to *her*, to the White Witch. He has betrayed us all."

"Oh, surely – oh, really!" said Susan, "he can't have done that."

"Can't he?" said Mr Beaver, looking very hard at the three children, and everything they wanted to say died on their lips, for each felt suddenly quite certain inside that this was exactly what Edmund had done.

"But will he know the way?" said Peter.

"Has he been in this country before?" asked Mr Beaver. "Has he ever been here alone?"

"Yes," said Lucy, almost in a whisper. "I'm afraid he has."

"And did he tell you what he'd done or who he'd met?"

"Well, no, he didn't," said Lucy.

"Then mark my words," said Mr Beaver, "he has already met the White Witch and joined her side, and been told where she lives. I didn't like to mention it before (he being your brother and all) but the moment I set eyes on that brother of yours I said to myself 'Treacherous'. He had the look of one who has been with the Witch and eaten her food. You can always tell them if you've lived long in Narnia; something about their eyes."

"All the same," said Peter in a rather choking sort of voice, "we'll still have to go and look for him. He is our brother after all, even if he is rather a little beast. And he's only a kid."

"Go to the Witch's House?" said Mrs Beaver. "Don't you see that the only chance of saving either him or yourselves is to keep away from her?"

"How do you mean?" said Lucy.

"Why, all she wants is to get all four of you (she's thinking all the time of those four thrones at Cair Paravel). Once you were all four inside her House her job would be done – and there'd be four new statues in her collection before you'd had time to speak. But she'll keep him alive as long as he's the only one she's got, because she'll want to use him as a decoy; as bait to catch the rest of you with."

"Oh, can *no* one help us?" wailed Lucy.

"Only Aslan," said Mr Beaver, "we must go on and meet him. That's our only chance now."

"It seems to me, my dears," said Mrs Beaver, "that it is very important to know just *when* he slipped away. How much he can tell her depends on how much he heard. For instance, had we started talking of Aslan before he left? If not, then we may do very well, for she won't know that Aslan has come to Narnia, or that we are meeting him, and will be quite off her guard as far as *that* is concerned."

"I don't remember his being here when we were talking about Aslan –" began Peter, but Lucy interrupted him.

"Oh yes, he was," she said miserably; "don't you remember, it was he who asked whether the Witch couldn't turn Aslan into stone too?"

"So he did, by Jove," said Peter; "just the sort of thing he would say, too!"

"Worse and worse," said Mr Beaver, "and the next thing is this. Was he still here when I told you that the place for meeting Aslan was the Stone Table?"

And of course no one knew the answer to this question.

"Because, if he was," continued Mr Beaver, "then she'll simply sledge down in that direction and get between us and the Stone Table and catch us on our way down. In fact we shall be cut off from Aslan."

"But that isn't what she'll do first," said Mrs Beaver, "not if I know her. The moment that Edmund tells her that we're all here she'll set out to catch us this very night, and if he's been gone about half an hour, she'll be here in about another twenty minutes."

"You're right, Mrs Beaver," said her husband, "we must all get away from here. There's not a moment to lose."

CHAPTER NINE

IN THE WITCH'S HOUSE

And now of course you want to know what had happened to Edmund. He had eaten his share of the dinner, but he hadn't really enjoyed it because he was thinking all the time about Turkish Delight – and there's nothing that spoils the taste of good ordinary food half so much as the memory of bad magic food. And he had heard the conversation, and hadn't enjoyed it much either, because he kept on thinking that the others were taking no notice of him and trying to give him the cold shoulder. They weren't, but he imagined it. And then he had listened until Mr Beaver told them about Aslan and until he had heard the whole arrangement for meeting Aslan at the Stone Table. It was then that he began very quietly to edge himself under the curtain which hung over the door. For the mention of Aslan gave him a mysterious and horrible feeling just as it gave the others a mysterious and lovely feeling.

Just as Mr Beaver had been repeating the rhyme about *Adam's flesh and Adam's bone* Edmund had been very quietly turning the door-handle; and just before Mr Beaver had begun telling them that the White Witch wasn't really human at all but half a Jinn and half a giantess, Edmund had got outside into the snow and cautiously closed the door behind him.

You mustn't think that even now Edmund was quite so bad that he actually wanted his brother and sisters to be turned into stone. He did want Turkish Delight and to be a Prince (and later a King) and to pay Peter out for calling him a beast. As for what the Witch would do with the others, he didn't want her to be particularly nice to them – certainly not to put them on the same level as himself; but he managed to believe, or to pretend he believed, that she wouldn't do anything very bad to them, "Because," he said to himself, "all these people who say nasty things about her are her enemies and probably half of it isn't true. She was jolly nice to me, anyway, much nicer than they are. I expect she is the rightful Queen really. Anyway, she'll be better than that awful Aslan!" At least, that was the excuse he made in his own mind for what he was doing. It wasn't a very good excuse, however, for deep down inside him he really knew that the White Witch was bad and cruel.

The first thing he realized when he got outside and found the snow falling all round him, was that he had left his coat behind in the Beavers' house. And of course there was no chance of going back to get it now. The next thing he realized was that the daylight was almost gone, for it had been nearly three o'clock when they sat down to dinner and the winter days were short. He hadn't reckoned on this; but he had to make the best of it. So he turned up his collar and shuffled across the top of the dam (luckily it wasn't so slippery since the snow had fallen) to the far side of the river.

It was pretty bad when he reached the far side. It was growing darker every minute and what with that and the snowflakes swirling all round him he could hardly see three feet ahead. And then too there was no road. He kept slipping into deep drifts of snow, and skidding on frozen puddles, and tripping over fallen tree-trunks, and sliding down steep banks, and barking his shins against rocks, till he was wet and cold and bruised all over. The silence and the loneliness were dreadful. In fact I really think he might have given up the whole plan and gone back and owned up and made friends with the others, if he hadn't happened to say to himself, "When I'm King of Narnia the first thing I shall do will be to make some decent roads." And of course that set him off thinking about being a King and all the other things he would do and this cheered him up a good deal. He had just settled in his mind what sort of palace he would have and how many cars and all about his private cinema and where the principal railways would run and what laws he would make against beavers and dams and was putting the finishing touches to some schemes for keeping Peter in his place, when the weather changed. First the snow stopped. Then a wind sprang up and it became freezing cold. Finally, the clouds rolled away and the moon came out. It was a full moon and, shining on all that snow, it made everything almost as bright as day – only the shadows were rather confusing.

He would never have found his way if the moon hadn't come

out by the time he got to the other river – you remember he had seen (when they first arrived at the Beavers') a smaller river flowing into the great one lower down. He now reached this and turned to follow it up. But the little valley down which it came was much steeper and rockier than the one he had just left and much overgrown with bushes, so that he could not have managed it at all in the dark. Even as it was, he got wet through for he had to stoop under branches and great loads of snow came sliding off on to his back. And every time this happened he thought more and more how he hated Peter – just as if all this had been Peter's fault.

But at last he came to a part where it was more level and the valley opened out. And there, on the other side of the river, quite close to him, in the middle of a little plain between two hills, he saw what must be the White Witch's House. And the moon was shining brighter than ever. The House was really

a small castle. It seemed to be all towers; little towers with long pointed spires on them, sharp as needles. They looked like huge dunce's caps or sorcerer's caps. And they shone in the moonlight and their long shadows looked strange on the snow. Edmund began to be afraid of the House.

But it was too late to think of turning back now. He crossed the river on the ice and walked up to the House. There was nothing stirring; not the slightest sound anywhere. Even his own feet made no noise on the deep newly fallen snow. He walked on and on, past corner after corner of the House, and past turret after turret to find the door. He had to go right round to the far side before he found it. It was a huge arch but the great iron gates stood wide open.

Edmund crept up to the arch and looked inside into the courtyard, and there he saw a sight that nearly made his heart stop beating. Just inside the gate, with the moonlight shining on it, stood an enormous lion crouched as if it was ready to spring. And Edmund stood in the shadow of the arch, afraid to go on and afraid to go back, with his knees knocking together. He stood there so long that his teeth would have been chattering with cold even if they had not been chattering with fear. How long this really lasted I don't know, but it seemed to Edmund to last for hours.

Then at last he began to wonder why the lion was standing so still – for it hadn't moved one inch since he first set eyes on it. Edmund now ventured a little nearer, still keeping in the shadow of the arch as much as he could. He now saw from the way the lion was standing that it couldn't have been looking at him at all. ("But supposing it turns its head?" thought Edmund.) In fact it was staring at something else – namely a little dwarf who stood with his back to it about four feet away. "Aha!" thought Edmund. "When it springs at the dwarf then will be my chance to escape." But still the lion never moved, nor did the dwarf. And now at last Edmund remembered what the others had said about the White Witch turning people into stone. Perhaps this was only a stone lion. And as soon as he had thought of that he noticed that the lion's back and the top of its head were covered with snow. Of course it must be only a statue! No living animal would have let itself get covered with snow. Then very slowly and with his heart beating as if it would burst, Edmund ventured to go up to the lion. Even now he hardly dared to touch it, but at last he put out his hand, very quickly, and did. It was cold stone. He had been frightened of a mere statue!

The relief which Edmund felt was so great that in spite of the cold he suddenly got warm all over right down to his toes, and at the same time there came into his head what seemed a perfectly lovely idea. "Probably," he thought, "this is the great Lion Aslan that they were all talking about. She's caught him already and turned him into stone. So *that's* the end of all their fine ideas about him! Pooh! Who's afraid of Aslan?"

And he stood there gloating over the stone lion, and presently he did something very silly and childish. He took a stump of lead pencil out of his pocket and scribbled a moustache on the lion's upper lip and then a pair of spectacles on its eyes. Then he said, "Yah! Silly old Aslan! How do you like being a stone? You thought yourself mighty fine, didn't you?" But in spite of the scribbles on it the face of the great stone beast still looked so terrible, and sad, and noble, staring up in the moonlight, that Edmund didn't really get any fun out of jeering at it. He turned away and began to cross the courtyard.

As he got into the middle of it he saw that there were dozens of statues all about – standing here and there rather as the pieces stand on a chess-board when it is half-way through the game. There were stone satyrs, and stone wolves, and bears and foxes and cat-a-mountains of stone. There were lovely stone shapes that looked like women but who were really the spirits of trees. There was the great shape of a centaur and a winged horse and a long lithe creature that Edmund took to be a dragon. They

'He turned away and began to cross the courtyard'

all looked so strange standing there perfectly life-like and also perfectly still, in the bright cold moonlight, that it was eerie work crossing the courtyard. Right in the very middle stood a huge shape like a man, but as tall as a tree, with a fierce face and a shaggy beard and a great club in its right hand. Even though he knew that it was only a stone giant and not a live one, Edmund did not like going past it.

He now saw that there was a dim light showing from a doorway on the far side of the courtyard. He went to it, there was a flight of stone steps going up to an open door. Edmund went up them. Across the threshold lay a great wolf.

"It's all right, it's all right," he kept saying to himself; "it's only a stone wolf. It can't hurt me," and he raised his leg to step over it. Instantly the huge creature rose, with all the hair bristling along its back, opened a great, red mouth and said in a growling voice:

"Who's there? Who's there? Stand still, stranger, and tell me who you are."

"If you please, sir," said Edmund, trembling so that he could hardly speak, "my name is Edmund, and I'm the Son of Adam that Her Majesty met in the wood the other day and I've come to bring her the news that my brother and sisters are now in Narnia – quite close in the Beavers' house. She – she wanted to see them."

"I will tell Her Majesty," said the Wolf. "Meanwhile, stand still on the threshold, as you value your life." Then it vanished into the house.

Edmund stood and waited, his fingers aching with cold and his heart pounding in his chest, and presently the grey wolf, Maugrim, the Chief of the Witch's Secret Police, came bounding back and said, "Come in! Come in! Fortunate favourite of the Queen – or else not so fortunate."

And Edmund went in, taking great care not to tread on the Wolf's paws.

He found himself in a long gloomy hall with many pillars, full, as the courtyard had been, of statues. The one nearest the door was a little faun with a very sad expression on its face, and Edmund couldn't help wondering if this might be Lucy's friend. The only light came from a single lamp and close beside this sat the White Witch.

"I'm come, your Majesty," said Edmund, rushing eagerly forward.

"How dare you come alone?" said the Witch in a terrible

voice. "Did I not tell you to bring the others with you?"

"Please, your Majesty," said Edmund, "I've done the best I can. I've brought them quite close. They're in the little house on top of the dam just up the river – with Mr and Mrs Beaver."

A slow cruel smile came over the Witch's face.

"Is this all your news?" she asked.

"No, your Majesty," said Edmund, and proceeded to tell her all he had heard before leaving the Beavers' house.

"What! Aslan?" cried the Queen, "Aslan! Is this true? If I find you have lied to me –"

"Please, I'm only repeating what they said," stammered Edmund.

But the Queen, who was no longer attending to him, clapped her hands. Instantly the same dwarf whom Edmund had seen with her before appeared.

"Make ready our sledge," ordered the Witch, "and use the harness without bells."

CHAPTER TEN

THE SPELL BEGINS TO BREAK

Now we must go back to Mr and Mrs Beaver and the three other children. As soon as Mr Beaver said, "There's no time to lose," everyone began bundling themselves into coats, except Mrs Beaver, who started picking up sacks and laying them on the table and said: "Now, Mr Beaver, just reach down that ham. And here's a packet of tea, and there's sugar, and some matches. And if someone will get two or three loaves out of the crock over there in the corner."

"What *are* you doing, Mrs Beaver?" exclaimed Susan.

"Packing a load for each of us, dearie," said Mrs Beaver very coolly. "You didn't think we'd set out on a journey with nothing to eat, did you?"

"But we haven't time!" said Susan, buttoning the collar of her coat. "She may be here any minute."

"That's what I say," chimed in Mr Beaver.

"Get along with you all," said his wife. "Think it over, Mr Beaver. She can't be here for quarter of an hour at least."

"But don't we want as big a start as we can possibly get," said Peter, "if we're to reach the Stone Table before her?"

"You've got to remember *that*, Mrs Beaver," said Susan. "As soon as she has looked in here and finds we're gone she'll be off at top speed."

"That she will," said Mrs Beaver. "But we can't get there

before her whatever we do, for she'll be on a sledge and we'll be walking."

"Then – have we no hope?" said Susan.

"Now don't you get fussing, there's a dear," said Mrs Beaver, "but just get half a dozen clean handkerchiefs out of the drawer. 'Course we've got a hope. We can't get there *before* her but we can keep under cover and go by ways she won't expect and perhaps we'll get through."

"That's true enough, Mrs Beaver," said her husband. "But it's time we were out of this."

"And don't *you* start fussing either, Mr Beaver," said his wife. "There. That's better. There's five loads and the smallest for the smallest of us: that's you, my dear," she added, looking at Lucy.

"Oh, do please come on," said Lucy.

"Well, I'm nearly ready now," answered Mrs Beaver at last, allowing her husband to help her into her snow-boots. "I suppose the sewing machine's too heavy to bring?"

"Yes. It *is*," said Mr Beaver. "A great deal too heavy. And you don't think you'll be able to use it while we're on the run, I suppose?" "I can't abide the thought of that Witch fiddling with it," said Mrs Beaver, "and breaking it or stealing it, as likely as not."

"Oh, please, please, please, do hurry!" said the three children. And so at last they all got outside and Mr Beaver locked the door ("It'll delay her a bit," he said) and they set off, all carrying their loads over their shoulders.

The snow had stopped and the moon had come out when they began their journey. They went in single file – first Mr Beaver, then Lucy, then Peter, then Susan, and Mrs Beaver last of all. Mr Beaver led them across the dam and on to the right bank of the river and then along a very rough sort of path among the trees right down by the river-bank. The sides of the valley, shining in the moonlight, towered up far above them on either hand. "Best keep down here as much as possible," he said. "She'll have to keep to the top, for you couldn't bring a sledge down here."

It would have been a pretty enough scene to look at it through a window from a comfortable armchair; and even as things were, Lucy enjoyed it at first. But as they went on walking and walking – and walking – and as the sack she was carrying felt heavier and heavier, she began to wonder how she was going to keep up at all. And she stopped looking at the dazzling brightness of the frozen river with all its waterfalls of ice and at the white masses of the tree-tops and the great glaring moon and the countless stars and could only watch the little short legs of Mr Beaver going pad-pad-pad-pad through the snow in front of her as if they were never going to stop. Then the moon disappeared and the snow began to fall once more. And at last Lucy was so tired that she was almost asleep and walking at the same time when suddenly she found that Mr Beaver had turned away from the river-bank to the right and was leading them steeply uphill into the very thickest bushes. And then as she came fully awake she found that Mr Beaver was just vanishing into a little hole in the bank which had been almost hidden under the bushes until you were quite on top of it. In fact, by the time she realized what was happening, only his short flat tail was showing.

Lucy immediately stooped down and crawled in after him. Then she heard noises of scrambling and puffing and panting behind her and in a moment all five of them were inside.

"Wherever is this?" said Peter's voice, sounding tired and pale in the darkness. (I hope you know what I mean by a voice sounding pale.)

"It's an old hiding-place for beavers in bad times," said Mr Beaver, "and a great secret. It's not much of a place but we must get a few hours' sleep."

"If you hadn't all been in such a plaguey fuss when we were starting, I'd have brought some pillows," said Mrs Beaver.

It wasn't nearly such a nice cave as Mr Tumnus's, Lucy thought – just a hole in the ground but dry and earthy. It was very small so that when they all lay down they were all a bundle of clothes together, and what with that and being warmed up by their long walk they were really rather snug. If only the floor of the cave had been a little smoother! Then Mrs Beaver handed round in the dark a little flask out of which everyone drank something – it made one cough and splutter a little and stung the throat, but it also made you feel deliciously warm after you'd swallowed it – and everyone went straight to sleep.

It seemed to Lucy only the next minute (though really it was hours and hours later) when she woke up feeling a little cold and dreadfully stiff and thinking how she would like a hot bath.

Then she felt a set of long whiskers tickling her cheek and saw the cold daylight coming in through the mouth of the cave. But immediately after that she was very wide awake indeed, and so was everyone else. In fact they were all sitting up with their mouths and eyes wide open listening to a sound which was the very sound they'd all been thinking of (and sometimes imagining they heard) during their walk last night. It was a sound of jingling bells.

Mr Beaver was out of the cave like a flash the moment he heard it. Perhaps you think, as Lucy thought for a moment, that this was a very silly thing to do? But it was really a very sensible one. He knew he could scramble to the top of the bank among bushes and brambles without being seen; and he wanted above all things to see which way the Witch's sledge went. The others all sat in the cave waiting and wondering. They waited nearly five minutes. Then they heard something that frightened them very much. They heard voices. "Oh," thought Lucy, "he's been seen. She's caught him!" Great was their surprise when a little later, they heard Mr Beaver's voice calling to them from just outside the cave.

"It's all right," he was shouting. "Come out, Mrs Beaver. Come out, Sons and Daughters of Adam. It's all right! It isn't *Her*!" This was bad grammar of course, but that is how beavers talk when they are excited; I mean, in Narnia – in our world they usually don't talk at all.

So Mrs Beaver and the children came bundling out of the cave, all blinking in the daylight, and with earth all over them, and looking very frowsty and unbrushed and uncombed and with the sleep in their eyes.

"Come on!" cried Mr Beaver, who was almost dancing with delight. "Come and see! This is a nasty knock for the Witch! It looks as if her power is already crumbling."

"What *do* you mean, Mr Beaver?" panted Peter as they all scrambled up the steep bank of the valley together.

"Didn't I tell you," answered Mr Beaver, "that she'd made it always winter and never Christmas? Didn't I tell you? Well, just come and see!"

And then they were all at the top and did see.

It *was* a sledge, and it *was* reindeer with bells on their harness. But they were far bigger than the Witch's reindeer, and they were not white but brown. And on the sledge sat a person whom everyone knew the moment they set eyes on him. He was a huge man in a bright red robe (bright as hollyberries) with a hood that had fur inside it and a great white beard that fell like a foamy waterfall over his chest. Everyone knew him because, though you see people of his sort only in Narnia, you see pictures of them and hear them talked about even in our world – the world on this side of the wardrobe door. But when you really see them in Narnia it is rather different. Some of the pictures of Father Christmas in our world make him look only funny and jolly. But now that the children actually stood looking at him they didn't find it quite like that. He was so big, and so glad, and so real, that they all became quite still. They felt very glad, but also solemn.

"I've come at last," said he. "She has kept me out for a long time, but I have got in at last. Aslan is on the move. The Witch's magic is weakening."

And Lucy felt running through her that deep shiver of

gladness which you only get if you are being solemn and still.

"And now," said Father Christmas, "for your presents. There is a new and better sewing machine for you, Mrs Beaver. I will drop it in your house as I pass."

"If you please, sir," said Mrs Beaver, making a curtsey. "It's locked up."

"Locks and bolts make no difference to me," said Father Christmas. "And as for you, Mr Beaver, when you get home you will find your dam finished and mended and all the leaks stopped and a new sluice-gate fitted."

Mr Beaver was so pleased that he opened his mouth very wide and then found he couldn't say anything at all.

"Peter, Adam's Son," said Father Christmas.

"Here, sir," said Peter.

"These are your presents," was the answer, "and they are tools not toys. The time to use them is perhaps near at hand. Bear them well." With these words he handed to Peter a shield and a sword. The shield was the colour of silver and across it there ramped a red lion, as bright as a ripe strawberry at the moment when you pick it. The hilt of the sword was of gold and it had a sheath and a sword belt and everything it needed, and it was just the right size and weight for Peter to use. Peter was silent and solemn as he received these gifts, for he felt they were a very serious kind of present.

"Susan, Eve's Daughter," said Father Christmas. "These are for you," and he handed her a bow and a quiver full of arrows and a little ivory horn. "You must use the bow only in great need," he said, "for I do not mean you to fight in the battle. It does not easily miss. And when you put this horn to your

'Peter was silent and solemn as he received these gifts'

lips and blow it, then, wherever you are, I think help of some kind will come to you."

Last of all he said, "Lucy, Eve's Daughter," and Lucy came forward. He gave her a little bottle of what looked like glass (but people said afterwards that it was made of diamond) and a small dagger. "In this bottle," he said, "there is a cordial made of the juice of one of the fire-flowers that grow in the mountains of the sun. If you or any of your friends is hurt, a few drops of this will restore them. And the dagger is to defend yourself at great need. For you also are not to be in the battle."

"Why, sir?" said Lucy. "I think – I don't know – but I think I could be brave enough."

"That is not the point," he said. "But battles are ugly when women fight. And now" – here he suddenly looked less grave – "here is something for the moment for you all!" and he brought out (I suppose from the big bag at his back, but nobody quite saw him do it) a large tray containing five cups and saucers, a bowl of lump sugar, a jug of cream, and a great big teapot all sizzling and piping hot. Then he cried out "Merry Christmas! Long live the true King!" and cracked his whip, and he and the reindeer and the sledge and all were out of sight before anyone realized that they had started.

Peter had just drawn his sword out of its sheath and was showing it to Mr Beaver, when Mrs Beaver said:

"Now then, now then! Don't stand talking there till the tea's got cold. Just like men. Come and help to carry the tray down and we'll have breakfast. What a mercy I thought of bringing the bread-knife."

So down the steep bank they went and back to the cave,

and Mr Beaver cut some of the bread and ham into sandwiches and Mrs Beaver poured out the tea and everyone enjoyed themselves. But long before they had finished enjoying themselves Mr Beaver said, "Time to be moving on now."

CHAPTER ELEVEN

ASLAN IS NEARER

Edmund meanwhile had been having a most disappointing time. When the dwarf had gone to get the sledge ready he expected that the Witch would start being nice to him, as she had been at their last meeting. But she said nothing at all. And when at last Edmund plucked up his courage to say, "Please, your Majesty, could I have some Turkish Delight? You – you – said –" she answered, "Silence, fool!" Then she appeared to change her mind and said, as if to herself, "And yet it will not do to have the brat fainting on the way," and once more clapped her hands. Another dwarf appeared.

"Bring the human creature food and drink," she said.

The dwarf went away and presently returned bringing an iron bowl with some water in it and an iron plate with a hunk of dry bread on it. He grinned in a repulsive manner as he set them down on the floor beside Edmund and said: "Turkish Delight for the little Prince. Ha! Ha! Ha!"

"Take it away," said Edmund sulkily. "I don't want dry bread." But the Witch suddenly turned on him with such a terrible expression on her face that he apologized and began to nibble at the bread, though it was so stale he could hardly get it down.

"You may be glad enough of it before you taste bread again," said the Witch.

While he was still chewing away the first dwarf came back and announced that the sledge was ready. The White Witch rose and went out, ordering Edmund to go with her. The snow was again falling as they came into the courtyard, but she took no notice of that and made Edmund sit beside her on the sledge. But before they drove off she called Maugrim and he came bounding like an enormous dog to the side of the sledge.

"Take with you the swiftest of your wolves and go at once to the house of the Beavers," said the Witch, "and kill whatever you find there. If they are already gone, then make all speed to the Stone Table, but do not be seen. Wait for me there in hiding. I meanwhile must go many miles to the West before I find a place where I can drive across the river. You may overtake these humans before they reach the Stone Table. You will know what to do if you find them!"

"I hear and obey, O Queen," growled the Wolf, and immediately he shot away into the snow and darkness, as quickly as a horse can gallop. In a few minutes he had called another wolf and was with him down on the dam sniffing at the Beavers' house. But of course they found it empty. It would have been a dreadful thing for the Beavers and the children if the night had remained fine, for the wolves would then have been able to follow their trail – and ten to one would have overtaken them before they had got to the cave. But now that the snow had begun again the scent was cold and even the footprints were covered up.

Meanwhile the dwarf whipped up the reindeer, and the Witch and Edmund drove out under the archway and on and away into the darkness and the cold. This was a terrible journey for Edmund, who had no coat. Before they had been going quarter of an hour all the front of him was covered with snow – he soon stopped trying to shake it off because, as quickly as he did that, a new lot gathered, and he was so tired. Soon he was wet to the skin. And oh, how miserable he was! It didn't look now as if the Witch intended to make him a King. All the things he had said to make himself believe that she was good and kind and that her side was really the right side sounded to him silly now. He would have given anything to meet the others at this moment – even Peter! The only way to comfort himself now was to try to believe that the whole thing was a dream and that he might wake up at any moment. And as they went on, hour after hour, it did come to seem like a dream.

This lasted longer than I could describe even if I wrote pages and pages about it. But I will skip on to the time when the snow had stopped and the morning had come and they were racing along in the daylight. And still they went on and on, with no sound but the everlasting swish of the snow and the creaking of the reindeer's harness. And then at last the Witch said, "What have we here? Stop!" and they did.

How Edmund hoped she was going to say something about breakfast! But she had stopped for quite a different reason. A little way off at the foot of a tree sat a merry party, a squirrel and his wife with their children and two satyrs and a dwarf and an old dog-fox, all on stools round a table. Edmund couldn't quite see what they were eating, but it smelled lovely and there seemed to be decorations of holly and he wasn't at all sure that he didn't see something like a plum pudding. At the moment when the sledge stopped, the Fox, who was obviously the oldest person present, had just risen to its feet, holding a glass in its right paw as if it was going to say something. But when the whole party saw the sledge stopping and who was in it, all the gaiety went out of their faces. The father squirrel stopped eating with his fork half-way to his mouth and one of the satyrs stopped with its fork actually in its mouth, and the baby squirrels squeaked with terror.

"What is the meaning of this?" asked the Witch Queen. Nobody answered.

"Speak, vermin!" she said again. "Or do you want my dwarf to find you a tongue with his whip? What is the meaning of all this gluttony, this waste, this self-indulgence? Where did you get all these things?"

"Please, your Majesty," said the Fox, "we were given them. And if I might make so bold as to drink your Majesty's very good health – "

"Who gave them to you?" said the Witch.

"F-F-F-Father Christmas," stammered the Fox.

"What?" roared the Witch, springing from the sledge and taking a few strides nearer to the terrified animals. "He has not been here! He cannot have been here! How dare you – but no. Say you have been lying and you shall even now be forgiven."

At that moment one of the young squirrels lost its head completely.

"He has – he has – he has!" it squeaked, beating its little spoon on the table. Edmund saw the Witch bite her lips so that a drop of blood appeared on her white cheek. Then she raised her wand. "Oh, don't, don't, please don't," shouted Edmund, but even while he was shouting she had waved her wand and instantly where the merry party had been there were only statues of creatures (one with its stone fork fixed forever half-way to its stone mouth) seated round a stone table on which there were stone plates and a stone plum pudding.

"As for you," said the Witch, giving Edmund a stunning blow on the face as she re-mounted the sledge, "let that teach you to ask favour for spies and traitors. Drive on!" And Edmund for the first time in this story felt sorry for someone besides himself. It seemed so pitiful to think of those little stone figures sitting there all the silent days and all the dark nights, year after year, till the moss grew on them and at last even their faces crumbled away.

Now they were steadily racing on again. And soon Edmund noticed that the snow which splashed against them as they rushed through it was much wetter than it had been all last night. At the same time he noticed that he was feeling much less cold. It was also becoming foggy. In fact every minute it grew foggier and warmer. And the sledge was not running nearly as well as it had been running up till now. At first he thought this was because the reindeer were tired, but soon he saw that that couldn't be the real reason. The sledge jerked, and skidded and kept on jolting as if it had struck against stones. And however the dwarf whipped the poor reindeer the sledge went slower and slower. There also seemed to be a curious noise all round them, but the noise of their driving and jolting and the dwarf's shouting at the reindeer prevented Edmund from hearing what it was, until suddenly the sledge stuck so fast that it wouldn't go on at all. When that happened there was a moment's silence. And in that silence Edmund could at last listen to the other noise properly. A strange, sweet, rustling, chattering noise – and yet not so strange, for he'd heard it before – if only he could remember where! Then all at once he did remember. It was the noise of running water. All round them though out of sight, there were streams, chattering, murmuring, bubbling, splashing and even (in the distance) roaring. And his heart gave a great leap (though he hardly knew why) when he realized that the frost was over. And much nearer there was a drip-drip-drip from the branches of all the trees. And then, as he looked at one tree he saw a great load of snow slide off it and for the first time since he had entered Narnia he saw the dark green of a fir tree. But he hadn't time to listen or watch any longer, for the Witch said:

"Don't sit staring, fool! Get out and help."

And of course Edmund had to obey. He stepped out into the snow – but it was really only slush by now – and began helping the dwarf to get the sledge out of the muddy hole it had got into. They got it out in the end, and by being very cruel to the reindeer the dwarf managed to get it on the move again, and they drove a little further. And now the snow was really melting in earnest and patches of green grass were beginning to appear in every direction. Unless you have looked at a world of snow as long as Edmund had been looking at it, you will hardly be able to imagine what a relief those green patches were after the endless white. Then the sledge stopped again.

"It's no good, your Majesty," said the dwarf. "We can't sledge in this thaw."

"Then we must walk," said the Witch.

"We shall never overtake them walking," growled the dwarf. "Not with the start they've got."

"Are you my counsellor or my slave?" said the Witch. "Do as you're told. Tie the hands of the human creature behind it and keep hold of the end of the rope. And take your whip. And cut the harness of the reindeer; they'll find their own way home."

The dwarf obeyed, and in a few minutes Edmund found himself being forced to walk as fast as he could with his hands tied behind him. He kept on slipping in the slush and mud and wet grass, and every time he slipped the dwarf gave him a curse and sometimes a flick with the whip. The Witch walked behind the dwarf and kept on saying, "Faster! Faster!"

Every moment the patches of green grew bigger and the patches of snow grew smaller. Every moment more and more of the trees shook off their robes of snow. Soon, wherever you looked, instead of white shapes you saw the dark green of firs or the black prickly branches of bare oaks and beeches and elms. Then the mist turned from white to gold and presently cleared away altogether. Shafts of delicious sunlight struck down on to the forest floor and overhead you could see a blue sky between the tree tops.

Soon there were more wonderful things happening. Coming suddenly round a corner into a glade of silver birch trees Edmund saw the ground covered in all directions with little yellow flowers – celandines. The noise of water grew louder. Presently they actually crossed a stream. Beyond it they found snowdrops growing.

"Mind your own business!" said the dwarf when he saw that Edmund had turned his head to look at them; and he gave the rope a vicious jerk.

But of course this didn't prevent Edmund from seeing. Only five minutes later he noticed a dozen crocuses growing round the foot of an old tree – gold and purple and white. Then came a sound even more delicious than the sound of the water. Close beside the path they were following a bird suddenly chirped from the branch of a tree. It was answered by the chuckle of another bird a little further off. And then, as if that had been a signal, there was chattering and chirruping in every direction, and then a moment of full song, and within five minutes the whole wood was ringing with birds' music, and wherever Edmund's eyes turned he saw birds alighting on branches, or sailing overhead or chasing one another or having their little quarrels or tidying up their feathers with their beaks.

"Faster! Faster!" said the Witch.

There was no trace of the fog now. The sky became bluer and bluer, and now there were white clouds hurrying across it from time to time. In the wide glades there were primroses. A light breeze sprang up which scattered drops of moisture from the swaying branches and carried cool, delicious scents against the faces of the travellers. The trees began to come fully alive. The larches and birches were covered with green, the laburnums with gold. Soon the beech trees had put forth their delicate, transparent leaves. As the travellers walked under them the light also became green. A bee buzzed across their path.

"This is no thaw," said the dwarf, suddenly stopping. "This is *Spring*. What are we to do? Your winter has been destroyed, I tell you! This is Aslan's doing."

"If either of you mention that name again," said the Witch, "he shall instantly be killed."

'as if that had been a signal, there was chattering and chirruping in every direction'

CHAPTER TWELVE

PETER'S FIRST BATTLE

While the dwarf and the White Witch were saying this, miles away the Beavers and the children were walking on hour after hour into what seemed a delicious dream. Long ago they had left the coats behind them. And by now they had even stopped saying to one another, "Look! there's a kingfisher," or "I say, bluebells!" or "What was that lovely smell?" or "Just listen to that thrush!" They walked on in silence drinking it all in, passing through patches of warm sunlight into cool, green thickets and out again into wide mossy glades where tall elms raised the leafy roof far overhead, and then into dense masses of flowering currant and among hawthorn bushes where the sweet smell was almost overpowering.

They had been just as surprised as Edmund when they saw the winter vanishing and the whole wood passing in a few hours or so from January to May. They hadn't even known for certain (as the Witch did) that this was what would happen when Aslan came to Narnia. But they all knew that it was her spells which had produced the endless winter; and therefore they all knew when this magic spring began that something had gone wrong, and badly wrong, with the Witch's schemes. And after the thaw had been going on for some time they all realized that the Witch would no longer be able to use her sledge. After that they didn't hurry so much and they allowed themselves more rests and longer ones. They were pretty tired by now of course; but not what I'd call bitterly tired – only slow and feeling very dreamy and quiet inside as one does when one is coming to the end of a long day in the open. Susan had a slight blister on one heel.

They had left the course of the big river some time ago; for one had to turn a little to the right (that meant a little to the south) to reach the place of the Stone Table. Even if this had not been their way they couldn't have kept to the river valley once the thaw began, for with all that melting snow the river was soon in flood – a wonderful, roaring, thundering yellow flood – and their path would have been under water.

And now the sun got low and the light got redder and the shadows got longer and the flowers began to think about closing.

"Not long now," said Mr Beaver, and began leading them uphill across some very deep, springy moss (it felt nice under their tired feet) in a place where only tall trees grew, very wide apart. The climb, coming at the end of the long day, made them all pant and blow. And just as Lucy was wondering whether she could really get to the top without another long rest, suddenly they *were* at the top. And this is what they saw.

They were on a green open space from which you could look down on the forest spreading as far as one could see in every direction – except right ahead. There, far to the East, was something twinkling and moving. "By gum!" whispered Peter to Susan, "the sea!" In the very middle of this open hill-top was the Stone Table. It was a great grim slab of grey stone supported on four upright stones. It looked very old; and it was cut all over with strange lines and figures that might be the letters of an unknown language. They gave you a curious feeling when you looked at them. The next thing they saw was a pavilion pitched on one side of the open place. A wonderful pavilion it was – and especially now when the light of the setting sun fell upon it – with sides of what looked like yellow silk and cords of crimson and tent-pegs of ivory; and high above it on a pole a banner which bore a red rampant lion fluttering in the breeze which was blowing in their faces from the far-off sea. While they were looking at this they heard a sound of music on their right; and turning in that direction they saw what they had come to see.

Aslan stood in the centre of a crowd of creatures who had grouped themselves round him in the shape of a half-moon. There were Tree-Women there and Well-Women (Dryads and Naiads as they used to be called in our world) who had stringed instruments; it was they who had made the music. There were four great centaurs. The horse part of them was like huge English farm horses, and the man part was like stern but beautiful giants. There was also a unicorn, and a bull with the head of a man, and a pelican, and an eagle, and a great Dog. And next to Aslan stood two leopards of whom one carried his crown and the other his standard.

But as for Aslan himself, the Beavers and the children didn't know what to do or say when they saw him. People who have not been in Narnia sometimes think that a thing cannot be good and terrible at the same time. If the children had ever thought so, they were cured of it now. For when they tried to look at Aslan's face they just caught a glimpse of the golden mane and

'Aslan stood in the centre of a crowd of creatures who had grouped themselves round him'

the great, royal, solemn, overwhelming eyes; and then they found they couldn't look at him and went all trembly.

"Go on," whispered Mr Beaver.

"No," whispered Peter, "you first."

"No, Sons of Adam before animals," whispered Mr Beaver back again.

"Susan," whispered Peter, "What about you? Ladies first."

"No, you're the eldest," whispered Susan. And of course the longer they went on doing this the more awkward they felt. Then at last Peter realized that it was up to him. He drew his sword and raised it to the salute and hastily saying to the others "Come on. Pull yourselves together," he advanced to the Lion and said:

"We have come – Aslan."

"Welcome, Peter, Son of Adam," said Aslan. "Welcome, Susan and Lucy, Daughters of Eve. Welcome He-Beaver and She-Beaver."

His voice was deep and rich and somehow took the fidgets out of them. They now felt glad and quiet and it didn't seem awkward to them to stand and say nothing.

"But where is the fourth?" asked Aslan.

"He has tried to betray them and joined the White Witch, O Aslan," said Mr Beaver. And then something made Peter say,

"That was partly my fault, Aslan. I was angry with him and I think that helped him to go wrong."

And Aslan said nothing either to excuse Peter or to blame him but merely stood looking at him with his great unchanging eyes. And it seemed to all of them that there was nothing to be said.

"Please – Aslan," said Lucy, "can anything be done to save Edmund?"

"All shall be done," said Aslan. "But it may be harder than you think." And then he was silent again for some time. Up to that moment Lucy had been thinking how royal and strong and peaceful his face looked; now it suddenly came into her head that he looked sad as well. But next minute that expression was quite gone. The Lion shook his mane and clapped his paws together ("Terrible paws," thought Lucy, "if he didn't know how to velvet them!") and said,

"Meanwhile, let the feast be prepared. Ladies, take these Daughters of Eve to the pavilion and minister to them."

When the girls had gone Aslan laid his paw – and though it was velveted it was very heavy – on Peter's shoulder and said, "Come, Son of Adam, and I will show you a far-off sight of the castle where you are to be King."

And Peter with his sword still drawn in his hand went with the Lion to the eastern edge of the hilltop. There a beautiful sight met their eyes. The sun was setting behind their backs. That meant that the whole country below them lay in the evening light – forest and hills and valleys and, winding away like a silver snake, the lower part of the great river. And beyond all this, miles away, was the sea, and beyond the sea the sky, full of clouds which were just turning rose colour with the reflection of the sunset. But just where the land of Narnia met the sea – in fact, at the mouth of the great river – there was something on a little hill, shining. It was shining because it was a castle and of course the sunlight was reflected from all the windows which looked towards Peter and the sunset; but to Peter it looked like a great star resting on the seashore.

"That, O Man," said Aslan, "is Cair Paravel of the four thrones, in one of which you must sit as King. I show it to you because you are the first-born and you will be High King over all the rest."

And once more Peter said nothing, for at that moment a

strange noise woke the silence suddenly. It was like a bugle, but richer.

"It is your sister's horn," said Aslan to Peter in a low voice; so low as to be almost a purr, if it is not disrespectful to think of a Lion purring.

For a moment Peter did not understand. Then, when he saw all the other creatures start forward and heard Aslan say with a wave of his paw, "Back! Let the Prince win his spurs," he did understand, and set off running as hard as he could to the pavilion. And there he saw a dreadful sight.

The Naiads and Dryads were scattering in every direction. Lucy was running towards him as fast as her short legs would carry her and her face was as white as paper. Then he saw Susan make a dash for a tree, and swing herself up, followed by a huge grey beast. At first Peter thought it was a bear. Then he saw that it looked like an Alsatian, though it was far too big to be a dog. Then he realized that it was a wolf – a wolf standing on its hind legs, with its front paws against the tree-trunk, snapping and snarling. All the hair on its back stood up on end. Susan had not been able to get higher than the second big branch. One of her legs hung down so that her foot was only an inch or two above the snapping teeth. Peter wondered why she did not get higher or at least take a better grip; then he realized that she was just going to faint and that if she fainted she would fall off.

Peter did not feel very brave; indeed, he felt he was going to be sick. But that made no difference to what he had to do. He rushed straight up to the monster and aimed a slash of his sword at its side. That stroke never reached the Wolf. Quick as lightning it turned round, its eyes flaming, and its mouth wide open in a howl of anger. If it had not been so angry that it simply had to howl it would have got him by the throat at once. As it was – though all this happened too quickly for Peter to think at all – he had just time to duck down and plunge his sword, as hard as he could, between the brute's forelegs into its heart. Then came a horrible, confused moment like something in a nightmare. He was tugging and pulling and the Wolf seemed neither alive nor dead, and its bared teeth knocked against his forehead, and everything was blood and heat and hair. A moment later he found that the monster lay dead and he had drawn his sword out of it and was straightening his back and rubbing the sweat off his face and out of his eyes. He felt tired all over.

Then, after a bit, Susan came down the tree. She and Peter felt pretty shaky when they met and I won't say there wasn't kissing and crying on both sides. But in Narnia no one thinks any the worse of you for that.

"Quick! Quick!" shouted the voice of Aslan. "Centaurs! Eagles! I see another wolf in the thickets. There – behind you. He has just darted away. After him, all of you. He will be going to his mistress. Now is your chance to find the Witch and rescue the fourth Son of Adam." And instantly with a thunder of hoofs and beating of wings a dozen or so of the swiftest creatures disappeared into the gathering darkness.

Peter, still out of breath, turned and saw Aslan close at hand.

"You have forgotten to clean your sword," said Aslan.

It was true. Peter blushed when he looked at the bright

blade and saw it all smeared with the Wolf's hair and blood. He stooped down and wiped it quite clean on the grass, and then wiped it quite dry on his coat.

"Hand it to me and kneel, Son of Adam," said Aslan. And when Peter had done so he struck him with the flat of the blade and said, "Rise up, Sir Peter Wolf's-Bane. And, whatever happens, never forget to wipe your sword."

CHAPTER THIRTEEN

DEEP MAGIC FROM THE DAWN OF TIME

Now we must get back to Edmund. When he had been made to walk far further than he had ever known that anybody *could* walk, the Witch at last halted in a dark valley all overshadowed with fir trees and yew trees. Edmund simply sank down and lay on his face doing nothing at all and not even caring what was going to happen next provided they would let him lie still. He was too tired even to notice how hungry and thirsty he was. The Witch and the dwarf were talking close beside him in low tones.

"No," said the dwarf, "it is no use now, O Queen. They must have reached the Stone Table by now."

"Perhaps the Wolf will smell us out and bring us news," said the Witch.

"It cannot be good news if he does," said the dwarf.

"Four thrones in Cair Paravel," said the Witch. "How if only three were filled? That would not fulfil the prophecy."

"What difference would that make now that *He* is here?" said the dwarf. He did not dare, even now, to mention the name of Aslan to his mistress.

"He may not stay long. And then – we would fall upon the three at Cair."

"Yet it might be better," said the dwarf, "to keep this one" (here he kicked Edmund) "for bargaining with."

"Yes! and have him rescued," said the Witch scornfully.

"Then," said the dwarf, "we had better do what we have to do at once."

"I would like to have it done on the Stone Table itself," said the Witch. "That is the proper place. That is where it has always been done before."

"It will be a long time now before the Stone Table can again be put to its proper use," said the dwarf.

"True," said the Witch; and then, "Well, I will begin."

At that moment with a rush and a snarl a Wolf rushed up to them.

"I have seen them. They are all at the Stone Table, with Him. They have killed my captain, Maugrim. I was hidden in the thickets and saw it all. One of the Sons of Adam killed him. Fly! Fly!"

"No," said the Witch. "There need be no flying. Go quickly. Summon all our people to meet me here as speedily as they can. Call out the giants and the werewolves and the spirits of those trees who are on our side. Call the Ghouls, and the Boggles, the Ogres and the Minotaurs. Call the Cruels, the Hags, the Spectres, and the people of the Toadstools. We will fight. What? Have I not still my wand? Will not their ranks turn into stone even as they come on? Be off quickly, I have a little thing to finish here while you are away."

The great brute bowed its head, turned, and galloped away.

"Now!" she said, "we have no table – let me see. We had better put it against the trunk of a tree."

Edmund found himself being roughly forced to his feet. Then the dwarf set him with his back against a tree and bound him

'At that very moment he heard loud shouts from every direction'

fast. He saw the Witch take off her outer mantle. Her arms were bare underneath it and terribly white. Because they were so very white he could see them, but he could not see much else, it was so dark in this valley under the dark trees.

"Prepare the victim," said the Witch. And the dwarf undid Edmund's collar and folded back his shirt at the neck. Then he took Edmund's hair and pulled his head back so that he had to raise his chin. After that Edmund heard a strange noise – whizz – whizz – whizz. For a moment he couldn't think what it was. Then he realized. It was the sound of a knife being sharpened.

At that very moment he heard loud shouts from every direction – a drumming of hoofs and a beating of wings – a scream from the Witch – confusion all round him. And then he found he was being untied. Strong arms were round him and he heard big, kind voices saying things like –

"Let him lie down – give him some wine – drink this – steady now – you'll be all right in a minute."

Then he heard the voices of people who were not talking to him but to one another. And they were saying things like "Who's got the Witch?" "I thought you had her." "I didn't see her after I knocked the knife out of her hand – I was after the dwarf – do you mean to say she's escaped?" "– A chap can't mind everything at once – what's that? Oh, sorry, it's only an old stump!" But just at this point Edmund went off in a dead faint.

Presently the centaurs and unicorns and deer and birds (they were of course the rescue party which Aslan had sent in the last chapter) all set off to go back to the Stone Table, carrying

Edmund with them. But if they could have seen what happened in that valley after they had gone, I think they might have been surprised.

It was perfectly still and presently the moon grew bright; if you had been there you would have seen the moonlight shining on an old tree-stump and on a fair-sized boulder. But if you had gone on looking you would gradually have begun to think there was something odd about both the stump and the boulder. And next you would have thought that the stump did look really remarkably like a little fat man crouching on the ground. And if you had watched long enough you would have seen the stump walk across to the boulder and the boulder sit up and begin talking to the stump; for in reality the stump and the boulder were simply the Witch and the dwarf. For it was part of her magic that she could make things look like what they aren't, and she had the presence of mind to do so at the very moment when the knife was knocked out of her hand. She had kept hold of her wand, so it had been kept safe, too.

When the other children woke up next morning (they had been sleeping on piles of cushions in the pavilion) the first thing they heard – from Mrs Beaver – was that their brother had been rescued and brought into camp late last night; and was at that moment with Aslan. As soon as they had breakfasted they all went out, and there they saw Aslan and Edmund walking together in the dewy grass, apart from the rest of the court. There is no need to tell you (and no one ever heard) what Aslan was saying, but it was a conversation which Edmund never forgot. As the others drew nearer Aslan turned to meet them, bringing Edmund with him.

"Here is your brother," he said, "and – there is no need to talk to him about what is past."

Edmund shook hands with each of the others and said to each of them in turn, "I'm sorry," and everyone said, "That's all right." And then everyone wanted very hard to say something which would make it quite clear that they were all friends with him again – something ordinary and natural – and of course no one could think of anything in the world to say. But before they had time to feel really awkward one of the leopards approached Aslan and said,

"Sire, there is a messenger from the enemy who craves audience."

"Let him approach," said Aslan.

The leopard went away and soon returned leading the Witch's dwarf.

"What is your message, Son of Earth?" asked Aslan.

"The Queen of Narnia and Empress of the Lone Islands desires a safe conduct to come and speak with you," said the dwarf, "on a matter which is as much to your advantage as to hers."

"Queen of Narnia, indeed!" said Mr Beaver. "Of all the cheek –"

"Peace, Beaver," said Aslan. "All names will soon be restored to their proper owners. In the meantime we will not dispute about them. Tell your mistress, Son of Earth, that I grant her safe conduct on condition that she leaves her wand behind her at that greak oak."

This was agreed to and two leopards went back with the dwarf to see that the conditions were properly carried out. "But supposing she turns the two leopards into stone?" whispered Lucy to Peter. I think the same idea had occurred to the leopards themselves; at any rate, as they walked off their fur was all standing up on their backs and their tails were bristling – like a cat's when it sees a strange dog.

"It'll be all right," whispered Peter in reply. "He wouldn't send them if it weren't."

A few minutes later the Witch herself walked out on to the top of the hill and came straight across and stood before Aslan. The three children who had not seen her before felt shudders running down their backs at the sight of her face; and there were low growls among all the animals present. Though it was bright sunshine everyone felt suddenly cold. The only two people present who seemed to be quite at their ease were Aslan and the Witch herself. It was the oddest thing to see those two faces – the golden face and the dead-white face – so close together. Not that the Witch looked Aslan exactly in his eyes; Mrs Beaver particularly noticed this.

"You have a traitor there, Aslan," said the Witch. Of course everyone present knew that she meant Edmund. But Edmund had got past thinking about himself after all he'd been through and after the talk he'd had that morning. He just went on looking at Aslan. It didn't seem to matter what the Witch said.

"Well," said Aslan. "His offence was not against you."

"Have you forgotten the Deep Magic?" asked the Witch.

"Let us say I have forgotten it," answered Aslan gravely.

"Tell us of this Deep Magic."

"Tell you?" said the Witch, her voice growing suddenly shriller. "Tell you what is written on that very Table of Stone which stands beside us? Tell you what is written in letters deep as a spear is long on the fire-stones on the Secret Hill? Tell you what is engraved on the sceptre of the Emperor-beyond-the-Sea? You at least know the Magic which the Emperor put into Narnia at the very beginning. You know that every traitor belongs to me as my lawful prey and that for every treachery I have a right to a kill."

"Oh," said Mr Beaver. "So *that's* how you came to imagine yourself a queen – because you were the Emperor's hangman. I see."

"Peace, Beaver," said Aslan, with a very low growl.

"And so," continued the Witch, "that human creature is mine. His life is forfeit to me. His blood is my property."

"Come and take it then," said the Bull with the man's head in a great bellowing voice.

"Fool," said the Witch with a savage smile that was almost a snarl, "do you really think your master can rob me of my rights by mere force? He knows the Deep Magic better than that. He knows that unless I have blood as the Law says all Narnia will be overturned and perish in fire and water."

"It is very true," said Aslan, "I do not deny it."

"Oh, Aslan!" whispered Susan in the Lion's ear, "can't we – I mean, you won't, will you? Can't we do something about the Deep Magic? Isn't there something you can work against it?"

"Work against the Emperor's Magic?" said Aslan, turning to her with something like a frown on his face. And nobody ever made that suggestion to him again.

Edmund was on the other side of Aslan, looking all the time at Aslan's face. He felt a choking feeling and wondered if he ought to say something; but a moment later he felt that he was not expected to do anything except to wait, and do what he was told.

"Fall back, all of you," said Aslan, "and I will talk to the Witch alone."

They all obeyed. It was a terrible time this – waiting and wondering while the Lion and the Witch talked earnestly together in low voices. Lucy said, "Oh, Edmund!" and began to cry. Peter stood with his back to the others looking out at the distant sea. The Beavers stood holding each other's paws with their heads bowed. The centaurs stamped uneasily with their hoofs. But everyone became perfectly still in the end, so that you noticed even small sounds like a bumble-bee flying past, or the birds in the forest down below them, or the wind rustling the leaves. And still the talk between Aslan and the White Witch went on.

At last they heard Aslan's voice, "You can all come back," he said. "I have settled the matter. She has renounced the claim on your brother's blood." And all over the hill there was a noise as if everyone had been holding their breath and had now begun breathing again, and then a murmur of talk.

The Witch was just turning away with a look of fierce joy on her face when she stopped and said,

"But how do I know this promise will be kept?"

"Haa-a-arrh!" roared Aslan, half rising from his throne; and his great mouth opened wider and wider and the roar grew louder and louder, and the Witch, after staring for a moment with her lips wide apart, picked up her skirts and fairly ran for her life.

CHAPTER FOURTEEN

THE TRIUMPH OF THE WITCH

As soon as the Witch had gone Aslan said, "We must move from this place at once, it will be wanted for other purposes. We shall encamp tonight at the Fords of Beruna."

Of course everyone was dying to ask him how he had arranged matters with the witch; but his face was stern and everyone's ears were still ringing with the sound of his roar and so nobody dared.

After a meal, which was taken in the open air on the hill-top (for the sun had got strong by now and dried the grass), they were busy for a while taking the pavilion down and packing things up. Before two o'clock they were on the march and set off in a north-easterly direction, walking at an easy pace for they had not far to go.

During the first part of the journey Aslan explained to Peter his plan of campaign. "As soon as she has finished her business in these parts," he said, "the Witch and her crew will almost certainly fall back to her House and prepare for a siege. You may or may not be able to cut her off and prevent her from reaching it." He then went on to outline two plans of battle – one for fighting the Witch and her people in the wood and another for assaulting her castle. And all the time he was advising Peter how to conduct the operations, saying things like, "You must put your Centaurs in such and such a place" or "You must post scouts to see that she doesn't do so-and-so," till at last Peter said,

"But you will be there yourself, Aslan."

"I can give you no promise of that," answered the Lion. And he continued giving Peter his instructions.

For the last part of the journey it was Susan and Lucy who saw most of him. He did not talk very much and seemed to them to be sad.

It was still afternoon when they came down to a place where the river valley had widened out and the river was broad and shallow. This was the Fords of Beruna and Aslan gave orders to halt on this side of the water. But Peter said,

"Wouldn't it be better to camp on the far side – for fear she should try a night attack or anything?"

Aslan, who seemed to have been thinking about something else, roused himself with a shake of his magnificent mane and said, "Eh? What's that?" Peter said it all over again.

"No," said Aslan in a dull voice, as if it didn't matter. "No. She will not make an attack to-night." And then he sighed deeply. But presently he added, "All the same it was well thought of. That is how a soldier ought to think. But it doesn't really matter." So they proceeded to pitch their camp.

Aslan's mood affected everyone that evening. Peter was feeling uncomfortable too at the idea of fighting the battle on his own; the news that Aslan might not be there had come as a great shock to him. Supper that evening was a quiet meal. Everyone felt how different it had been last night or even that morning. It was as if the good times, having just begun, were already drawing to their end.

This feeling affected Susan so much that she couldn't get to sleep when she went to bed. And after she had lain counting sheep and turning over and over she heard Lucy give a long sigh and turn over just beside her in the darkness.

"Can't you get to sleep either?" said Susan.

"No," said Lucy. "I thought you were asleep. I say, Susan!"

"What?"

"I've a most horrible feeling – as if something were hanging over us."

"Have you? Because, as a matter of fact, so have I."

"Something about Aslan," said Lucy. "Either some dreadful thing is going to happen to him, or something dreadful that he's going to do."

"There's been something wrong with him all afternoon," said Susan. "Lucy! What was that he said about not being with us at the battle? You don't think he could be stealing away and leaving us tonight, do you?"

"Where is he now?" said Lucy. "Is he here in the pavilion?"

"I don't think so."

"Susan! Let's go outside and have a look round. We might see him."

"All right. Let's," said Susan; "we might just as well be doing that as lying awake here."

Very quietly the two girls groped their way among the other sleepers and crept out of the tent. The moonlight was bright and everything was quite still except for the noise of the river chattering over the stones. Then Susan suddenly caught Lucy's arm and said, "Look!" On the far side of the camping ground, just where the trees began, they saw the Lion slowly walking away from them into the wood. Without a word they both followed him.

He led them up the steep slope out of the river valley and then slightly to the right – apparently by the very same route which they had used that afternoon in coming from the Hill of the Stone Table. On and on he led them, into dark shadows and out into pale moonlight, getting their feet wet with the heavy dew. He looked somehow different from the Aslan they knew. His tail and his head hung low and he walked slowly as if he were very, very tired. Then, when they were crossing a wide open place where there were no shadows for them to hide in, he stopped and looked round. It was no good trying to run away so they came towards him. When they were closer he said,

"Oh, children, children, why are you following me?"

"We couldn't sleep," said Lucy – and then felt sure that she need say no more and that Aslan knew all they had been thinking.

"Please, may we come with you – wherever you're going?" asked Susan.

"Well –" said Aslan, and seemed to be thinking. Then he said, "I should be glad of company tonight. Yes, you may come, if you will promise to stop when I tell you, and after that leave me to go on alone."

"Oh, thank you, thank you. And we will," said the two girls.

Forward they went again and one of the girls walked on each side of the Lion. But how slowly he walked! And his great, royal head drooped so that his nose nearly touched the grass.

Presently he stumbled and gave a low moan.

"Aslan! Dear Aslan!" said Lucy, "what is wrong? Can't you tell us?"

"Are you ill, dear Aslan?" asked Susan.

"No," said Aslan. "I am sad and lonely. Lay your hands on my mane so that I can feel you are there and let us walk like that."

And so the girls did what they would never have dared to do without his permission, but what they had longed to do ever since they first saw him – buried their cold hands in the beautiful sea of fur and stroked it and, so doing, walked with him. And presently they saw that they were going with him up the slope of the hill on which the Stone Table stood. They went up at the side where the trees came furthest up, and when they got to the last tree (it was one that had some bushes about it) Aslan stopped and said,

"Oh, children, children. Here you must stop. And whatever happens, do not let yourselves be seen. Farewell."

And both the girls cried bitterly (though they hardly knew why) and clung to the Lion and kissed his mane and his nose and his paws and his great, sad eyes. Then he turned from them and walked out on to the top of the hill. And Lucy and Susan, crouching in the bushes, looked after him, and this is what they saw.

A great crowd of people were standing all round the Stone Table and though the moon was shining many of them carried torches which burned with evil-looking red flames and black smoke. But such people! Ogres with monstrous teeth, and wolves, and bull-headed men; spirits of evil trees and poisonous

plants; and other creatures whom I won't describe because if I did the grown-ups would probably not let you read this book – Cruels and Hags and Incubuses, Wraiths, Horrors, Efreets, Sprites, Orknies, Wooses, and Ettins. In fact here were all those who were on the Witch's side and whom the Wolf had summoned at her command. And right in the middle, standing by the Table, was the Witch herself.

A howl and a gibber of dismay went up from the creatures when they first saw the great Lion pacing towards them, and for a moment even the Witch seemed to be struck with fear. Then she recovered herself and gave a wild fierce laugh.

"The fool!" she cried. "The fool has come. Bind him fast."

Lucy and Susan held their breaths waiting for Aslan's roar and his spring upon his enemies. But it never came. Four Hags, grinning and leering, yet also (at first) hanging back and half afraid of what they had to do, had approached him. "Bind him, I say!" repeated the White Witch. The Hags made a dart at him and shrieked with triumph when they found that he made no resistance at all. Then others – evil dwarfs and apes – rushed in to help them, and between them they rolled the huge Lion over on his back and tied all his four paws together, shouting and cheering as if they had done something brave, though, had the Lion chosen, one of those paws could have been the death of them all. But he made no noise, even when the enemies, straining and tugging, pulled the cords so tight that they cut into his flesh. Then they began to drag him towards the Stone Table.

"Stop!" said the Witch. "Let him first be shaved."

Another roar of mean laughter went up from her followers as

'many of them carried torches which burned with evil-looking red flames and black smoke' an ogre with a pair of shears came forward and squatted down by Aslan's head. Snip-snip-snip went the shears and masses of curling gold began to fall to the ground. Then the ogre stood back and the children, watching from their hiding-place, could see the face of Aslan looking all small and different without its mane. The enemies also saw the difference.

"Why, he's only a great cat after all!" cried one.

"Is *that* what we were afraid of?" said another.

And they surged round Aslan, jeering at him, saying things like "Puss, Puss! Poor Pussy," and "How many mice have you caught today, Cat?" and "Would you like a saucer of milk, Pussums?"

"Oh, how *can* they?" said Lucy, tears streaming down her cheeks. "The brutes, the brutes!" for now that the first shock was over the shorn face of Aslan looked to her braver, and more beautiful, and more patient than ever.

"Muzzle him!" said the Witch. And even now, as they worked about his face putting on the muzzle, one bite from his jaws would have cost two or three of them their hands. But he never moved. And this seemed to enrage all that rabble. Everyone was at him now. Those who had been afraid to come near him even after he was bound began to find their courage, and for a few minutes the two girls could not even see him – so thickly was he surrounded by the whole crowd of creatures kicking him, hitting him, spitting on him, jeering at him.

At last the rabble had had enough of this. They began to drag the bound and muzzled Lion to the Stone Table, some pulling and some pushing. He was so huge that even when they got him there it took all their efforts to hoist him on to the surface of it. Then there was more tying and tightening of cords.

"The cowards! The cowards!" sobbed Susan. "Are they *still* afraid of him, even now?"

When once Aslan had been tied (and tied so that he was really a mass of cords) on the flat stone, a hush fell on the crowd. Four Hags, holding four torches, stood at the corners of the Table. The Witch bared her arms as she had bared them the previous night when it had been Edmund instead of Aslan. Then she began to whet her knife. It looked to the children, when the gleam of the torchlight fell on it, as if the knife were made of stone, not of steel, and it was of a strange and evil shape.

At last she drew near. She stood by Aslan's head. Her face was working and twitching with passion, but his looked up at the sky, still quiet, neither angry nor afraid, but a little sad. Then, just before she gave the blow, she stooped down and said in a quivering voice,

"And now, who has won? Fool, did you think that by all this you would save the human traitor? Now I will kill you instead of him as our pact was and so the Deep Magic will be appeased. But when you are dead what will prevent me from killing him as well? And who will take him out of my hand *then*? Understand that you have given me Narnia forever, you have lost your own life and you have not saved his. In that knowledge, despair and die."

The children did not see the actual moment of the killing. They couldn't bear to look and had covered their eyes.

CHAPTER FIFTEEN

DEEPER MAGIC FROM BEFORE THE DAWN OF TIME

While the two girls still crouched in the bushes with their hands over their faces, they heard the voice of the Witch calling out,

"Now! Follow me all and we will set about what remains of this war! It will not take us long to crush the human vermin and the traitors now that the great Fool, the great Cat, lies dead."

At this very moment the children were for a few seconds in very great danger. For with wild cries and a noise of skirling pipes and shrill horns blowing, the whole of that vile rabble came sweeping off the hill-top and down the slope right past their hiding-place. They felt the Spectres go by them like a cold wind and they felt the ground shake beneath them under the galloping feet of the Minotaurs; and overhead there went a flurry of foul wings and a blackness of vultures and giant bats. At any other time they would have trembled with fear; but now the sadness and shame and horror of Aslan's death so filled their minds that they hardly thought of it.

As soon as the wood was silent again Susan and Lucy crept out onto the open hill-top. The moon was getting low and thin clouds were passing across her, but still they could see the shape of the Lion lying dead in his bonds. And down they both knelt in the wet grass and kissed his cold face and stroked his beautiful

fur – what was left of it – and
cried till they could cry no
more. And then they looked
at each other and held each
other's hands for mere loneliness
and cried again; and then
again were silent. At last Lucy
said, "I can't bear to look
at that horrible muzzle. I
wonder could we take it off?"

So they tried. And after a lot of working at it (for their
fingers were cold and it was now the darkest part of the night)
they succeeded. And when they saw his face without it they
burst out crying again and kissed it and fondled it and wiped
away the blood and the foam as well as they could. And it
was all more lonely and hopeless and horrid than I know how
to describe.

"I wonder could we untie him as well?" said Susan presently.
But the enemies, out of pure spitefulness, had drawn the cords
so tight that the girls could make nothing of the knots.

I hope no one who reads this book has been quite as miserable as Susan and Lucy were that night; but if you have been – if you've been up all night and cried till you have no more tears left in you – you will know that there comes in the end a sort of quietness. You feel as if nothing was ever going to happen again. At any rate that was how it felt to these two. Hours and hours seemed to go by in this dead calm, and they hardly noticed that they were getting colder and colder. But at last Lucy noticed two other things. One was that the sky on the east side of the hill was a little less dark than it had been an hour ago. The other was some tiny movement going on in the grass at her feet. At first she took no interest in this. What did it matter? Nothing mattered now! But at last she saw that whatever-it-was had begun to move up the upright stones of the Stone Table. And now whatever-they-were were moving about on Aslan's body. She peered closer. They were little grey things.

"Ugh!" said Susan from the other side of the Table. "How beastly! There are horrid little mice crawling over him. Go away, you little beasts." And she raised her hand to frighten them away.

"Wait!" said Lucy, who had been looking at them more closely still. "Can you see what they're doing?"

Both girls bent down and stared.

"I do believe –" said Susan. "But how queer! They're nibbling away at the cords!"

"That's what I thought," said Lucy. "I think they're friendly mice. Poor little things – they don't realize he's dead. They think it'll do some good untying him."

It was quite definitely lighter by now. Each of the girls noticed for the first time the white face of the other. They could see the mice nibbling away; dozens and dozens, even hundreds, of little field mice. And at last, one by one, the ropes were all gnawed through.

The sky in the East was whitish by now and the stars were getting fainter – all except one very big one low down on the eastern horizon. They felt colder than they had been all night. The mice crept away again.

The girls cleared away the remains of the gnawed ropes. Aslan looked more like himself without them. Every moment his dead face looked nobler, as the light grew and they could see it better.

In the wood behind them a bird gave a chuckling sound. It had been so still for hours and hours that it startled them. Then another bird answered it. Soon there were birds singing all over the place.

It was quite definitely early morning now, not late night.

"I'm so cold," said Lucy.

"So am I," said Susan. "Let's walk about a bit."

They walked to the eastern edge of the hill and looked down.

The one big star had almost disappeared. The country all looked dark grey, but beyond, at the very end of the world, the sea showed pale. The sky began to turn red. They walked to and fro more times than they could count between the dead Aslan and the eastern ridge, trying to keep warm; and oh, how tired their legs felt. Then at last, as they stood for a moment looking out towards the sea and Cair Paravel (which they could now just make out) the red turned to gold along the line where the sea and the sky met and very slowly up came the edge of the sun. At that moment they heard from behind them a loud noise – a great cracking, deafening noise as if a giant had broken a giant's plate.

"What's that?" said Lucy, clutching Susan's arm.

"I – I feel afraid to turn round," said Susan; "something awful is happening."

"They're doing something worse to *Him*," said Lucy. "Come on!" And she turned, pulling Susan round with her.

The rising of the sun had made everything look so different – all colours and shadows were changed – that for a moment they didn't see the important thing. Then they did. The Stone Table was broken into two pieces by a great crack that ran down it from end to end; and there was no Aslan.

"Oh, oh, oh!" cried the two girls, rushing back to the Table.

"Oh, it's *too* bad," sobbed Lucy; "they might have left the body alone."

"Who's done it?" cried Susan. "What does it mean? Is it magic?"

"Yes!" said a great voice behind their backs. "It is more magic." They looked round. There, shining in the sunrise, larger than they had seen him before, shaking his mane (for it had apparently grown again) stood Aslan himself.

"Oh, Aslan!" cried both the children, staring up at him, almost as much frightened as they were glad.

"Aren't you dead then, dear Aslan?" said Lucy.

"Not now," said Aslan.

"You're not – not a – ?" asked Susan in a shaky voice. She couldn't bring herself to say the word *ghost*. Aslan stooped his golden head and licked her forehead. The warmth of his breath and a rich sort of smell that seemed to hang about his hair came all over her.

"Do I look it?" he said.

"Oh, you're real, you're real! Oh, Aslan!" cried Lucy, and both girls flung themselves upon him and covered him with kisses.

"But what does it all mean?" asked Susan when they were somewhat calmer.

"It means," said Aslan, "that though the Witch knew the Deep Magic, there is a magic deeper still which she did not know. Her knowledge goes back only to the dawn of time. But if she could have looked a little further back, into the stillness and the darkness before Time dawned, she would have read there a different incantation. She would have known that when a willing victim who had committed no treachery was killed in a traitor's stead, the Table would crack and Death itself would start working backwards. And now –"

"Oh yes. Now?" said Lucy, jumping up and clapping her hands.

"Oh, children," said the Lion, "I feel my strength coming back to me. Oh, children, catch me if you can!" He stood for a second, his eyes very bright, his limbs quivering, lashing himself with his tail. Then he made a leap high over their heads and landed on the other side of the Table. Laughing, though she didn't know why, Lucy scrambled over it to reach him. Aslan leaped again. A mad chase began. Round and round the hill-top he led them, now hopelessly out of their reach, now letting them almost catch his tail, now diving between them, now tossing them in the air with his huge and beautifully velveted paws and catching them again, and now stopping unexpectedly so that all three of them rolled over together in a happy laughing heap of fur and arms and legs. It was such a romp as no one has ever had except in Narnia; and whether it was more like playing with a thunderstorm or playing with a kitten Lucy could never make up her mind. And the funny thing was that when all three finally lay together panting in the sun the girls no longer felt in the least tired or hungry or thirsty.

"And now," said Aslan presently, "to business. I feel I am going to roar. You had better put your fingers in your ears."

And they did. And Aslan stood up and when he opened his

mouth to roar his face became so terrible that they did not dare to look at it. And they saw all the trees in front of him bend before the blast of his roaring as grass bends in a meadow before the wind. Then he said,

"We have a long journey to go. You must ride on me." And he crouched down and the children climbed on to his warm, golden back, and Susan sat first, holding on tightly to his mane and Lucy sat behind holding on tightly to Susan. And with a great heave he rose underneath them and then shot off, faster than any horse could go, down hill and into the thick of the forest.

That ride was perhaps the most wonderful thing that happened to them in Narnia. Have you ever had a gallop on a horse? Think of that; and then take away the heavy noise of the hoofs and the jingle of the bits and imagine instead the almost noiseless padding of the great paws. Then imagine instead of the black or grey or chestnut back of the horse the soft roughness of golden fur, and the mane flying back in the wind. And then imagine you are going about twice as fast as the fastest racehorse. But this is a mount that doesn't need to be guided and never grows tired. He rushes on and on, never missing his footing, never hesitating, threading his way with perfect skill between tree trunks, jumping over bush and briar and the smaller streams, wading the larger, swimming the largest of all. And you are riding not on a road nor in a park nor even on the downs, but right across Narnia, in spring, down solemn avenues of beech and across sunny glades of oak, through wild orchards of snow-white cherry trees, past roaring waterfalls and mossy rocks and echoing caverns, up windy slopes alight with gorse bushes, and across the shoulders of heathery mountains and along giddy ridges and down, down, down again into wild valleys and out into acres of blue flowers.

It was nearly midday when they found themselves looking down a steep hillside at a castle – a little toy castle it looked from where they stood – which seemed to be all pointed towers. But the Lion was rushing down at such a speed that it grew larger every moment and before they had time even to ask themselves what it was they were already on a level with it. And now it no longer looked like a toy castle but rose frowning in front of them. No face looked over the battlements and the gates were fast shut. And Aslan, not at all slacking his pace, rushed straight as a bullet towards it.

"The Witch's home!" he cried. "Now, children, hold tight."

Next moment the whole world seemed to turn upside down, and the children felt as if they had left their insides behind them; for the Lion had gathered himself together for a greater leap than any he had yet made and jumped – or you may call it flying rather than jumping – right over the castle wall. The two girls, breathless but unhurt, found themselves tumbling off his back in the middle of a wide stone courtyard full of statues.

'That ride was perhaps the most wonderful thing that happened to them in Narnia'

CHAPTER SIXTEEN

What happened about the statues

"What an extraordinary place!" cried Lucy. "All those stone animals – and people too! It's – it's like a museum."

"Hush," said Susan, "Aslan's doing something."

He was indeed. He had bounded up to the stone lion and breathed on him. Then without waiting a moment he whisked round – almost as if he had been a cat chasing its tail – and breathed also on the stone dwarf, which (as you remember) was standing a few feet from the lion with his back to it. Then he pounced on a tall stone dryad which stood beyond the dwarf, turned rapidly aside to deal with a stone rabbit on his right, and rushed on to two centaurs. But at that moment Lucy said,

"Oh, Susan! Look! Look at the lion."

I expect you've seen someone put a lighted match to a bit of newspaper which is propped up in a grate against an unlit fire. And for a second nothing seems to have happened; and then you notice a tiny streak of flame creeping along the edge of the newspaper. It was like that now. For a second after Aslan had breathed upon him the stone lion looked just the same. Then a tiny streak of gold began to run along his white marble back – then it spread – then the colour seemed to lick all over him as the flame licks all over a bit of paper – then, while his hindquarters were still obviously stone, the lion shook his mane and all the heavy, stone folds rippled into living hair.

Then he opened a great red mouth, warm and living, and gave a prodigious yawn. And now his hind legs had come to life. He lifted one of them and scratched himself. Then, having caught sight of Aslan, he went bounding after him and frisking round him whimpering with delight and jumping up to lick his face.

Of course the children's eyes turned to follow the lion; but the sight they saw was so wonderful that they soon forgot about *him*. Everywhere the statues were coming to life. The courtyard looked no longer like a museum; it looked more like a zoo. Creatures were running after Aslan and dancing round him till he was almost hidden in the crowd. Instead of all that deadly white the courtyard was now a blaze of colours; glossy chestnut sides of centaurs, indigo horns of unicorns, dazzling plumage of birds, reddy-brown of foxes, dogs and satyrs, yellow stockings and crimson hoods of dwarfs; and the birch-girls in silver, and the beech-girls in fresh, transparent green, and the larch-girls in green so bright that it was almost yellow. And instead of the deadly silence the whole place rang with the sound of happy roarings, brayings, yelpings, barkings, squealings, cooings, neighings, stampings, shouts, hurrahs, songs and laughter.

"Oh!" said Susan in a different tone. "Look! I wonder – I mean, is it safe?"

Lucy looked and saw that Aslan had just breathed on the feet of the stone giant.

"It's all right!" shouted Aslan joyously. "Once the feet are put right, all the rest of him will follow."

"That wasn't exactly what I meant," whispered Susan to Lucy. But it was too late to do anything about it now even if Aslan would have listened to her. The change was already creeping up the Giant's legs. Now he was moving his feet. A moment later he lifted his club off his shoulder, rubbed his eyes and said, "Bless me! I must have been asleep. Now! Where's that dratted little Witch that was running about on the ground. Somewhere just by my feet it was." But when everyone had shouted up to him to explain what had really happened, and when the Giant had put his hand to his ear and got them to repeat it all again so that at last he understood, then he bowed down till his head was no further off than the top of a haystack and touched his cap repeatedly to Aslan, beaming all over his honest ugly face. (Giants of any sort are now so rare in England and so few giants are good-tempered that ten to one you have never seen a giant when his face is beaming. It's a sight well worth looking at.)

"Now for the inside of this house!" said Aslan. "Look alive, everyone. Up stairs and down stairs and in my lady's chamber! Leave no corner unsearched. You never know where some poor prisoner may be concealed."

And into the interior they all rushed and for several minutes the whole of that dark, horrible, fusty old castle echoed with the opening of the windows and with everyone's voices crying out at once, "Don't forget the dungeons – Give us a hand with this door! – Here's another little winding stair – Oh! I say. Here's a poor kangaroo. Call Aslan – Phew! How it smells in here – Look out for trap-doors – Up here! There are a whole lot more on the landing!" But the best of all was when Lucy came rushing upstairs shouting out,

"Aslan! Aslan! I've found Mr Tumnus. Oh, do come quick."

A moment later Lucy and the little Faun were holding each other by both hands and dancing round and round for joy. The little chap was none the worse for having been a statue and was of course very interested in all she had to tell him.

But at last the ransacking of the Witch's fortress was ended. The whole castle stood empty with every door and window open and the light and the sweet spring air flooding into all the dark and evil places which needed them so badly. The whole crowd of liberated statues surged back into the courtyard. And it was then that someone (Tumnus, I think) first said,

"But how are we going to get out?" for Aslan had got in by a jump and the gates were still locked.

"That'll be all right," said Aslan; and then, rising on his

hind-legs, he bawled up at the Giant. "Hi! You up there," he roared. "What's your name?"

"Giant Rumblebuffin, if it please your honour," said the Giant, once more touching his cap.

"Well then, Giant Rumblebuffin," said Aslan, "just let us out of this, will you?"

"Certainly, your honour. It will be a pleasure," said Giant Rumblebuffin. "Stand well away from the gates, all you little 'uns." Then he strode to the gate himself and bang – bang – bang went his huge club. The gates creaked at the first blow, cracked at the second, and shivered at the third. Then he tackled the towers on each side of them and after a few minutes of crashing and thudding both the towers and a good bit of the wall on each side went thundering down in a mass of hopeless rubble; and when the dust cleared it was odd, standing in that dry, grim, stony yard, to see through the gap all the grass and waving trees and sparkling streams of the forest, and the blue hills beyond that and beyond them the sky.

"Blowed if I ain't all in a muck sweat," said the Giant, puffing like the largest railway engine. "Comes of being out of condition. I suppose neither of you young ladies has such a thing as a pocket-handkerchee about you?"

"Yes, I have," said Lucy, standing on tip-toes and holding her handkerchief up as far as she could reach.

"Thank you, Missie," said Giant Rumblebuffin, stooping down. Next moment Lucy got rather a fright for she found herself caught up in mid-air between the Giant's finger and thumb. But just as she was getting near his face he suddenly started and then put her gently back on the ground muttering,

"Bless me! I've picked up the little girl instead. I beg your pardon, Missie, I thought you *was* the handkerchee!"

"No, no," said Lucy laughing, "here it is!" This time he managed to get it but it was only about the same size to him that a saccharine tablet would be to you, so that when she saw him solemnly rubbing it to and fro across his great red face, she said, "I'm afraid it's not much use to you, Mr Rumblebuffin."

"Not at all. Not at all," said the giant politely. "Never met a nicer handkerchee. So fine, so handy. So – I don't know how to describe it."

"What a nice giant he is!" said Lucy to Mr Tumnus.

"Oh yes," replied the Faun. "All the Buffins always were. One of the most respected of all the giant families in Narnia. Not very clever, perhaps (I never knew a giant that was), but an old family. With traditions, you know. If he'd been the other sort she'd never have turned him into stone."

At this point Aslan clapped his paws together and called for silence.

"Our day's work is not yet over," he said, "and if the Witch is to be finally defeated before bed-time we must find the battle at once."

"And join in, I hope, sir!" added the largest of the centaurs.

"Of course," said Aslan. "And now! Those who can't keep up – that is, children, dwarfs, and small animals – must ride on the backs of those who can – that is, lions, centaurs, unicorns, horses, giants and eagles. Those who are good with their noses must come in front with us lions to smell out where the battle is. Look lively and sort yourselves."

And with a great deal of bustle and cheering they did. The

most pleased of the lot was the other lion who kept running about everywhere pretending to be very busy but really in order to say to everyone he met. "Did you hear what he said? *Us Lions*. That means him and me. *Us Lions*. That's what I like about Aslan. No side, no stand-off-ishness. *Us Lions*. That meant him and me." At least he went on saying this till Aslan had loaded him up with three dwarfs, one dryad, two rabbits, and a hedgehog. That steadied him a bit.

When all were ready (it was a big sheep-dog who actually helped Aslan most in getting them sorted into their proper order) they set out through the gap in the castle wall. At first the lions and dogs went nosing about in all directions. But then suddenly one great hound picked up the scent and gave a bay. There was no time lost after that. Soon all the dogs and lions and wolves and other hunting animals were going at full speed with their noses to the ground, and all the others, streaked out for about half a mile behind them, were following as fast as they could. The noise was like an English fox-hunt only better because every now and then with the music of the hounds was mixed the roar of the other lion and sometimes the far deeper and more awful roar of Aslan himself. Faster and faster they went as the scent became easier and easier to follow. And then, just as they came to the last curve in a narrow, winding valley, Lucy heard above all these noises another noise – a different one, which gave her a queer feeling inside. It was a noise of shouts and shrieks and of the clashing of metal against metal.

Then they came out of the narrow valley and at once she saw the reason. There stood Peter and Edmund and all the rest of Aslan's army fighting desperately against the crowd of

'It was a noise of shouts and shrieks and of the clashing of metal against metal'

horrible creatures whom she had seen last night; only now, in the daylight, they looked even stranger and more evil and more deformed. There also seemed to be far more of them. Peter's army – which had their backs to her – looked terribly few. And there were statues dotted all over the battlefield, so apparently the Witch had been using her wand. But she did not seem to be using it now. She was fighting with her stone knife. It was Peter she was fighting – both of them going at it so hard that Lucy could hardly make out what was happening; she only saw the stone knife and Peter's sword flashing so quickly that they looked like three knives and three swords. That pair were in the centre. On each side the line stretched out. Horrible things were happening wherever she looked.

"Off my back, children," shouted Aslan. And they both tumbled off. Then with a roar that shook all Narnia from the western lamp-post to the shores of the eastern sea the great beast flung himself upon the White Witch. Lucy saw her face lifted towards him for one second with an expression of terror and amazement. Then Lion and Witch had rolled over together but with the Witch underneath; and at the same moment all war-like creatures whom Aslan had led from the Witch's house rushed madly on the enemy lines, dwarfs with their battleaxes, dogs with teeth, the Giant with his club (and his feet also crushed dozens of the foe), unicorns with their horns, centaurs with swords and hoofs. And Peter's tired army cheered, and the newcomers roared, and the enemy squealed and gibbered till the wood re-echoed with the din of that onset.

CHAPTER SEVENTEEN

THE HUNTING OF THE WHITE STAG

The battle was all over a few minutes after their arrival. Most of the enemy had been killed in the first charge of Aslan and his companions; and when those who were still living saw that the Witch was dead they either gave themselves up or took to flight. The next thing that Lucy knew was that Peter and Aslan were shaking hands. It was strange to her to see Peter looking as he looked now – his face was so pale and stern and he seemed so much older.

"It was all Edmund's doing, Aslan," Peter was saying. "We'd have been beaten if it hadn't been for him. The Witch was turning our troops into stone right and left. But nothing would stop him. He fought his way through three ogres to where she was just turning one of your leopards into a statue. And when he reached her he had sense to bring his sword smashing down on her wand instead of trying to go for her directly and simply getting made a statue himself for his pains. That was the mistake all the rest were making. Once her wand was broken we began to have some chance – if we hadn't lost so many already. He was terribly wounded. We must go and see him."

They found Edmund in charge of Mrs Beaver a little way back from the fighting line. He was covered with blood, his mouth was open, and his face a nasty green colour.

"Quick, Lucy," said Aslan.

And then, almost for the first time, Lucy remembered the precious cordial that had been given her for a Christmas present. Her hands trembled so much that she could hardly undo the stopper, but she managed it in the end and poured a few drops into her brother's mouth.

"There are other people wounded," said Aslan while she was still looking eagerly into Edmund's pale face and wondering if the cordial would have any result.

"Yes, I know," aid Lucy crossly. "Wait a minute."

"Daughter of Eve," said Aslan in a graver voice, "others also are at the point of death. Must *more* people die for Edmund?"

"I'm sorry, Aslan," said Lucy, getting up and going with him. And for the next half-hour they were busy – she attending to the wounded while he restored those who had been turned into stone. When at last she was free to come back to Edmund she found him standing on his feet and not only healed of his wounds but looking better than she had seen him look – oh, for ages; in fact ever since his first term at that horrid school which was where he had begun to go wrong. He had become his real old self again and could look you in the face. And there on the field of battle Aslan made him a knight.

"Does he know," whispered Lucy to Susan, "what Aslan did for him? Does he know what the arrangement with the Witch really was?"

"Hush! No. Of course not," said Susan.

"Oughtn't he to be told?" said Lucy.

"Oh, surely not," said Susan. "It would be too awful for him. Think how you'd feel if you were he."

"All the same I think he ought to know," said Lucy. But at

that moment they were interrupted.

That night they slept where they were. How Aslan provided food for them all I don't know; but somehow or other they found themselves all sitting down on the grass to a fine high tea at about eight o'clock. Next day they began marching eastward down the side of the great river. And the next day after that, at about teatime, they actually reached the mouth. The castle of Cair Paravel on its little hill towered up above them; before them were the sands, with rocks and little pools of salt water, and seaweed, and the smell of the sea and long miles of bluish-green waves breaking for ever and ever on the beach. And oh, the cry of the sea-gulls! Have you heard it? Can you remember?

That evening after tea the four children all managed to get down to the beach again and get their shoes and stockings off and feel the sand between their toes. But next day was more solemn. For then, in the Great Hall of Cair Paravel – that wonderful hall with the ivory roof and the west wall hung with peacock's feathers and the eastern door which looks towards the sea, in the presence of all their friends and to the sound of trumpets, Aslan solemnly crowned them and led them to the four thrones amid deafening shouts of, "Long Live King Peter! Long Live Queen Susan! Long Live King Edmund! Long Live Queen Lucy!"

"Once a king or queen in Narnia, always a king or queen. Bear it well, Sons of Adam! Bear it well, Daughters of Eve!" said Aslan.

And through the eastern door, which was wide open, came the voices of the mermen and the mermaids swimming close to the shore and singing in honour of their new Kings and Queens.

So the children sat on their thrones and sceptres were put into their hands and they gave rewards and honours to all their friends, to Tumnus the Faun, and to the Beavers, and Giant Rumblebuffin, to the leopards, and the good centaurs, and the good dwarfs, and to the lion. And that night there was a great feast in Cair Paravel, and revelry and dancing, and gold flashed and wine flowed, and answering to the music inside, but stranger, sweeter, and more piercing, came the music of the sea people.

But amidst all these rejoicings Aslan himself quietly slipped away. And when the Kings and Queens noticed that he wasn't there they said nothing about it. For Mr Beaver had warned them, "He'll be coming and going," he had said. "One day you'll see him and another you won't. He doesn't like being tied down – and of course he has other countries to attend to.

It's quite all right. He'll often drop in. Only you mustn't press him. He's wild, you know. Not like a *tame* lion."

And now, as you see, this story is nearly (but not quite) at an end. These two Kings and two Queens governed Narnia well, and long and happy was their reign. At first much of their time was spent in seeking out the remnants of the White Witch's army and destroying them, and indeed for a long time there would be news of evil things lurking in the wilder parts of the forest – a haunting here and a killing there, a glimpse of a werewolf one month and a rumour of a hag the next. But in the end all that foul brood was stamped out. And they made good laws and kept the peace and saved good trees from being unnecessarily cut down, and liberated young dwarfs and young satyrs from being sent to school, and generally stopped busybodies and interferers and encouraged ordinary people who wanted to live and let live. And they drove back the fierce giants (quite a different sort from Giant Rumblebuffin) on the north of Narnia when these ventured across the frontier. And they entered into friendship and alliance with countries beyond the sea and paid them visits of state and received visits of state from them. And they themselves grew and changed as the years passed over them. And Peter became a tall and deep-chested man and a great warrior, and he was called King Peter the Magnificent. And Susan grew into a tall and gracious woman with black hair that fell almost to her feet and the kings of the countries beyond the sea began to send ambassadors asking for her hand in marriage. And she was called Susan the Gentle. Edmund was a graver and quieter man than Peter, and great in council and judgement. He was called King Edmund the Just.

'So the children sat on their thrones and sceptres were put into their hands'

But as for Lucy, she was always gay and golden-haired, and all princes in those parts desired her to be their Queen, and her own people called her Queen Lucy the Valiant.

So they lived in great joy and if ever they remembered their life in this world it was only as one remembers a dream. And one year it fell out that Tumnus (who was a middle-aged Faun by now and beginning to be stout) came down river and brought them news that the White Stag had once more appeared in his parts – the White Stag who would give you wishes if you caught him. So these two Kings and two Queens with the principal members of their court, rode a-hunting with horns and hounds in the Western Woods to follow the White Stag. And they had not hunted long before they had a sight of him. And he led them a great pace over rough and smooth and through thick and thin, till the horses of all the courtiers were tired out and these four were still following. And they saw the stag enter into a thicket where their horses could not follow. Then said King Peter (for they talked in quite a different style now, having been Kings and Queens for so long), "Fair Consorts, let us now alight from our horses and follow this beast into the thicket; for in all my days I never hunted a nobler quarry."

"Sir," said the others, "even so let us do."

So they alighted and tied their horses to trees and went on into the thick wood on foot. And as soon as they had entered it Queen Susan said,

"Fair friends, here is a great marvel, for I seem to see a tree of iron."

"Madam," said King Edmund, "if you look well upon it you shall see it is a pillar of iron with a lantern set on the top thereof."

"By the Lion's Mane, a strange device," said King Peter, "to set a lantern here where the trees cluster so thick about it and so high above it that if it were lit it should give light to no man!"

"Sir," said Queen Lucy. "By likelihood when this post and this lamp were set here there were smaller trees in the place, or fewer, or none. For this is a young wood and the iron post is old." And they stood looking upon it. Then said King Edmund,

"I know not how it is, but this lamp on the post worketh upon me strangely. It runs in my mind that I have seen the like before; as it were in a dream, or in the dream of a dream."

"Sir," answered they all, "it is even so with us also."

"And more," said Queen Lucy, "for it will not go out of my mind that if we pass this post and lantern either we shall find strange adventures or else some great change of our fortunes."

"Madam," said King Edmund, "the like foreboding stirreth in my heart also."

"And in mine, fair brother," said King Peter.

"And in mine too," said Queen Susan. "Wherefore by my counsel we shall lightly return to our horses and follow this White Stag no further."

"Madam," said King Peter, "therein I pray thee to have me excused. For never since we four were Kings and Queens in Narnia have we set our hands to any high matter, as battles, quests, feats of arms, acts of justice, and the like, and then given over; but always what we have taken in hand, the same we have achieved."

"Sister," said Queen Lucy, "my royal brother speaks rightly. And it seems to me we should be shamed if for any fearing or foreboding we turned back from following so noble a beast as now we have in chase."

"And so say I," said King Edmund. "And I have such desire to find the signification of this thing that I would not by my good will turn back for the richest jewel in all Narnia and all the islands."

"Then in the name of Aslan," said Queen Susan, "if ye will all have it so, let us go on and take the adventure that shall fall to us."

So these Kings and Queens entered the thicket, and before they had gone a score of paces they all remembered that the thing they had seen was called a lamp-post, and before they had gone twenty more they noticed that they were making their way not through branches but through coats. And next moment they all came tumbling out of a wardrobe door into the empty room, and they were no longer Kings and Queens in their hunting array but just Peter, Susan, Edmund and Lucy in their old clothes. It was the same day and the same hour of the day on which they had all gone into the wardrobe to hide. Mrs Macready and the visitors were still talking in the passage; but luckily they never came into the empty room and so the children weren't caught.

And that would have been the very end of the story if it hadn't been that they felt they really must explain to the Professor why four of the coats out of his wardrobe were missing. And the Professor, who was a very remarkable man, didn't tell them not to be silly or not to tell lies, but believed the whole story. "No," he said, "I don't think it will be any good trying to go back through the wardrobe door to get the coats. You won't get into Narnia again by *that* route. Nor would the coats be much use by now if you did! Eh? What's that? Yes, of course you'll get back to Narnia again some day. Once a King in Narnia, always a King in Narnia. But don't go trying to use the same route twice. Indeed, don't *try* to get there at all. It'll happen when you're not looking for it. And don't talk too much about it even among yourselves. And don't mention it to anyone else unless you find that they've had adventures of the same sort themselves. What's that? How will you know? Oh, you'll *know* all right. Odd things they say – even their looks – will let the secret out. Keep your eyes open. Bless me, what *do* they teach them at these schools?

And that is the very end of the adventure of the wardrobe. But if the Professor was right it was only the beginning of the adventures of Narnia.